The General Law of Capitalist Accumulation in Latin America and Beyond

The General Law of Capitalist Accumulation in Latin America and Beyond

Actuality and Pertinence

Edited by
Lorenzo Fusaro and
Leinad Johan Alcalá Sandoval

LEXINGTON BOOKS
Lanham • Boulder • New York • London

Published by Lexington Books
An imprint of The Rowman & Littlefield Publishing Group, Inc.
4501 Forbes Boulevard, Suite 200, Lanham, Maryland 20706
www.rowman.com

86–90 Paul Street, London EC2A 4NE

Translations by Petch, Fionn, CM Idiomas and Segovia, Rafael, CM Idiomas.

British Library Cataloguing in Publication Information Available

Library of Congress Cataloging-in-Publication Data Available

ISBN: 978-1-7936-3823-6 (cloth)
ISBN: 978-1-7936-3824-3 (electronic)

Contents

List of Figures

Introduction

The General Law of Capitalist Accumulation: Actuality and Pertinence

Lorenzo Fusaro and Leinad Alcalá Sandoval*

In 1930, as the Great Depression was causing deep economic and social distress, leading to the questioning of the capitalist economic order, Keynes proposed to take the wings to the future and asked: "What can we reasonably expect the level of our economic life to be a hundred years hence? What are the economic possibilities for our grandchildren?" (Keynes 1930). He further replied to these questions arguing that the pessimistic views he confronted should be dismissed. For thanks to capital accumulation and, along with it, technological improvements and compound interest rates, the future, according to the British economist, looked bright. His overall assessment can be summarized by his prediction that human beings would face, eventually, the "problem" of how to use their freedom from economic concerns. In his words:

> Man will be faced with his real, his permanent problem—how to use his freedom from pressing economic cares, how to occupy the leisure, which science and compound interest will have won for him, to live wisely and agreeably and well. (Keynes 1930)

It should be noted that his comments omitted people living in subordinated nations and that they focused mostly on the United Kingdom and the United

* We wish to express our deepest thanks to all the authors who have contributed to this volume and to those who participated in our seminar series dedicated to the General law of capitalist accumulation—in particular, considering that we were all working in very difficult circumstances due to the Covid-19 pandemic. This project would not have been possible without the professionalism and patience shown by Nicolette Amstutz and Alexandra Rallo from Lexington Books / Rowman & Littlefield who accompanied us throughout the process that led to the publication of this book. Also, we are grateful to our research assistants Ana Lilia Barrera Arandula and Andrea Jiménez Valle for their great help in preparing the manuscript.

States. He recognized that in both countries, fast technological improvements were creating the anomaly of widespread unemployment as "the increase of technical efficiency has been taking place faster than we can deal with the problem of labour absorption" (Keynes 1930). However, Keynes remained confident that this was a temporary maladjustment that could be overcome.

Hence when praising the benefits of compound interest rates that capital accumulation grants, he focused in particular on foreign investments and their contribution to national wealth. Openly stating what several Marxists and *Dependentistas* would perhaps agree with—though not criticizing such developments—Keynes estimated that foreign investment "yields us [the UK] an income at the rate of about 6 1/2 per cent. Half of this we bring home and enjoy; the other half, namely, 3 1/4 per cent, we leave to accumulate abroad at compound interest. Something of this sort has now been going on for about 250 years" (Keynes 1930). Interestingly, Keynes had no problem admitting that the origin of foreign investment was "the treasure which Drake stole from Spain in 1580." This, eventually, Keynes reconstructed, enabled Queen Elizabeth to balance the budget, to finance the Levant Company, and, out of the profits of the latter, to finance the East India Company he, finally, referred to as the foundation of England's ensuing foreign investments. Hence, he concluded by calculating that "every £1 which Drake brought home in 1580 has now [in 1930] become £100,000. Such is the power of compound interest" (Keynes 1930).

ONE HUNDRED YEARS ON: "DIALECTICAL INVERSION" AND MULTIPLE CRISES

Keynes comments in the discussed article do not do justice to the complexities of his overall intellectual contribution. Yet they succinctly summarize a view about the future of capitalism that is shared by many while discussing important elements that Marx's general law of capitalist accumulation addresses—albeit reaching very different conclusions. Before turning to Marx's general law, it should be noted that contrary to the views adopted by the British economist, roughly one century after he wrote "Economic Possibilities for our Grandchildren," the capitalist world economy is (again) going through a period of deep multiple crises: economic, and ecological (and we subsume here the many facets of the contemporary crisis under these headings). Latin America, for example, with an historically gloomy record, exhibited increasing poverty, unemployment, and the deterioration of the living conditions of very large sections of population during the past years (CEPAL 2020) while being exposed to the effects of climate change. This amplified migratory flows, shattered social reproduction, and caused deep social and political crises—all elements that might have also contributed to the emergence of the likes of Bolsonaro. However, these multiple crises and increased polarization do not just concern the "periphery" as they are increasingly permeating the "center." Paradigmatic are contemporary observations on the United States. Thus, concerned about political developments in the United States, even the *Financial Times*' Martin Wolf recently wrote about "the strange death of American democracy." To the question "Why this is happening?," Wolf replies:

> The answer is a mix of greed, ambition and anger in a country that has grown increasingly diverse and an *economy that has failed to give secure prosperity to a large proportion of the population.* This has created a familiar coalition built on 'othering' outsiders, glorifying the nation, protecting the wealthy and worshipping a great leader. (Wolf 2021, own emphasis)

As we shall see, by arguing that the economy has failed to provide a safe future for a major segment of the population, Martin Wolf is partially paraphrasing nothing but Marx's general law.

Some contemporary Marxists are returning to the idea of an "age of catastrophe" (Foster and Suvandi 2020; Callinicos 2021) when analyzing the contemporary situation recalling Hobsbawm's investigation of the 1930s (Hobsbawm 1994). What differentiates the Marxist vantage point is to see that these multiple crises are related and endogenous, and that they hence result from specific relations of production, namely capitalist relations of production. The latter cannot be emphasized enough. Current developments cannot, therefore, be understood as external shocks nor are they a consequence of human behavior as such. Crucially, Marx uses the concept of "dialectical inversion" in order to portray how even potentially progressive elements, such as technological change as envisaged by Keynes, turn into their opposite within capitalist relations of production. As Marx states when discussing the general law, "… all means for the development of production undergo a dialectical inversion so that they become means of domination and exploitation of the producers" (*Marx-Engels-Werke*, Bd. 23, 674).[1] The workings of this dialectical inversion are perhaps concisely stated in *Capital*'s chapter on machinery that dwells on the consequences of the development of the productive forces, which represents an essential element of Marx's general law. As Marx writes:

> Machinery in itself shortens the hours of labor, but when employed by capital it lengthens them; . . . in itself it lightens labour, but when employed by capital it heightens its intensity; . . . in itself it is a victory of man over the forces of nature but in the hands of capital it makes man the slave of those forces; . . . in itself it

> increases the wealth of the producers, but in the hands of capital it makes them into paupers. (*Marx-Engels-Werke*, Bd. 23, 465)

Thus, contrary to the view adopted by Keynes (he went as far as imagining "three-hour shifts or a fifteen-hour week"), technological improvements (under capitalist relations of production) are not leading to a shortening of the working day. It is already well documented—just taking up a recent example—that technologies that allowed remote working during the pandemic have led to the lengthening of the working day and not its shortening (NBER 2021). Again, the still ongoing pandemic shows the pertinence of Marx's comments on human beings' relation to the "forces of nature" under capitalist relations of production. For also in this case, the development and application of technology within capital relations of production have not led to the victory of human beings over the forces of nature. On the contrary, and as is well known, it led to the current environmental and biological crisis (IPCC 2021; UN 2020). Finally, as many studies on inequality show, the latter remains astonishingly high and persistent within and between regions (Oxfam 2020). It is important to stress that, following also Maddison's historical revision, the capitalist mode of production conveys unprecedented levels of inequality: while the ratio between the richest and poorest regions stood at roughly 1:1 in the year 1000 and 3:1 in 1820, it jumped to 19:1 in 1998 (Maddison 2006, 126).

The reason for why under capitalist relations of production, we observe this "dialectical inversion" is, eventually, related to the law of value that is itself a product of capitalist relations of production. Overall, development and human beings' existence within capitalist relations of production are hence conditioned by the *law of value* that Marx outlines at the very beginning of *Capital*. Starting from the analysis of commodities and their "secrets," Marx arrives at the presentation of his conception of value and the law of value that serves as a "regulative law" of the capitalist mode of production. As Marx puts it, "The labour-time socially necessary to produce them [commodities] asserts itself [violently, *gewaltsam*] as a regulative law of nature. In the same way, the law of gravity asserts itself when a person's house collapses on top of him" (*Marx-Engels-Werke*, Bd. 23, 89). Yet, unlike the law of gravity associated with natural dynamics, the law of value has a social base and belongs exclusively to the capitalist mode of production. Although without realizing it, we participate so much in the creation and execution of the law of value. And notwithstanding the foregoing, we remain subordinate to its effects: the houses that fall on us—retaking the previous quote—are represented by, for example, ecological crises, recurrent economic crises, the loss of work, precariousness, the need to migrate to other places, and so on. This is a consequence of the fact that necessary social labour time to produce commodities (and hence value that works as a regulative law) changes constantly—and even more so during crises as changes in value become particularly vicious. Unfortunately, these variations in value occur behind the back of the producers. On the one hand, competition and the ensuing necessary "ceaseless" accumulation of capital tend to increase the productivity of labour thereby constantly changing the value of commodities and capital, of course. On the other hand, the same processes also constantly modify habits, tastes, and so on, in short, what society considers as needs—affecting again value.

THE GENERAL LAW OF CAPITALIST ACCUMULATION

We have already mentioned how technological change, under capitalist relations of production, has unwanted consequences. But what are the long-term implications of the aforementioned "dialectical inversion" related to the operation of the law of value? When answering this question, it is important to stress that in his general law, Marx is presenting "the influence of the growth of capital on the fate of the working class" (*Marx-Engels-Werke*, Bd. 23, 640). Also, that Marx is looking at "total social capital" (*Marx-Engels-Werke*, Bd. 23, 642, 658, 668). He is therefore not analyzing a single nation, Mexico, as opposed to the United States or Germany or Argentina. On the contrary, we need to look at the world as a whole. Therefore, looking at the capitalist world as a whole and *pace* Keynes, Marx reaches the conclusion that

> accumulation of wealth at one pole is, therefore, at the same time accumulation of misery, agony of toil slavery, ignorance, brutality, mental degradation, at the opposite pole, *i.e.,* on the side of the class that produces its own product in the form of capital. (*Marx-Engels-Werke*, Bd. 23, 675)

In its more detailed formulation, the general law, finally, reads as follows:

> The greater the social wealth, the functioning capital, the extent and energy of its growth, and therefore also the greater the absolute mass of the proletariat and the productivity of its labour, the greater is the industrial reserve army. The same causes which develop the expansive power of capital, also develop the labour-power at its disposal. The relative mass of the industrial reserve army thus increases with the potential energy of wealth. But the greater this reserve army in proportion to the active labour-army, the greater is the mass of a consolidated surplus population, whose misery is in inverse ratio to the amount of torture it has to undergo in the form of labour. The more extensive, finally,

> the pauperized sections of the working class and the industrial reserve army, the greater is official pauperism. *This is the absolute general law of capitalist accumulation.* Like all other laws, it is modified in its working by many circumstances, the analysis of which does not concern us here. (Marx-Engels-Werke, Bd. 23, 673–674)

Hence, the tendency for the development of the productive forces under, and fostered by, capitalist relations of production results in a series of deep contradictions. Next, we present just some of those, pointing to a number of themes that, in our view, might be addressed following Marx's reflections in chapter 23:

i. Nature. While one might be accused of attempting to read too much into Marx's general law, it is worth pointing to the fact that several exemplifications of the impact of the development of the productive forces on nature (under capitalist relations of production) can be found in section 5 of chapter 23 ("Illustrations of the General Law of Capitalist Accumulation"). Here, the "dialectical inversion" mentioned previously and the deleterious impact on the development of the productive forces under capitalist relations of production upon nature are discussed.
ii. Population, relative surplus population, and the Reserve Army of Labour. Marx outlines the specificities of demographic development within capitalism, arguing that capital accumulation is accompanied by an increase of the proletariat (understood, simply, as persons who do not control the means of production and might just be able to sell their labour-power): "The same causes which develop the expansive power of capital, also develop the labour-power at its disposal" (*Marx-Engels-Werke*, Bd. 23, 673). At the same time, the increase in the productivity of labour results in the fact that not all labour-power thus created is absorbed by capital. Hence, the creation of a *relative* surplus population—*relative* to the instant requirements of capital accumulation. As his analysis on the Industrial Reserve of Labour suggests and as different chapters within this volume show, the latter is far more complex and richer than the concept of "unemployment." Importantly, the process is also accompanied by the tendency to increase the organic composition of capital (the ratio between constant capital and variable capital). Note that these processes cannot be reduced to the introduction of new technology and machinery alone. As Marx shows, there are several means by which the productivity of labour might be increased (see especially chapters 11 and 12 of *Capital*, Volume I).
iii. The conditions of existence of the working class, including, but not limited to, poverty, inequality, migration, and social reproduction. The two

main conditions in capitalist production, according to Marx, are that (a) workers operate under the control of the capitalist and (b) that the product of their labour belongs to the capitalist (*Marx-Engels-Werke*, Bd. 23, 199). As is well known, workers are exploited because there is a difference between the *value of the commodity labour-power* capitalists buy (paying a wage) and the *value produced* by the commodity labour-power. The result is that the quota of the total riches produced that goes to the producers diminishes. This, jointly with point (ii), calls forth reflections on inequality, poverty, and social reproduction as well as the identification of the causes that lead to migration. While one might initially contemplate those excluded from the production process (i.e., the Reserve Army of Labour), it should be also noted that the nefarious effects of capital accumulation also apply to the "active working population" independently from their income as their subordinated relation persists (and subordinated persons cannot, of course, enjoy "freedom"). Higher wages or even better working conditions, as Marx writes in the same chapter:

> no more abolish the exploitation of the wage-laborer, and his situation of dependence, than do better clothing, food and treatment, and a larger *peculium*, in the case of the slave. A rise in the price of labor, as a consequence of the accumulation of capital, only means in fact that the length and weight of the golden chain the wage-laborer has already forged for himself allow it to be loosened somewhat. (*Marx-Engels-Werke*, Bd. 23, 646)

iv. Macroeconomic dynamics, wages, and competition. The chapter is useful for understanding and theorizing macroeconomic dynamics (though as Cámara observes in this volume, it is crucial to integrate organically the different sections of the chapter, and not to dwell exclusively on its individual sections). Also, as Mariña shows, it offers an important contribution to the theorization of the determination of wages. Finally, Marx needs to anticipate some considerations on the functioning of competition between capitals in chapter 10 ("The Concept of Relative Surplus Value") developing it further in *Capital*, volume III. Yet crucial aspects of the concrete workings of competition, related, for example, to the concentration and centralization of capital, are presented in chapter 23 as also Leinad Alcalá illustrates (see chapter 1).

v. Imperialism, dependency, and underdevelopment. Interestingly, some of the few explicit notes on these subjects in *Capital*, in particular Marx's comments on Ireland and its subordinated position to Britain, are to be found within the historical section of chapter 23. In this volume, it is argued that Marx's general law might be understood as a pioneering contribution to the understanding of the development of underdevelopment.

Further, imperialist practices are crucial for understanding how the relative surplus population is both concretely forged and channeled.

vi. Multiple crises. The chapter does not offer a theory of capitalist breakdown. Rather, it offers hints to a series of contradictions (some of which pointed out earlier) that might result in crises. Hence and as highlighted, it provides clues for understanding ecological crises while also contributing to explain inequality and poverty and possible crises of social reproduction. Moreover, and as is known, the same causes that lead to the general law—an increase in the productivity of labour and the rise in the organic composition of capital—are also crucial for The Law of the Tendency of the Rate of Profit to Fall (see English translation of Capital, Vol III) of the general rate of profit that contributes to the understanding of economic crises. Finally, and relatedly, the chapter tenders important elements for analyzing social and political crises.

As we can discern from the aforementioned text, the general law of capitalist accumulation is central to the understanding of the capitalist mode of production, its dynamics, and its (multiple) crises. Simon Clarke went as far as to argue—perhaps correctly—that the general law represents "the culmination of the analysis of Volume One of *Capital,* and which is for Marx politically the most important consequence of the contradictory form of capitalist production" (Clarke 1994, 251). As also Cámara (see chapter 3) states in this volume, "the general law of capitalist accumulation is an indispensable theoretical foundation for the analysis of the macrodynamics of capitalist accumulation in Marxist economic theory."

While there are notable exceptions (e.g., Foster, McChesney and Jonna 2011; Mateo 2018; Merrifield 2019; Bahçe 2020; Bernards and Soederberg 2020), it is quite remarkable that despite the growing interest in Marxism that occurred in light of the Long Depression (using Michael Roberts' labeling of the otherwise called Great Recession) (Roberts 2016), only few analyses refer explicitly to the importance of Marx's general law of capitalist accumulation. Interestingly, this was not always the case. Independently from the point of view one might share or not, the great (heated) debates that occurred in the late 19th century and thereafter were based on an assessment of Marx's general law and its political implications. Famously, Karl Kautsky's political assessments were largely based on Marx's general law. As Jukka Gronow has recently highlighted, in Kautsky's view,

> The general law of capitalist accumulation was a central law of capitalism. To Kautsky it was a historical, empirical law predicting the future development of capitalism toward the increasing concentration of capital in the hands of the capitalist class. As a result, the increasing numbers of wage workers who constituted the great majority of the population faced diminishing numbers

> of capitalists who accumulated increasing amounts of capital in their hands. Together with its other side, the immiseration of the working class, the law predicted the polarization of the bourgeois society into two antagonistic social classes. (Kautsky 1907–1908). This became the basic doctrine of the inevitability of the coming socialist revolution. (Gronow 2021, 67)

Revisionist arguments as those developed by Eduard Bernstein, while leading to different interpretations and political conclusions, were also based on reflections upon Marx's general law (Howard and King 1989, 76). It is also noteworthy that even Antonio Gramsci related what he referred to as the "organic crisis" to Marx's general law of capitalist accumulation and the law of the tendencial fall of the general rate of profit (Fusaro 2020). Classical theories of imperialism also evoked aspects of Marx's general law. Moreover, in the 1960 and 1970s, at least a selected reading of chapter 23 influenced the theorization of *Monopoly Capital* (Baran and Sweezy 1966) and important debates on unemployment and the business cycle (Goodwin, 1967).

At the same time, it is striking that opponents of Marxism attacked exactly Marx's general law. Thus, while even claiming to sharing some of Marx's insights, Popper stated:

> [Marx's] law that misery must increase together with accumulation does not hold. Means of production have accumulated and the productivity of labour has increased since his day to an extent which even he would hardly have thought possible. But child labour, working hours, the agony of toil, and the precariousness of the worker's existence, have not increased; they have declined. . . . Experience shows that Marx's prophecies were false. (Popper 1945, 391–392, quoted in Fuchs 2016, 297)

Following the previous discussion, it can be stated that the interpretation proposed by Popper is misleading. For as we have shown, Marx's insights are exactly based on an increase of the productivity of labour. It is not its lack, or its slow increase, that brings about the nasty scenario Popper does not want to see. As illustrated, due to the "dialectical inversion" under capitalist relations of production that we highlighted, the rise in the productivity of labour results in unwanted consequences. Despite this, it appears that Western Marxism willy-nilly accepted the aforementioned critique, neglecting Marx's central law. This has been somewhat different in Latin America where in the 1960s, some *Dependentistas*, drawing on and discussing of chapter 23, coined the concept of *marginalidad* (Quijano 1966; Nun 1969) referring to that part of the surplus population that, in their view, is "afunctional" or "dysfunctional" to capital accumulation. Turning to contemporary and influential Marxist contributions, as, for example, those provided by David Harvey (2010) and

Michael Heinrich (2012), we notice that they do not grant great attention to Marx's general law. Partially this might be due to the fact that they dismiss the validity of some crucial theoretical blocks, as, for example, the tendency for the organic composition of capital to rise, that are crucial to Marx's general law of capitalist accumulation and, as mentioned previously, also related the law of the tendency of the rate of profit to fall. Denying the existence of the former tendency makes it intellectually difficult to grant importance to Marx's general law of capitalist accumulation.

THE CONTRIBUTION OF THE PRESENT VOLUME

It is starting from this background that our Research Group in Political Economy (*Área de Sociedad y Acumulación Capitalista* [ASAC]), based at the Universidad Autónoma Metropolitana in Mexico City, jointly with other colleagues from other universities interested in this topic, has decided to take up the theme of Marx's general law and discuss it in periodical seminars resulting in this book project. This, after having gone through a similar successful process on another topic in critical political economy between 2016 and 2018, that resulted in a further collected book titled *La naturaleza contradictoria del capitalismo contemporanéo* that has been published in 2020 (Cámara 2020).

As emerged from our debates, and as has been detailed earlier, Marx's general law is essential for understanding and characterizing the main economic dynamics of the capitalist mode of production, and, at the same time, a helpful analytical tool for discerning and interpreting social and political developments that characterize the contemporary world economy. The aim of this collected volume is then to offer readers an in-depth analysis of Marx's general law and to show its fruitful application to the analysis of contemporary capitalism with a particular focus on Latin America, albeit drawing also on further examples beyond this region.

The book, made up of 11 chapters that engage with Marx's general law, is divided into two parts. The first part, Revisiting Marx's General Law presents an in-depth (re)reading of Marx's work starting with Leinad Alcalá's chapter "The General Law of Capitalist Accumulation: A Methodological Analysis from the Theory of Capital" that situates Marx's General law within the overall architecture of his work from the perspective of the concept of capital. In the next chapter, Roberto Fineschi introduces the idea of "crepuscular capitalism," pointing to ongoing profound political transformations that result from the General law of capitalist accumulation. Sergio Cámara's contribution "The General Law of Capitalist Accumulation and a Theory of Labor-Shortage Business Cycles" argues that the law is an indispensable theoretical foundation for analyzing macroeconomic dynamics and even short-term macrodynamics, provided that the chapter is interpreted in its integrity and different time frames are considered. This first part of the book concludes with Abelardo Mariña's and Sibyl Italia Pineda Salazar's chapters that turn to the theme of labour examining how the general law is helpful in determining the value of labour-power, in analyzing wage fluctuations, and (re)interpreting the idea of precarious labour.

The second part of the collected volume Underdevelopment, Imperialism, and the Industrial Reserve Army of Labour in Latin America and Beyond explores important topics in political economy focusing especially, but not exclusively, on Latin America from the perspective of Marx's law. This part of the book opens with Fusaro's contribution that argues that Marx's general law offers an important analytical tool for understanding the "development of underdevelopment." Lucia Pradella and Rossana Cillo assert that imperialism and colonialism have played and still play a crucial role in the expansion of the Industrial Reserve Army of Labour. Historically, as Matari Pierre outlines in his chapter engaging with Marini's "Dialectics of Dependency," the creation of a relative surplus population has made "susper-explotation" possible. However, Matari argues, the latter process has been unsustainable in the long run. Still, as William Robinson argues, digitalization is expected to increase exponentially the surplus labour population and might represent a dangerous and politically explosive group. Felipe Docoa's chapter explores the actual composition of the Industrial Reserve Army for the case of Mexico. Finally, Carlos Alberto Duque Garcia's chapter analyzes the dynamics of unpaid domestic work and social reproduction in Mexico within Marx's general law. Through this collected volume, we therefore hope to exhibit the pertinence and actuality of Marx's general law and to stimulate academic and political debates in Latin America and beyond.

NOTE

1. Throughout the introduction, we follow the German original within the *Marx-Engels Werke*, providing the English translation. Unlike the English editions of *Capital*, both within the *Marx-Engels Werke* and the Spanish edition, the chapter titled "The General Law of Capitalist Accumulation" is chapter 23 (and not 25, as in the English editions).

BIBLIOGRAPHY

Baran, Paul A. and Sweezy, Paul M. *Monopoly Capital*. New York and London: Monthly Review Press.

Bernards, Nick and Soederberg, Susanne. 2020. "Relative Surplus Populations and the Crises of Contemporary Capitalism: Reviving, Revisiting, Recasting." *Geoforum*. Online: https://www.sciencedirect.com/science/article/abs/pii/S0016718520302931?via%3Dihub.

Bahçe, Serdal. 2019. "Is 'The General Law of Capitalist Accumulation' Still Valid? An Analysis Based on Direct and Indirect Marxian Effects." *Munich Personal RePEc Archive*. Online: https://mpra.ub.uni-muenchen.de/101266/1/MPRA_paper_101266.pdf.

Callinicos, Alex. 2021. "Neoliberal Capitalism Implodes: Global Catastrophe and the Far Right Today." *International Socialism*, 170. Online: http://isj.org.uk/implodes-catastrophe/.

Cámara, Sergio (ed.). 2020. *La naturaleza contradictoria del capitalismo contemporáneo*. México: UAM.

CEPAL (Comisión Económica para América Latina; Economic Commission for Latin America). 2020. "Enfrentar los efectos cada vez mayores del COVID-19 para la reactivación con igualdad: nuevas proyecciones." *Informe Especial COVID-10*. Online: https://www.cepal.org/es/publicaciones/45782-enfrentar-efectos-cada-vez-mayores-covid-19-reactivacion-igualdad-nuevas.

Clarke, Simon. 1994. *Marx's Theory of Crisis*. New York: St. Martin's Press.

Foster, Bellamy and Suvandi, Intan. 2020. "Covid 19 and Catastrophe Capitalism." *Monthly Review,* 72, 2. Online: https://monthlyreview.org/2020/06/01/covid-19-and-catastrophe-capitalism/.

Foster, John Bellamy, McChesney, Robert and Jonna, Jamil. (2011). "The Global Reserve Army of Labor and the New Imperialism." *Monthly Review*. Online: https://monthlyreview.org/2011/11/01/the-global-reserve-army-of-labor-and-the-new-imperialism/.

Fuchs, Christian. 2016. *Reading Marx in the Information Age*. London: Routledge.

Fusaro, Lorenzo. 2020. "The *Gramscian Moment* in International Political Economy." In *Revisiting Gramsci's Notebooks*, edited by Francesca Antonini, Aaron Bernstein, Lorenzo Fusaro and Robert Jackson. Leiden and Boston: Brill.

Goodwin, Richard. 1967. "A Growth Cycle." In *Socialism, Capitalism, and Economic Growth. Essays Presented to Maurice Dobb*, edited by Charles Feinstein, 54–59. Cambridge: Cambridge University Press.

Gronow, Jukka. 2021. "Karl Kautsky." In *Routledge Handbook of Marxism and Post-Marxism*, edited by Alex Callinicos, Stathiks Kouvelakis and Lucia Pradella. London: Routledge.

Harvey, David. 2010. *A Companion to Marx's Capital*. London: Verso.

Heinrich, Michael. 2004. *An Introduction to the Three Volumes of Karl Marx's* Capital. New York: Monthly Review Press.

Hobsbawm, Eric. 1994. *Age of Extremes: The Short Twentieth Century, 1914–1991*. London: Michael Joseph; New York: Viking Penguin.

Howard, Michael Charles, and John Edward King. 1989. *A History of Marxian Economics, Volume I, 1883–1929*. Princeton, NJ: Princeton University Press.

IPCC (Intergovernmental Panel on Climate Change). 2021. Climate Change 2021. Online: https://www.ipcc.ch/report/ar6/wg1/downloads/report/IPCC_AR6_WGI_Full_Report_smaller.pdf.

Keynes, John Maynard. 1930. "Economic Possibilities for our Grandchildren." Online: https://www.marxists.org/reference/subject/economics/keynes/1930/our-grandchildren.htm.

Maddison, Angus. 2006. *The World Economy, Volume 1: A Millennial Perspective; Volume 2: Historical Statistics*. Paris: OECD.

Marx, Karl, and Friedrich Engels. 1956–1990. *Marx-Engels-Werke (forty-three volumes)*. Berlin: Dietz Verlag.

Mateo, Juan Pablo. 2018. "Capital, trabajo y la ley general de la acumulación." In *Sociología Histórica*, 9, 507–534.

Merrifield, Andy. 2019. "Notes on Marx's General Law of Capitalist Accumulation." *Monthly Review*. Online. Online: https://mronline.org/2019/06/19/notes-on-marxs-general-law-of-capitalist.

NBER (National Bureau of Economic Research). 2021. "Collaborating During Coronavirus: The Impact of COVID-19 on the Nature of Work" by Evan DeFilippis, Stephen Michael Impink, Madison Singell, Jeffrey T. Polzer & Raffaella Sadun. Online: https://www.nber.org/papers/w27612.

Nun, José. 1969. "Superpoblacion relativa, ejercito industrial de reserva y masa marginal." *Revista lationamericana de sociologia*, 66, 178–123.

Oxfam. 2020. "Tiempo para el cuidado: El trabajo de cuidados y la crisis global de desigualdad." *Informe de Oxfam*. Online: https://oxfamilibrary.openrepository.com/bitstream/handle/10546/620928/bp-time-to-care-inequality-200120-es.pdf.

Quijano, Anibal. 1966. "Notas sobre el concepto de marginalidad social." CEPAL, octubre 1966.

Roberts, Michael. 2016. *The Long Depression. Marxism and the Global Crisis of Capitalism*. Chicago: Haymarket Books.

UN United Nations. 2020. "Introduction." *United Nation Summit on Biodiversity*. Online: https://www.un.org/pga/75/united-nations-summit-on-biodiversity/.

Wolf, Martin. 2021. "The Strange Death of American Democracy." *Financial Times 28.09.2021*. Online: https://www.ft.com/content/a2e499d0-10f0-4fa2-8243-e23eedc4f9f4.

Part I

REVISITING MARX'S GENERAL LAW

Chapter 1

The General Law of Capitalist Accumulation

A Comprehensive Reading from the Perspective of the Systematic Structure of Capital

Leinad Johan Alcalá Sandoval

The *general law of capitalist accumulation* (GLCA) is one of the most significant contributions to the examination of the dynamics of the capitalist mode of production. The analysis of the law and its implications has been studied by several Marxist authors. In general, at least two approaches can be identified for interpreting and analyzing the implications of the GLCA. First, the approach that considers necessary to adopt a methodological perspective based on a reading of *Capital* as a work organized into systematically articulated levels of abstraction (*see* Smith 1990; Reuten, 2004; Fineschi 2018); and second, the approach that examines and interprets the law without considering this methodological perspective (*see* Fine and Saad-Filho 2004; Harvey 2010; Guerrero 2010). This chapter considers that a methodological interpretation based on the systematic structure of capital enables a comprehensive reading of the GLCA.

The aim of this chapter is to show that exposition of the GLCA is fundamental to the development of the structure of capital and consistent with the systematic ordering employed by Marx in *Capital*. In this way, a comprehensive reading of the law in relation to the levels of abstraction is proposed, one that makes it possible to show the systematic connections, examining the methodological limits and indicating the analytical implications. The rest of the chapter is organized into four additional sections. In the second section, arguments are presented to show that *Capital* is a work organized in different levels of abstraction, emphasizing the importance of the development of the concept of capital in order to study the capitalist mode of production as a totality. In the third section, a theoretical framework is put forward to examine the methodological implications of the analysis of accumulation in volume I, together with its relationship with the systematic structure of capital. The fourth section makes a methodological evaluation of the GLCA to identify the theoretical elements involved in a comprehensive reading. Finally, the fifth section presents the conclusion.

CAPITAL: A BOOK ORGANIZED INTO DIFFERENT LEVELS OF ABSTRACTION

In *Capital*, Marx aims to investigate the capitalist mode of production and to "bring to light the economic law that governs the movement of modern society" (Marx 1867 [2013], 21). The book is a *critique of political economy*[1] organized as a theoretical project of *investigation* and *presentation* of the capitalist mode of production.[2] The *investigation* consists of the collection of empirical data. It is an analytical process of critical appropriation of the empirical perception of the capitalist mode of production as a totality. The outcome is the identification of the economic categories that describe the functioning of capitalist society.[3] Having reached this point, the *presentation* involves the systematic ordering of the research results. It orders the economic categories that describe the movement of the capitalist mode of production, that is, a synthetic reconstruction of what is being investigated as a representation of the "totality of many determinations and relationships" (Marx 1857/1858 [2011], 21). Dialectical logic is the method of presenting the totality represented by capital.[4]

The development of the concept of capital consists in the progression of *moments*[5] structured at different levels of abstraction. The logical progression of categories provides a systematic structure based on the conceptual reproduction of the concrete in successive stages,[6] that is, a movement of *overcoming* from abstract and simple categories to increasingly concrete and complex one.[7] From the perspective of dialectical logic, the *overcoming* of categories is a process in which these are regressively based, that is, the categories are determined progressively while preserving the determinations of the preceding ones. In this way, it is shown that all the categories are necessary for the progression and that they are mutually conditioned (*see* Robles & Escorcia 2013). This results in a systematic ordering organized in levels of abstraction that correspond to the development of the presentation of capital.

The concept of capital is the basis for studying capitalist society; it is "the economic power of bourgeois society, which dominates everything. It must constitute the point of departure and of arrival" (Marx 1857/1858 [2011],

28). In this way, the concept provides a systematic structure to examine the capitalist mode of production from the logical progression of categories articulated in levels of abstraction. For this reason, it is necessary to

> produce a precise analysis of the concept of capital, since it is the basic concept of modern economics just as capital itself, which is its abstract reflection, is the basis of bourgeois society. From a clear perception of the basic premise of the relationship all the contradictions of bourgeois production must emerge as also the limit at which it progresses beyond itself. (Marx 1857/1858 [2011], 273)

In *Capital*, the most complete exposition of the theory of capital is found.[8] Each volume has a specific objective related to the conceptual development of capital. Thus, volume I (1867) is subtitled *The Process of Production of Capital*, which reflects the fact that its central objective is to analyze the conditions of capital production as a result of the formation of surplus value. The work is complemented by the analysis of *The Process of Circulation of Capital*, the objective of volume II (1885) and, finally, the analysis of *The Process of Capitalist Production as a Whole*, which corresponds to volume III (1893). In this way, the division of the work aims to analyze each *moment* necessary for the configuration of capital as a *process*.[9] This is pointed out by Marx in part 1 of volume III:

> In *Book I we analysed* the phenomena which constitute the *process of capitalist production* as such, as the immediate productive *process*, with no regard for any of the secondary effects of outside influences. But this immediate *process* of production does not exhaust the life span of capital. It is supplemented in the *actual world by the process of circulation*, which was the *object of study in Book II*. In the latter, namely in *Part III*, which treated the *process* of circulation as a medium for the *process* of social reproduction, it developed that the *capitalist process of production* taken as a *whole* represents *a synthesis of the processes of production and circulation*. Considering what this *third book treats*, it cannot confine itself to general reflection relative to this synthesis. On the contrary, it must locate and *describe the concrete forms which grow out of the movements of capital* as a *whole*. In their *actual movement capitals confront each other in such concrete shape*, for which the form of capital in the immediate *process* of production, just as its form in the process of circulation, *appear only as special instances*. The various forms of capital, as evolved in this book, thus approach step by step the form which they *assume on the surface of society*, in the action of different *capitals upon one another*, in *competition*, and in the ordinary consciousness of the agents of production themselves. (Marx 1894 [2011], 29–30, emphasis added)

The systematic structure of the concept of capital is organized into three levels of abstraction in *Capital*, namely, universality, particularity, and singularity (Fineschi 2001).[10] The first begins with the exposition of the *emergence of capital from money* and incorporates the relationship between capital and labour. At this level of abstraction, capital is considered in its general form, that is, as *capital in general*, which is the "one and all at the same time, it develops until the profit is produced, for which it is divided into more than one" (Fineschi 2018, 319). The second corresponds to the study of the different forms that capital adopts to compete among itself for a share of the surplus value. At this level of abstraction, the action of each capital brings into "existence previously developed universal laws" (Fineschi 2018). The final level is the complete fetishization of capital, "money that creates more money" (Marx 1894 [2011], 500), which takes the form of interest-bearing capital as a "particular that acts as a universal" (Fineschi 2018).

The formulation of the GLCA is presented by Marx in universality.[11] Indeed, the analysis of the *capital accumulation process* and of the GLCA corresponds to part 7 of volume I. The aim of this section is to examine accumulation without considering the *actual production conditions*, that is, leaving aside the analysis of the *Process of Circulation of Capital* and of the *Process of Capitalist Production as a Whole*. Thus, the objective is to analyze "accumulation in abstract terms" (Marx 1867 [2013], 692). However, it is in chapter 23[12] where the most important theoretical conclusions about the effect of the antagonistic nature of accumulation on the reproduction of the labour force are found, that is, the consequences of the *real conditions of the capitalist production process* about the working class.

The GLCA captures the movement of capital that structures capitalist society. For this reason, in the formulation of the law, categories and determinations that correspond to later levels of abstraction, namely particularity and singularity, are assumed. A comprehensive reading and methodological perspective shows that the categories that Marx incorporates for the formulation do not break with the ordering of the presentation that corresponds to the systematic structure of capital.

THE ANALYSIS OF ACCUMULATION IN UNIVERSALITY: METHODOLOGICAL IMPLICATIONS

Universality aims to study the conditions for the *valorization* of capital; the emergence and conservation of capital is shown to be a *value in process*. In this way, the level of abstraction encompasses the analysis of the *process of production of capital* and the *process of circulation of capital*. The objective of the *process of production of capital* is to reveal the conditions that allow the valorization of value through the production of commodities and the formation of surplus value; in this way, the *process of circulation of capital* shows the movement of capital to ensure its reproduction. Both *processes* find in *living labor* the *mediation* that allows capital *to conserve its identity, reproduce itself, and constantly increase*, adding a surplus. This surplus is the result of the exploitation of labour-power,[13] of the constant production of surplus value to accumulate it in the form of capital. Accumulation takes place on the basis of the *antithetical relationship* between capital and labour.[14] In this way, the exploitation of labour-power is the productive and reproductive force of capital.

In this context, Marx begins the development of the analysis of accumulation in part 7 in correspondence with the methodological implications imposed by *capital in general*, that is, based on the assumptions and limitations that belong to this level of abstraction.[15] Indeed, universality entails analytical implications about what can or cannot be developed in the context of *capital in general*. In the first place, the analysis of accumulation is carried out considering an *average capital*, "thus abstracting from intra- and inter-branch differences, including differing production periods and compositions of capital" (Reuten 2004, 3). Second, the assumption is that commodities are always sold at their value. In this sense, capital accumulation is achieved when the capitalist manages to sell all the goods produced and to reconvert the money extracted from this process into capital again. Thus, supply coincides with demand, avoiding any problems with realization and crisis. Finally, the *transmuted forms of surplus value*, that is, the fractions into which surplus value can be divided (profit of enterprise, commercial profit, interest, and ground-rent).[16]

Accumulation in the Development of the Systematic Structure of Capital

Fineschi (2018) points out that Marx examines accumulation in universality dividing it into two parts. The first part is incorporated before the analysis of circulation (*Accumulation I*). The second part is incorporated with the analysis of circulation (*Accumulation II*).[17] In this way, *Accumulation I* corresponds to the analysis of accumulation as a *moment* of the immediate process of *production*, in which the conditions of the reproduction of individual capital in its simple and extended form are examined. Meanwhile, *Accumulation II* corresponds to the analysis of accumulation as a *moment* of the capital circulation process, in which the conditions of the reproduction of the *overall social capital* through the movement of multiple capitals are examined.[18] Both are constitutive moments of the whole, so there is a systematic connection that conditions their development.

Indeed, Marx anticipates with the analysis of *accumulation I* the articulation between individual capital and multiple capitals.[19] Individual capital requires the relationship with *other* capitals to be able to generate "the abstract conditions of its existence" (Fineschi 2018, 328). The *other* capitals are part of the reproduction of the *aggregate social capital*, that is, they constitute the movement of social capital.[20] In this way, *capital in general* is a structure that includes the "one-multiple relationship" (Fineschi 2018, 327)[21] because without multiple capitals, "it is not possible to think of accumulation and, therefore, of the very evolution of capital as a totality" (Fineschi 2018, 330). Therefore, the multiple capitals are

> necessary for the theorization of individual reproduction. Their interaction must be formalized before entering the world of competition, studying the pure formal and material proportionality through which their production and reproduction can take place. In essence, before capital and profit. Without this part of the theory, capital cannot yet lay out its presuppositions properly and completely. (Fineschi 2018, 329)[22]

The analysis of accumulation is key to the development of universality. The division of the exposition at this level of abstraction is necessary for the theorization of capital and therefore for the development of the subsequent levels of abstraction. Accumulation is a category that fulfills a methodological function, that of guaranteeing the articulation between the levels of abstraction that comprise the systematic structure of capital.

Accumulation articulates the levels of abstraction that make up the systematic structure of capital, that is, it provides the determinations that underlie the systematic connection between universality, particularity, and singularity, whereby the structure of capital is complete. In this regard, Fineschi (2018) points out that in its own *internal articulation*, accumulation produces "as its own results what were initially its unpositioned presuppositions. Achieving this means producing the 'positioned-presuppositions'" (Fineschi 2018, 317).[23]

Thus, the position of accumulation in universality *produces* the *presuppositions-positions* that allow the development of the systematic structure of capital. Without the presentation of the theory of accumulation at this level of abstraction, capital cannot "position its own presuppositions" (Fineschi 2018, 319), meaning that it is not configured either as a *process* or as a totality. Consequently, accumulation theory becomes "the true key to the development of Marx's theory" (Fineschi 2018, 317), so the author decides to present it systematically in part 7 of volume I:

> The structure that we find in Capital (the book) represents the final solution to this series of reconsiderations. Here Marx comes to the conclusion that it is not

> enough to think of the simple production of capital and reproduction of singular capital (the genus one and all at the same time), as it initially appeared, but also the conditions of reproduction of the multiples. It is a question of setting out the forms of continuity of this process of production of use value through value and of value through use value (the contradiction immanent to commodities). Production cannot be anything other than a process that is continuously repeated, hence it is reproduction (Marx 1991, 506; trans. Ital. 621; Marx 1976–80, 2243). (Fineschi 2018, 327)

Accumulation continues to develop at the subsequent levels of the theory of capital, namely, in particularity, with the exposition of competition, and in singularity, "where real accumulation . . . and fictitious accumulation occur in parallel" (Fineschi 2018, 331). However, for reasons of space, it is not possible to present here in detail the link between accumulation and these levels of abstraction.[24] This chapter is limited to methodologically assessing part 7, where the GLCA is formulated.

Brief Methodological Evaluation of Part 7

Part 7 of volume I corresponds to the analysis of accumulation in connection with the *capital production process*, that is, with *Accumulation I*. In this regard, Smith (1990) demonstrates the systematic connections that exist between the production process and the accumulation process based on the dialectical reconstruction of the categories that belong to the *form of capital*.[25] This reconstruction shows that the analysis of the capital production process culminates with the incorporation of accumulation; therefore, the result is consistent with the ordering and logical progression that "is clearly found at the end of the first volume of *Capital*" (Smith 1990, 144).

Likewise, Reuten (2004) performs a methodological assessment of part 7 and points out that, at this level of abstraction, Marx is considering accumulation "merely as a *moment* of the immediate process of production" (Reuten 2004, 1, emphasis added), that is, he analyzes it in the context of "the *capital-labor relation in general*" (Reuten 2004, 4, emphasis added). In this way, part 7 is limited to examining only the *inner mechanism of capital accumulation* (Reuten 2004)[26] consistent with the "systematic-dialectical methodology" (Reuten 2004, 18).

Consequently, Smith (1990) and Reuten (2004) agree that the exposition of part 7 is consistent with the systematic ordering based on dialectical logic. Specifically, Reuten (2004) points out that the first three chapters of this part can be considered as *systematic chapters*.[27]

Indeed, Marx begins his analysis based on simplified notions of the process, that is, with *simple reproduction*; this is the "first step in a systematic grasp of 'accumulation' on this level of abstraction" (Smith 1990, 135). *Simple reproduction* is defined as "the reiteration of the production process on the same scale" (Marx 1867 [2013], 696). Subsequently, it incorporates the analysis of the *transformation of surplus value into capital*, that is, the *large-scale reproduction process*, the *elementary form of accumulation.*[28] This sets out how capital grows through the reinvestment of surplus value, that is, through the "use of surplus value as capital, or the reconversion of surplus value into capital" (Marx 1867 [2013], 713).[29] The third chapter of the section analyzes the consequences of the increase of capital on the working class, manifested in a general law of accumulation. A methodological evaluation of this chapter is the basis for developing a comprehensive reading of the GLCA.

THE GLCA AND THE SYSTEMATIC STRUCTURE OF CAPITAL: ELEMENTS FOR A COMPREHENSIVE READING

Chapter 23 is divided into five sections that set out how the GLCA develops and manifests itself.[30] These include categories and theoretical references that accompany the formulation of the law but that cannot be developed because they belong to later levels of abstraction. Indeed, Marx is aware that the use of the concepts is limited by the level of abstraction, so he cannot explore the implications to the full, and this leads him to simplify the analysis in order to present the main conclusions. This means that in the presentation of the chapter, there are categories with analytical implications that go beyond the objective of expounding universality; as a result, they are returned to in later levels of abstraction. In this way, Marx is showing that the GLCA is linked with the development of the systematic structure of capital.

The chapter states that there is a relationship between the accumulation process and the reproduction of the working class that is expressed in a *population law*, which is inherent in the capitalist mode of production. Indeed, in the capitalist mode of production, "the labourer exists to satisfy the needs of self-expansion" (Marx 1867 [2013], 769); consequently, it is the level of accumulation that regulates the absolute and relative changes in the amount of labour-power available and required. In this way, the effects of changes in the *composition of capital* and the increase of individual capital and global social capital, that is, of the *concentration* and *centralization* of capital,[31] in the reproduction of the labour force, are examined.

A comprehensive reading requires interpreting the conclusions of each section, methodologically evaluating which elements of the presentation are consistent with the corresponding level of abstraction, and which anticipate and are connected with the development of the theory of accumulation at subsequent levels of abstraction.

Attraction of Labour-Power

The objective of part 1 is to examine the effects of accumulation on the variable part of capital assuming that the *composition of capital* remains constant. Composition is considered in two ways, with respect to value (*value composition*) and with respect to the ratio between the mass of employed means of production and the amount of labour required for their employment (*technical composition*). The correlation between the two is expressed in the *organic composition of capital* (Marx 1867 [2013], 759).[32]

In this respect, Marx is ambiguous when it comes to clearly distinguishing the conceptual variations related to the *composition of capital*. In this chapter, the use of the definitions is not always consistent and sometimes the terms change as the analysis progresses (Reuten 2004).[33] So, at the beginning, Marx claims that "wherever I refer to the composition of capital, without further qualification, its organic composition is always understood" (Marx 1867 [2013], 760), without going at depth or explaining the meaning of this simplification.

The concept of *organic composition of capital* appears for the first time in the French edition of volume I (Fineschi 2018), and the development of the chapter does not go deeper into the justification of the concept, meaning that its incorporation can be seen as controversial (Reuten 2004). The analysis of the *composition of capital* is taken up again in part 2 of volume II (in the analysis of the *Turnover of Capital*)[34] (Marx 1885 [2011], 183) and, later, in the part 3 of volume III (when presenting the *Law of the Tendency of the Rate of Profit to Fall*) (Marx 1894 [2011], 269). The latter corresponds to the level of abstraction of particularity.[35]

The main conclusion of this section is that "*growth of capital* involves growth of its variable constituent or of the part invested in labour power" (Marx 1867 [2013], 759). In other words, the demand for labour increases proportionally to the increase in capital, causing a process of attraction of labour-power. In this context, Marx highlights some analytical implications related to the effects of capital accumulation.

Firstly, he shows that the accumulation of capital constantly reproduces, in an expanded way, the capitalist character of the production process[36]; therefore, as accumulation progresses, the relationship of dependency between capital and labour is also reinforced. In this way, "*Accumulation of capital is, therefore, increase of the proletariat*" (Marx 1867 [2013], 761). Secondly, he states that the course of accumulation leads to fluctuations in wage levels, and that the price of labour is always a function of the "needs of the self-expansion of capital" (Marx 1867 [2013], 769).[37] Thus, the conclusion of part 1 shows that, in the capitalist mode of production, it is the level of accumulation that regulates the demand for labour, as well as its price.[38]

The conclusion and analytical implications of part 1 correspond to the level of abstraction of universality. The analysis takes place in the context of accumulation as an immediate *moment* in the process of capital production, consistent with the determinations that correspond to *capital in general* and with the systematic structure of capital.

Repulsion of the Labour-Power and Formation of Global Social Capital

Part 2 examines the effects of the "Relative Diminution of the Variable Part of Capital Simultaneously with the Progress of Accumulation and of the Concentration that Accompanies it" (Marx 1867 [2011], 771). It sets out two themes that are central for the formulation of the GLCA. The first is related to the analysis of the demand for labour as the *technical composition of capital* increases; the second examines the process of *attraction* and *repulsion* of individual capitals.

Marx points out that in the course of accumulation, the *technical composition of capital* increases, altering the *social degree of labor productivity*[39]; this causes a decrease in the demand for labour, that is, the development of the productive force leads to the repulsion of the labour force.[40] This conclusion is consistent with the determinations of the corresponding level of abstraction. In this regard, Reuten asserts that, when analyzing the effects of variations in the *technical composition of capital* on the demand for labour, Marx is proposing an examination of the factors influencing the acceleration of accumulation in the context of the *capital-labor relation*:

> Marx first sets out the elementary shape of accumulation: extension or growth of capital. Next he shows how this growth accelerates in combination with the development of the productive forces of labor (section 2 below). And finally he introduces another accelerator: the technical composition of capital (section 3 below). All along his focus is on the dynamic consequences of this triple interaction on the *capital-labor relation*, and particularly on their propagation of a reserve army of unemployed labor which is a necessary condition for continuous accumulation of capital. (Reuten 2004, 2, emphasis added)

In this sense, Marx simplifies the analysis by only pointing out the link between the variations in the *technical composition of capital* with the demand for work in the context of the *capital-labor relation*.

At this point, Marx moves from the analysis of the accumulation of individual capital[41] to its relationship with *multiple individual capitals*, that is, he examines the increase of the many individual capitals as aliquot parts of the global social capital and the process of *concentration* and *centralization*. *Attraction* and *repulsion* are the movements that articulate the expanded reproduction of global social capital. *Centralization* means the *attraction* of *individual capitals*, and *concentration* is the mutual *repulsion* of *multiple capitals*; it is "concentration of capitals already formed, destruction of their individual independence, expropriation of capitalist by capitalist, transformation of many small into few large capitals" (Marx 1867 [2013], 777).

Thus, accumulation brings with it *attraction* and *repulsion* between the *multiple capitals*, giving rise to competition. Indeed, *centralization* emerges through competition and "always ends in the ruin of many small capitalists, whose capitals partly pass into the hands of their conquerors" (Marx 1867 [2013], 779). Competition is essential to analyze how the law operates; however, its inclusion represents a break with the limits imposed by universality. Marx is aware of this, and for this reason, he warns us:

> The laws of this concentration (in the 3rd and 4th editions: 'centralization') of capitals, or of the attraction of capital by capital, cannot be developed here. A brief hint at a few facts must suffice. The *battle of competition is fought by cheapening of commodities*. The cheapness of commodities demands, *caeteris paribus* [under otherwise equal conditions], on the productiveness of labour, and this again on the scale of production. Therefore, the larger capitals beat the smaller. (Marx 1867 [2013], 778, emphasis added)[42]

In this context, Marx also includes credit as another mechanism for the *centralization* of capital. Credit is considered, together with competition, as the "most powerful lever of centralization" (Marx 1867 [2013], 779). Indeed, credit facilitates the absorption of smaller capital, the *expropriation of one capitalist by another*, so it becomes "a new and terrible weapon in the battle of competition" (Marx 1867 [2013], 780).

The analysis of credit does not correspond to the level of abstraction of universality either. The exposition takes place in part 5 of volume III (the *Division of Profit into Interest and Profit of Enterprise*) (Marx 1894 [2011]),[43] which is a part of the level of singularity. The inclusion of competition and credit are theoretical references necessary to show how the *centralization* of capital functions and therefore are fundamental for the development of the theory of accumulation; their inclusion at the level of universality thus anticipates their analysis at later levels without breaking with de-systematic structure of capital.

Progressive Production of a Relative Surplus Population and Its Forms of Existence: Formulation of the GLCA

In the third section, the main result of the law is presented, namely, that accumulation reproduces a surplus working population always available to the *needs of capital valorization*; and the fourth section examines the *different forms* of the *relative surplus population.*[44] Thus, Marx examines the dynamics of the progress of accumulation that goes hand in hand with the development of the productive force and the *concentration* and *centralization* of capital. This progressively affects the demand for labour, which falls in proportion to the increase of global capital. Thus, as the expansive force of capital increases, so will the *absolute magnitude of the working population* and its *productive power*, so the "same causes which develop the expansive power of capital, develop also the labour power at its disposal" (Marx 1867 [2013], 803). This is the way the law operates, which is described by Marx as "the absolute general law of capitalist accumulation" (Marx 1867 [2013], 803).[45]

Thus, in these sections, Marx is focused on the effects of the dynamics of accumulation in the process of *attraction* and *repulsion* of the working population. The dynamic is presented as fluctuations guided by increases in the *composition of capital* and the process of *centralization* of capital. This characterizes the *movement* or *life course of modern industry*, which is founded on the continual formation of an *industrial reserve army.*[46] For this reason, the *surplus population* is a necessary product of accumulation; it is the "lever of capitalistic accumulation, nay, a condition of existence of the capitalist mode of production" (Marx 1867 [2013], 786).

In reality, in these sections, Marx does not introduce any new theoretical elements (Reuten 2004). The central contribution is the recognition that the progress of accumulation is empirically cyclical. He defines the *life cycle* of modern industry as a *10-year cycle*,[47] which is accompanied by "periods of average activity, production at high pressure, crisis and stagnation" (Marx 1867 [2013], 784).[48] However, Marx does not define the time horizon of these phases; meaning he incorporates an empirical phenomenon into the theory without further characterizing it. Specifically, he does not theorize the relationship between the transition phases of the different periods with changes in the *composition of capital*. This is also replicated when defining the *forms of existence* of the *relative surplus population* and establishing its link with the *phases of the industrial cycle*. In this regard, Marx limits himself to simplifying the analysis in order to present his main conclusions:

> Regardless of the formal *periodic* differences in the surplus population in the *changing phases of the industrial cycle*, in which it manifests itself (in the 4th edition he writes: 'Not taking into account the great *periodically* recurring

> forms that the *changing phases of the industrial cycle impress on it*,') now an acute form during the crisis, then again a chronic form during dull times—it has always three forms, the *floating*, the *latent*, the *stagnant* (Emphasis in original). (Marx 1867 [2013], 798)

Thus, in these sections, Marx uses categories, and anticipates theoretical references, which cannot be developed at the level of abstraction of volume I. Therefore, a point is reached in the theoretical exposition that is insufficient to go deeper into the analytical implications of the law. However, the formulation of the GLCA provides the conceptual foundations for reconstructing how it is articulated with the subsequent levels of abstraction[49]; therefore, its exposition at the level of universality is fundamental to identify the theoretical route that makes it possible to analyze the antagonistic character of the capitalist mode of production based on the systematic reconstruction of capital.

Illustration of the General Law of Capitalist Accumulation

Finally, the fifth section illustrates how the GLCA operates in modern society. An empirical analysis is presented with the results of the research into the forms that the law manifests itself in England in a given period. Thus, Marx begins by pointing out:

> No period of modern society is so favourable for the study of capitalist accumulation as the period of the last 20 years. It is as if this period had found Fortunatus' purse. But of all countrics England again furnishes the classical example, because it holds the foremost place in the world-market, because capitalist production is here alone completely developed, and lastly, because the introduction of the Free-trade millennium since 1846 has cut off the last retreat of vulgar economy. (Marx 1867 [2013], 808)

The aim of this section is to carry out a concrete analysis of how the GLCA operates in the fully developed capitalist mode of production. Marx illustrates how the antagonistic character of capitalist accumulation manifests itself in the conditions of reproduction of the working class, which is why the section includes significant empirical and historical content in terms of references and statistical data resulting from his research. He points to the relationship between increasing accumulation and the class struggle, analyzes the sanitary conditions of the working classes linked to the lowest paid classes, examines implications related to urban development, and exposes the problem of agricultural workers, to mention only a few examples. All these issues are linked to the forms of manifestation of the GLCA among the working class.[50]

The inclusion of empirical references in this section shows how Marx interrupts the systematic ordering to set out the concrete results of his research into the operation of the law. Historical and statistical considerations have an illustrative function; in a systematic argument, historical considerations can have only this function.[51] The inclusion of contingent facts does not mean that the systematic rigor of the theory is weakened, so a digression from the systematic ordering is possible. This is pointed out by Smith:

> The key point is that these historical illustrations may claim a place in *Capital* without undermining the systematic nature of the theory. Reference to historical matters thus does not replace the logical argument here. It complements it by providing empirical examples of a categorial structure. (Smith 1990, 130)

This section also shows that an illustration of the law requires the incorporation of categories that belong to all the levels of abstraction. Indeed, the forms of manifestation of the law are related to the categories and determinations that develop at the levels of particularity and singularity. These levels of abstraction make it possible to theoretically establish the relationship with capitalist competition for a fraction of surplus value, the role of credit as a lever of accumulation, the formation of joint-stock companies, and the effects of the crisis on relative surplus population, to mention only some of the implications. Thus, a comprehensive reading of the GLCA is related to the dynamics of capital accumulation that continues to be developed at subsequent levels of abstraction. In this way, the analysis of the relationship between the accumulation process and the reproduction of the working class parallels the development of the systematic structure of capital, and therefore requires the determinations that Marx sets out in the three volumes of *Capital* to be incorporated.

CONCLUSION

In this chapter, the GLCA is analyzed from the perspective of the systematic structure of capital. It argues that *Capital* is a work organized into levels of abstraction in which the concept of capital is structured and developed. Each level of abstraction imposes methodological limits that are overcome as the presentation of the argument progresses. In this context, the formulation of the GLCA pertains to the level of universality. Universality imposes limits on the theoretical scope and the analytical implications that can be developed. However, Marx is aware of this and sets out the theoretical elements related to the law, simplifying his analysis in order to reach the main conclusions, and using the categories and determinations that are developed at the levels of particularity and singularity. In this sense, the formulation also incorporates historical facts that illustrate how the law operates. The incorporation of these does not break with the systematic structure of capital.

Indeed, chapter 23 belongs to the *systematic chapters* of part 7, so the statement of the law is consistent with the systematic structure of capital. Methodological evaluation of the chapter reveals that a comprehensive reading can be connected to the development of levels of abstraction throughout the three volumes of *Capital*. In this way, the methodological perspective identifies the categories and analytical implications necessary to formulate the GLCA, thus highlighting its relevance in capturing the real movement of capital as it manifests itself in the antagonistic nature of capitalist accumulation.

NOTES

1. Marx's emphasis on the subtitle of *Capital, A Critique of Political Economy*, involves a reflection on the objective of the work. In general, it is understood to indicate that the objective of the project is to analyze capitalism based on a critique of the theoretical system of political economy by previous and contemporary authors. However, this does not mean that the main objective is to critically analyze the various existing theories, and thereby solely to present a new theory that remedies the theoretical confusions about political economy. This would be to understand the book in only a limited manner. In this regard, Heinrich formulates some ideas about understanding the meaning of critique in Marx.

For Marx it is more than a critique in this sense, since he does not limit himself to criticizing certain theories, but rather addresses political economy as a *whole*: it is a critique of the *categorical presuppositions* of a *whole* science. This general character of the critique is made clear by Marx as early as the late 1850s in a letter to Ferdinand Lassalle:

> The work I am presently concerned with is a Critique of Economic Categories or, if you like, a critical exposé of the system of the bourgeois economy. It is at once an exposé and, by the same token, a critique of the system (MEW 29, P. 550, underlined by Marx). (Heinrich 2008, 50)

Therefore, the use of the expression *critique* incorporates the aim of understanding the movement of the capitalist mode of production as a totality, as a social process with multiple determinations that can be examined on the basis of elaborating different economic categories. Likewise, it implies a critical stance toward bourgeois social relations and the role of the ruling class in the process of exploitation, as well as the basis for generating a class consciousness to reverse the process of domination.

2. In the epilogue to the second edition, Marx emphasizes the importance of identifying that the scientific method for analyzing the capitalist mode of production is made up of these two stages:

Of course the method of presentation must differ in form from that of inquiry. The latter has to appropriate the material in detail, to analyse its different forms of development, to trace out their inner connexion. Only after this work is done, can the actual movement be adequately described. (Marx 1867 [2013], 19)

3. It is important to note that the choice of these categories is the result of a specific social and historical context. Each category is an expression of the determinations that constitute the capitalist mode of production.

4. This is not to argue that Marx's dialectical exposition in *Capital* is the result of a literal application of the categories of Hegel's dialectical logic to the critique of political economy. Rather, it is about the construction of a categorical system that Marx develops to present the capitalist mode of production. This system makes use of Hegelian logic to present the internal connection between the economic categories.

There are different interpretations of Marx's scientific method and its relation to Hegel's dialectical philosophy. Although the influence of Hegel on Marx's thought is recognized, Marxist scholars' interpretation of this influence varies widely. Althusser (1965), in his book *Reading Capital*, considers that Hegel had an influence on Marx only during the "young Marx" period (*Economic and philosophical manuscripts*, 1844); however, once the author had devoted himself to the critique of classical political economy, the "mature Marx" (*Contribution to the Critique of Political Economy,* 1859) breaks with Hegel's language and method, and abandons Hegel's philosophy.

In a different vein, in the 1970s, a current led by Backhaus and Reichelt emerged in Germany, which aimed to carry out a "new reading of Marx" (Heinrich, 2008) based on a global analysis of Marx's works that include *Capital*, the *Grundrisse*, *Critique of Political Economy*, and the *Economic and Philosophical Manuscripts*, among others. The need for a "reconstruction" of the critique of political economy is argued on the basis of a methodological structure that emphasizes the influence of Hegel on Marx with regard to the dialectical exposition of categories. Based on this approach, a reading emerges of authors who belong to the "new dialectic" or "systematic dialectic" (see Reuten and Williams 1989; Robles 1990; Smith 1993; Arthur 1993; Fineschi 2001, 2005; among others).

5. A *moment* is a *dialectic-systematic* notion that refers to the components of each progression of the presentation, that is, it refers to a particular type of analysis within a level of abstraction (Reuten 2004).

6. In this regard, Marx points out:

The concrete is concrete because it is a *synthesis of many determinations*, thus a unity of the diverse. In thinking, it, therefore, appears as a process of summing-up, as a result, not as the starting point, although it is the real starting point, and thus also the starting point of perception and conception. (Marx 1859 [2013], 301, emphasis added)

7. Smith (1990) points out that the logical transition between the categories shifts from a structure of *unity* and *difference* toward one of *unity-in-difference*. *Unity* and *difference* are thus, simultaneously, the conditions for the categories to be overcome dialectically; likewise, *contradiction* and *denial* are logical operators that make it possible to sort the categories in a systematic way. In this way, the ordering proceeds

from a category of simple *unity*, through one of *difference*, to a final stage *of unity-in-the-difference* (Smith 1990).

8. Fineschi (2005) points out that the plan of the theory of capital outlined by Marx is found in three manuscripts; the first, the *Economic Manuscripts of 1857–58* sees him progressively define the structure of the full exposition of the concept of capital; this plan was later reorganized in the *Economic Manuscripts of 1861–63*, on the concepts of market value and production prices; finally, in the *Economic Manuscripts of 1864–65*, we find the only exposition on credit, the banking system, and fictitious capital. The development of these drafts is consummated in *Capital*.

9. The configuration of capital as a *process* means that it acquires the determinations that give it the ability to *increase itself* and the potentiality to *renew itself*, that is, of being a *value that values itself*. Every moment is necessary for this goal: "Capital is not a simple relation, but a *process*, in whose various moments it is always capital" (Marx 1857/1858 [2011], 198). Capital aims to be an *endless process*:

> The goal-determining activity of capital can only be that of growing wealthier, i.e. of magnification, of increasing itself. . . . Fixed as wealth, as the general form of wealth, as value which counts as value, it is therefore the constant drive to go beyond its quantitative limit: *an endless process*. (Marx 1857–1858 [2011], 211, emphasis added)

10. This interpretation takes as a reference the organic plan that Marx sets out in the *Economic Manuscripts of 1857–58*, the *Grundrisse*, in which he describes how the plan of the work is divided into three levels of abstraction. This triad would correspond to the core of dialectical exposition of capital, and, therefore, it uses dialectical logic for its presentation.

11. The presentation of universality begins in section 2 of volume I, covers volume II, and ends with the exposition of *Equalisation of the General Rate of Profit through Competition Market-Prices and Market-Values: Surplus-Profit* (Marx 1894 [2011], 219), that is, in chapter 10 of section 2 of volume III.

12. In the first German edition (1867) published by Marx, the GLCA is found in chapter 23. Later, Engels rearranged the English edition (1886) of volume I, dividing the *second section* into three chapters. As a result, the law moved to chapter 25. In this chapter, the Spanish edition is used as a reference, which is the translation of the German editions, meaning that the GLCA is found in chapter 23.

13. Labour-power is the set of physical and mental capacities found in the *living individual*. In the capitalist mode of production, labour-power is a special commodity held by the *free* worker and that he offers for sale in a *voluntary* way to the capitalist, who is the bearer of the money commodity. The capitalist and the worker confront each other as possessors of legally *equal* goods. It is a necessary condition for the existence of capital that the capitalist finds the *free worker holder* of his labour-power, that is, lacking other commodities to sell, "devoid, rid of all necessary things" (Marx 1867 [2013], 205) to ensure his reproduction.

14. Capital only guarantees its existence by confronting work, and work only produces value by confronting capital. This is characterized by Marx as an "antithetical relationship" (Marx 1857/1858 [2011], 231). Capital is only capital as *nonwork* and work is only work as *noncapital*. Work like *noncapital* is *living labor*, and is the

subjectivity of work as a pure form that "must be eliminated and overcome" in the "material objectivity of capital" (Marx 1857/1858 [2011], 238), that is, it must be subsumed in capital.

15. These assumptions are raised as the systematic reconstruction of capital progresses, that is, at subsequent levels of abstraction of particularity and singularity.

16. This is indicated by the author in chapter 23 of volume I (Marx 1867 [2011], 692) and in the *Grundrisse*, in the section titled "Necessary Work. Surplus Labor. Surplus Population: Surplus Capital" (Marx 1857/1858 [2011], 118).

17. The author reaches this conclusion after analyzing the different drafts of *Capital* found in the *Grundrisse*. These drafts show that Marx changes the position of accumulation several times. Initially, he locates it in particularity, that is, after presenting the analysis of the circulation of capital, prior to the development of the analysis of competition and concentration; later, he relocates it to universality. The detail of these changes, as well as the methodological examination that justifies them, is found in Fineschi (2018).

18. Although in volume I, there are elements related to *Accumulation II*, the argument is mainly developed in section 3 of volume II that deals with *The Reproduction and Circulation of the Aggregate Social Capital* (Marx 1885 [2011], 429–638).

19. In chapter 23, Marx anticipates this articulation by setting out the link between the increase in the multiple individual capitals and the increase in social capital (Marx 1867 [2013], 777).

20. In this regard, Marx points out:

> The movement of the social capital consists of the totality of the movements of its individualised fractional parts, the turnovers of the individual capitals. Just as the metamorphosis of the individual commodity is a link in the series of metamorphoses of the commodity-world—the circulation of commodities—so the metamorphosis of the individual capital, its turnover, is a link in the circuit described by social capital. (Marx 1885 [2011], 430)

21. This coincides with the dialectic of the *one* and the *multiple*, which Marx takes from Hegel. In this regard, Fineschi points out:

> It must be remembered that if production takes place entirely in a capitalist way, this does not mean that everything is produced by a single capital, in fact this is impossible, again due to the fundamental character of the category "goods," which implies autonomous and independent producers. This capital/capitals relationship is explicitly referred by Marx to the dynamics of one/multiple and to the categories of "attraction" and "repulsion" that evidently recall the Hegelian logic of being (cf. Marx 1976–1981, 353, 59–60). (Fineschi 2018, 329)

22. From this perspective, *Accumulation II* methodologically anticipates the analysis of the competition that emerges at the particularity level of abstraction.

23. Fineschi explains that the relationship *presupposition-position* is a concept in dialectical logic taken from Hegel to define a type of category that develops its own determinations of a totality that are not yet explained by it, that is, determinations that are *presuppositions* and that in their becoming *position* themselves as a result of

the whole. In this way, the position of the *presupposition-position* makes explicit the qualities of a totality:

> When in this text we indicate that something is a presupposition we refer to qualities or determinations of a totality that have not yet been generated or explained by it, but have been placed in advance, assumed. On the contrary, when we refer that something has been positioned it is because that something is already a result generated by the totality or by the system. The position implies making explicit all the qualities of a totality, that is, all the qualities that were assumed are now generated by the totality. This approach arises from an examination of two German verbs employed by Hegel: *setzen* and *voraussetzen*. The compound verb *voraussetzen* can be translated by the verbs *to suppose*, *to require*, *to assume* or *to presuppose*. However, it is worth dwelling on the elements it is comprised of: *voraus* translates as *go ahead* or *in front of*, while *setzen* translates as *set*, *place* or *sit*. (Fineschi s.f.)

Likewise, this relationship allows the theory to be developed without depending on external factors to maintain its coherence; so "thanks to it [the presupposition-position] the theory can move by itself" (Fineschi 2018, 318).

24. In this regard, Fineschi points out:

> In the capitalist mode of production, accumulation is established as the valorization of capital. Reconstructing the nexus between material content and social form at all the levels of abstraction through which that nexus develops is an operation that Marx began but did not complete. It is up to us to follow this path. (Fineschi 2018, 334)

25. In this regard, the author points out that there are categories that pertain to the problem of the dialectical reconstruction of the *form of capital*, and others to the *form of value*. The process of production and accumulation are part of the reconstruction of the *form of capital*. Therefore, the intention is to analyze the stages that make up the *dialectic of the production process* (Smith 1990, 127) to show that the systematic ordering is consistent with the use of dialectical logic.

26. For Reuten, it is important to emphasize that in this section, Marx limits himself to analyzing only the *internal mechanism* of accumulation, leaving aside external determinations. However, he points out that internal determinations are not more important than external determinations, because " 'inner' determinations are not more important than 'outer' determinations; the former have no existence without the latter; and the outer determinations may modify the actualization of the inner" (Reuten 2004, 1).

27. The last two chapters that belong to the section, namely, chapter 24, "So-Called Primitive Accumulation," and chapter 25, "Modern Theory of Colonization," are essentially chapters of a historical nature. For this reason, they are not part of the systematic ordering of the work. In this regard, Fineschi (2018, 333) points out that, although these chapters are found in part 7, they in fact belong to a separate part, as indicated by Marx in a letter. Similarly, Smith (1990) develops a methodological evaluation of the meaning of the inclusion of historical material in the final part of volume I.

28. In this sense, Smith (1990) points out that the systematic development of simple reproduction to expanded reproduction requires a shift from a category of

unity to one of *difference*. Consistent with the systematic derivation, the author concludes that the *accumulation fund* or *reserve fund* is the category that functions as a structure of *difference*. In this way, the *expanded form* incorporates a structure of *unity-in-difference*, as systematically required. In the author's words:

> Simple accumulation tends to advance to the point where a *reserve fund* will slowly accumulate. This fund, as it is not incorporated into simple accumulation, constitutes a moment of "difference" that is opposed to the structure of simple accumulation. Expanded accumulation would therefore incorporate this difference within a structure of *unity-in-difference*, as systematically required. This occurs when part of the surplus is productively invested in expanded means of production and labor power, leading to a higher level of production. This closes the dialectic of the forms of accumulation and of the production process itself. (Smith 1990, 136)

29. The law of capitalist appropriation is identified from the analysis of expanded accumulation. Indeed, the accumulation of capital is founded on the law of appropriation, or of private property; property is "the right to appropriate the unpaid work of others" (Marx 1867 [2011], 721) so the split between property and work "becomes the necessary consequence of a law that apparently originated in their identity" (Marx 1867 [2011], 722).

30. The objective is not to carry out an exegesis of the chapter but to identify and analyze the elements that correspond to the systematic structure of capital and that are present in the exposition of the GLCA.

31. The distinction between *concentration* and *centralization* appears for the first time in the French edition of Volume I produced by Marx in 1872 and 1875 (see Fineschi 2018).

32. This is pointe out by the author in the introduction to chapter 23 (*see* Marx 1867 [2011], 759–760).

33. This is analyzed by Reuten (2004) in section Brief Methodological Evaluation of Part 7.

34. Specifically, it is taken up in chapter 11, which deals with *Theories of Fixed and Circulating Capital. Ricardo* (Marx 1885 [2011], 261–276), and in chapter 14, which analyzes *Time of Circulation* (Marx 1885 [2011], 303–313).

35. Where the effect of the increase in labour productivity on competition between capitals is analyzed.

36. This is indicated by the author when he states that "reproduction on a progressive scale, i.e., accumulation, reproduces the capital relation on a progressive scale, more capitalists or larger capitalists at this pole, more wage workers at that" (Marx 1867 [2013], 761).

37. The ultimate goal of capitalist production is the production of surplus value, for which the capitalist has as his sole objective:

> Augmentation of his capital, production of commodities containing more labour than he pays for, containing therefore a portion of value that costs him nothing, and that is nevertheless realised when the commodities are sold. . . . Labour power is only saleable so far as it preserves the means of production in their capacity of capital, reproduces its

own value as capital, and yields in unpaid labour a source of additional capital. (Marx 1867 [2013], 767)

38. Or as noted by the author: "To put it mathematically: the rate of accumulation is the independent, not the dependent, variable, the rate of wages, the dependent, not the independent, variable" (Marx 1867 [2013], 769).

39. Marx points out that "the degree of productivity of labour, in a given society, is expressed in the relative extent of the means of production that one labourer, during a given time, with the same tension of labour power, turns into products" (Marx 1867 [2013], 772).

40. Given that "as the growth of capital becomes more productive, the demand for labor falls in relation to the magnitude of capital itself" (Marx 1867 [2013], 774).

41. The accumulation of individual capital is defined as *simple concentration*:

> Every individual capital is a larger or smaller concentration of means of production, with a corresponding command over a larger or smaller labour-army. With the increasing mass of wealth which functions as capital, accumulation increases the concentration of that wealth in the hands of individual capitalists, and thereby widens the basis of production on a large scale and of the specific methods of capitalist production. (Marx 1867 [2013], 777)

42. Also, in part 4 of volume I, Marx already anticipated the analysis of competition. When analyzing the *Production of Relative Surplus Value*, he notes:

> It is not our intention to consider, here, the way in which the *laws, immanent in capitalist production*, manifest themselves in the movements of individual masses of capital, where they assert themselves as coercive *laws of competition*, and are brought home to the mind and consciousness of the individual capitalist as the directing motives of his operations. But this much is clear; a scientific analysis of competition is not possible, before we have a conception of the inner nature of capital, just as the apparent motions of the heavenly bodies are not intelligible to any but him, who is acquainted with their real motions, motions which are not directly perceptible by the senses. Nevertheless, for the better comprehension of the production of relative surplus-value, we may add the following remarks, in which we assume nothing more than the results we have already obtained. (Marx 1867 [2013], 384)

43. The analysis of credit is developed in part 5 of volume III.

44. Marx asserts that the *relative surplus population* "exists in every possible form. Every labourer belongs to it during the time when he is only partially employed or wholly unemployed" (Marx 1867 [2013], 797); but for simplicity's sake, he focuses on the surplus population that is directly or indirectly related to the dynamics or changes of the industrial cycle (Marx 1867 [2013], 797). Thus, the *forms of existence of the relative surplus population* continually take three forms, namely, the *floating*, the *latent*, and the *stagnant*. The surplus population in its floating form is one that can be analyzed cyclically, that is, it is directly linked to the *industrial cycle*. This *surplus population* is made up of workers who "sometimes repelled, sometimes attracted again in greater masses . . . although in a constantly decreasing proportion to the scale of production" (Marx 1867 [2013], 798). The surplus population in its *latent* form is made up of the surplus population that flows

from agricultural to industrial work. The *latent* form represents labour-power that has not yet been directly exploited by capital, so Marx links it to a part of the agricultural population that is "on the point of passing over into an urban or manufacturing proletariat" (Marx 1867 [2013], 798). This form of surplus population flows constantly, but its "constant flow towards the towns presupposes, in the country itself, a constant latent surplus population" (Marx 1867 [2013], 800–801). The *stagnant* form of the surplus population is "a part of the active labour army, but with extremely irregular employment" (Marx 1867 [2013], 801). This is the part of the working class whose "conditions of life sink below the average normal level of the working class" and is characterized by a "maximum of working-time, and minimum of wages" (Marx 1867 [2013], 801).

45. This law, Marx affirms, "is modified in its working by many circumstances, the analysis of which does not concern us here" (Marx 1867 [2013], 803).

46. This is pointed out by Marx when describing the modern *industry life cycle*:

> The course characteristic of modern industry, viz., a decennial cycle (interrupted by smaller oscillations), of periods of average activity, production at high pressure, crisis and stagnation, depends on the constant formation, the greater or less absorption, and the re-formation of the industrial reserve army or surplus population. (Marx 1867 [2013], 787)

47. It is worth noting that Reuten (2004) identifies Marx as one of the first theorists to recognize the existence of a 10-year cycle and include it in the research agenda of economists.

48. Some scholars have attempted to derive a theory of the cycle related to the scarcity of labour (*cf.* Itoh 1988). However, Reuten (2004) argues that, from the point of view of the systematic-dialectical methodology, it is not possible to identify a theory of the cycle in volume I; its development is possible, he claims, but requires "the terrains and concepts developed in Volumes II and III of *Capital*" (Reuten 2004, 18).

49. In accordance with the relevance of the accumulation category as *presupposition-position.*

50. In this regard, Marx recognizes that in order to gain a full understanding of how the law operates, it is necessary to examine the situation of the reproduction of the working class as a whole; however, he points out that the limits of the book force him to focus on the situation of the industrial and agricultural worker:

> But for a full elucidation of the law of accumulation, his condition outside the workshop must also be looked at, his condition as to food and dwelling. The limits of this book compel us to concern ourselves chiefly with the worst paid part of the industrial proletariat, and with the agricultural labourers, who together form the majority of the working class. (Marx 1867 [2013], 815)

Likewise, when analyzing the situation of the British agricultural proletariat, he points to the connection with the law:

Nowhere does the antagonistic character of capitalistic production and accumulation assert itself more brutally than in the progress of English agriculture (including cattle-breeding) and the retrogression of the English agricultural labourer. (Marx 1867 [2013], 839–840)

51. In this regard, Smith (1990) carries out an exhaustive analysis of the subject.

BIBLIOGRAPHY

Fausto, Ruy. "Dialética Marxista, Dialética Hegeliana. O capital e a Lógica de Hegel." In *Marx: Lógica e Política: investigacoes para uma reconstituicao do sentido da dialética*, edited by Ruy Fausto, 41–77. Paris: Université Paris VIII, 1993.

Fine, Ben, and Alfredo Saad-Filho. *Marx's 'Capital'*. London: Pluto Press, 2004.

Fineschi, Roberto. "Marx-Gesellschaft eV" October 29, 2005. http://www.marx-gesellschaft.de/Texte/1005_Fineschi_Four%20Levels_Abstraction.pdf (last accessed: 2014).

———. *Ripartire da Marx. Processo storico ed economia politica nella teoria del capitale.* La citta del Sole: Istituto Italiano per Gli Studi Filosofici, 2001.

———. "Una historia compleja. La teoría de la acumulación en Marx (Documento inédito)." n.d.

———. "Una storia complessa. La teoria dell'accumulazione in Marx. " *Consecutio Rerum*, 5 (2018): 317–336.

Guerrero, Diego. *Un resumen completo de El capital de Marx.* Madrid: Maia Editions, 2010.

Harvey, David. *A Companion to Marx's Capital.* New York: Verso, 2010.

Heinrich, Michael. "Capital in General and the Structure of Marx's Capital." *Capital & Class* 13, no. 2 (July 1989): 63–79.

———. *Crítica de la economía política. Una introducción a El capital de Marx.* Madrid: Escolar y Mayo Editores SL, 2008.

Itoh, Makoto. *The Basic Theory of Capitalism.* London: Macmillan, 1988.

Marx, Karl. *Contribución a la crítica de la economía política.* Mexico City: Siglo XXI editores, 1859 [2013].

———. *Capital.* Mexico: Siglo XXI, 1867 [2011].

———. *Capital.* Mexico: Siglo XXI, 1894 [2013].

———. *Capital.* Mexico: Siglo XXI, 1885 [2011].

———. *Elementos fundamentales para la crítica de la economía política (Grundrisse) Volume I.* Mexico: Siglo XXI editores, 1857/1858 [2011].

———. *Elementos fundamentales para la crítica de la economía política (Grundrisse) Volume II.* Mexico: Siglo XXI editores, 1857/1858 [2011].

Reuten, Geert. "The Inner Mechanism of the Accumulation of Capital: The Triple Acceleration. A Methodological Appraisal of Part Seven' of Marx's Capital I." In *The Constitution of Capital; Essays on Volume I of Marx's 'Capital'*, edited by Bellofiore and Taylor, 274–298. London/New York: Palgrave Macmillan, 2004.

———. "El trabajo difícil de una teoría del valor social: metáforas y dialéctica sistemática al principio de El capital en Marx." In *Dialéctica y Capital. Elementos para una reconstrucción de la crítica de la economía política*, edited by Mario Robles Báez, 31–58. Mexico: Universidad Autónoma Metropolitana, 2005.

Robles, Mario. *Marx: lógica y capital. La dialéctica de la tasa de ganancia y la forma-precio.* Mexico: Universidad Autónoma Metropolitana, 2011.

Robles, Mario, and Roberto Escorcia. *Dinero y Capital. Hacia una reconstrucción de la teoría de Marx sobre el dinero.* Mexico City: Universidad Autónoma Metropolitana, 2016.

Robles, Mario, and Roberto Escorcia. "La dialéctica del trabajo, valor y precio en la conceptualización del capital de Marx: Una reconstrucción." *Unpublished document, Metropolitan Autonomous University-Xochimilco*, 2013.

Smith, Tony. *The Logic of Marx's Capital: Replies to Hegelian Criticisms.* New York: State University of New York Press, Albany, 1990.

Chapter 2

Violence and Crepuscular Capitalism

Structural Dynamics and Superstructural Forms of the General Law of Capitalist Accumulation

Roberto Fineschi

PREMISES

The theme of violence can't be properly dealt with outside a theoretical framework, which defines the subjects that practice or suffer violence. If it is not explicitly outlined, one can unintentionally end up following worldviews that are in principle reactionary or philosophically untenable. The same applies to general concepts such as "power"; there is a risk of methodological individualism: if it is evident that, on the one hand, it seems possible to identify transhistorical structures connected with violence (the same as power, language, etc.), on the other, if these are fixed in their abstraction as substantial concepts outside their historical complex processuality, they turn out to be "hypostatizations":[1] typical elements of a peculiar historical period are transfigurated into transhistorical "essences."

If we don't conceive violence as a part of a theory of historical process, it easily happens to reduce the relationship of the subjects that are practicing/suffering violence to the dichotomy individuals-society, individuals-institutions, and individuals-state, where we can alternatively focus on the universal side—to which the individuals have to be subjugated or assimilated—or the particular one, where individuals will always be somehow negated by the "otherness" of society; its rules can be accepted or refused but are in the end conceived as something "alien" to each one's own individual essence.[2] Both extremes of authoritarianism and individualism seem to originate in the category of "person" as their philosophical foundation. Here, a peculiar category of the bourgeois exchange society is taken on as the concept of "human" as such, as "natural" social habit. The specific figures resulting from the commodity-money dialectics are hypostatized as universal forms of human action. It is then not philosophically consistent to criticize the violence of modern bourgeois society, of the capitalist mode of production, by claiming the universal concept of "person," or by using its same ideological forms; their use reconnects to capitalism instead of surpassing it.[3]

According to Marx, a theory based on abstract individuals, defined as such before and outside society, misunderstands phenomenal appearance (individuals who freely decide to exchange) with essence (exchange society): appearance is not taken as necessary manifestation of essence in a different form, but as essence itself; the *representation* that individuals *phenomenally* have of the process is mistaken as a *scientific* explanation of that process. This is an ideology, which is not mere deception, but a necessary, deformed form of perception; Marx thinks that exchange and commodities' language is spoken out in the subjects that realize it. Their "personality"—their alleged pre-social autonomy—exists only inasmuch as they are a moment of the complex and interconnected exchange process. This same process, however, lets them think that they are free and equal regardless of their connection; moreover: they think that they start the process as if it were the result of their own will. It is the typical dialectical inversion of essence and phenomenon that produces an "objective appearance." The universal Christian person (and its many philosophical variants) is, according to Marx, its most refined form.[4]

Marx's articulated and complex theory of Capital is an alternative to the abstract individual-society relationship based on the substantial character of "person." Historical subjects are here defined by the dialectics of function and conflict as *classes*, multiindividual subjects that are characterized through the role that they functionally have in the production relationships. These are their temporally determined forms of existence with which productive forces enter in contradiction at a certain level of development. This dialectics of function and conflict[5] articulated in the specific forms of the *fundamental law of capitalist accumulation* is still the key to investigate the concept of violence. In this theoretical setting, what is substantial is the social framework and its *diachronic* and *synchronic* dynamic. The latter permits us to investigate both material and ideal reproduction, which implies specific relationships between different subjects, and subjects and things; relationships that define their social role, and the way they become aware of it. The former allows us to think about the present as a nonstatic model, its dynamic in regard to a "before" and "after." Humanity as such is then not a summatory of given pre-social individuals, but a *process* through which they get defined, together with nature and as part of it. According to Marx, an individual-society relationship outside such a process is not conceivable or purely ideological. In Marx's theory, historical actors are not individuals, but classes.[6] Such a definition is not to be read in immediate, strict political terms. It is a "functional" definition based on their role in the historically determined social reproduction; in our case, the capitalist mode of production. The dynamic of each framework determines its development up to a certain level and implies a conflictuality, which is compatible with the system; there is, however, a turning point after which not only the different interests conflict but also conflict shakes the system's foundations themselves.[7]

Incidentally, I need to specify that the reference to Marx is not a generic revival of old-fashioned ideas from the past century. My starting point is the *new* Marx offered by the critical edition of his works; this has redefined not just past interpretations but also the same textual basis on which they can be developed. These changes are still not universally known.[8] The page to turn is the idea that saw just in the factory working class the only possible antagonist of capital. This misunderstanding was due to an inconvenient translation/interpretation of the German word *Arbeiter* with factory-worker, instead of wage-worker. In a determined period of capitalist development, this seemed a perfect description of the ongoing events: the "figure" of the factory-worker perfectly incarnated the "form" of movement of the social dynamics. But "forms" and "figures" are not identical: the latter is an empirically/theoretically determined actor in a historically determined factual stage of the general dynamics and represents the latter; form is instead the functionally/logically determined subject. Figures are determined representatives of forms. If figures change, this doesn't necessarily imply that forms do. The same forms (e.g., wage-work, partial character of the activity, and its subordination to an objective process of capital valorization) are well represented by the figure "factory-worker" but not only by it. Those forms work well also with other possible subjects (figures) in different sub-configurations of the system.[9]

If violence is violence of one class over another, the issue of violence has to be investigated as a moment of a historical process according to which classes, the forms of existence of productive forces, get configured as production relationships. This approach is more flexible and scientifically productive than the reductive perspective of individuals sociologically or empirically grouped as summatory of ones. A theory of historical process has a dynamic that allows to conceive trends and differentiated stages of social action for those figures that incarnate the forms of movement of the system. A legitimate use of violence exists as a historically determined relationship of law and law violation; state violence can be legitime within a determined historical framework but become illegitime inasmuch as social contradictions (class struggle) make it incompatible with the structural changes of the reproduction of society as a system.

FOR A THEORY OF CREPUSCULAR CAPITALISM

If we correctly understand an ontology based on a personal anthropology in terms of bourgeois ideology, and investigate the concept of violence in the perspective of Marx's theory of historical process, and in particular in relation to the general law of capital accumulation, what kind of answers do we find?

I would like to provisionally introduce the concept of "crepuscular capitalism." I don't mean the category that emerged in the context of the Frankfurt School or in the postwar period as "late capitalism," that is a capitalism "corrected" or "integrated" by state intervention and welfare state in anti-cyclical function (Adorno 1969, Habermas 1973), or in partially similar terms by Mandel (1972). I mean a hypothetical stage of the capitalist mode of production in which the dialectics of function and conflict have reached a conceptual breaking point: the capitalist mode of production has come to a determined level of development in which its intrinsic trend to the extromission of labour-power out of the production process, gradually in all branches, determines not only a dramatic increase of the technical composition and a probable fall of the rate of profit in the long run but also a fall of the mass of profit, since the material number of employed workers, and so the mass of surplus value, sinks. Even if the rate of exploitation grows to very high levels, the fall can't be compensated because of the lack of effectively active workers; the intrinsic logic of the system sets a trend to the mathematical limit of nothing. There are apparently *physical limits* to the extraction of surplus value (Marx 1991, 355 ff., 359 ff.). The mathematical concept of limit perfectly expresses this trend: it can't be reached, as not all workers can be excluded since surplus value exists only inasmuch as it is extracted on top of necessary labour; this is the fundamental condition of existence of the entire capitalist system. Here is the core contradiction of the capitalist mode of production: on the one hand, it creates infinite productivity, on the other, because of the same laws, it can be used only if it allows capital valorization, which, however, gradually becomes more and more difficult. This point is not conceived as a revival of the well-known break-down theory (Colletti 1975; Grossmann 1929), as one might think; this stage of capitalist development can indefinitely last, and implies specific social dynamics and, in particular, social actors that have a peculiar perception of their activity and the process they are part of.

The concept of the Reserve Army (Marx 1990, 781 ff.) gets here redefined: its elastic nature stops working. Since investments that can valorize capital become more and more difficult because of the intrinsic trend of capital toward overproduction and automation, workers get consistently excluded with an increasing low possibility (tending to nothing) of being reabsorbed in the same or other branches; they can't be in principle reinserted into the process. This does not mean that they are outside the capitalist system, but its utmost result: still (potential) wage-workers, functionally not employable because of the system itself. What is new here is not only that they start living as latent permanent unemployed but also *perceiving* their condition as stable. How does this determine their worldview and what new social praxis and self-consciousness emerge out of this stagnant reality?

(1) It becomes more and more difficult to find a job. The mechanization of all activities, starting to include some that were formerly considered intellectual, reduces the relevance of education in regular jobs (and now in part of the intellectual ones). Workers' personal skills are often unrelated to the job that happens to find or substantially indifferent; for this reason, hiring criteria become absolutely arbitrary. The relationship of hard work/merit/success, one of the fundamentals of bourgeois ideology, gets broken.
(2) Labour as source of value is by now a residual that the capitalist mode of production has made tending toward nothing; most of its development is now based on science and technological application of abstract knowledge. The nexus labour/wealth is broken not only in the sense already explained by Marx in the accumulation theory (labour produces not one's own but someone else's wealth): immediate human activity has become just a drop in the great ocean of wealth production. Its concrete, physical performance becomes less and less relevant, but still necessary.
(3) However we live in the ideological world of "person," freedom, and equality. But these qualities are effective only in social praxis inasmuch as the personal atom has the capacity to interact with other personal atoms; in a commodity society, this interaction is called exchange. However, without a job, wage, or money, it is impossible to practice one's own personality. This becomes impossible on the basis of the same laws that made personality the ideologically fundamental concept of bourgeois society. Its "human" universal value is negated not only, as a matter of fact, in the slavary of wage-work; this was compatible with the appearance of equal exchange and free choice (Marx 1990, 270ff., 713ff.). Now, it seems that the same personal formalism of bourgeois society enters a dramatic crisis and can't be practiced.
(4) In their social praxis, individuals perceive that the system imposes upon them their position. They perceived the unfairness of capitalistic exploitation, but now they experience even their existential disappearance as a person in the formalistic way of the exchange process. They face not just labour alienation—this respected formal freedom and equality—but the impossibility to practice what commodity circulation

continues to produce as their essence: personality, freedom, and equality. Those with money, as long as they are equal to them, shouldn't have more rights than them for personal realization. How did they get their money, in particular on the noncapitalist side? More and more not for their merits or work—because of job shortage—but often as a privilege (because of the generalization of recommendation policies). Then, if the practice of personality is possible just because of good fortune or privilege, it is linked to preconditions that deny the fundamental bourgeois concept of personality: *random or privileged access* means that universal equality and freedom are violated in order to be in the condition of practicing universal equality and freedom. This access is not just to apical positions but more and more to common jobs. If this attitude becomes structural, the violation of personality is necessary and due to the same rules that developed personality itself to ideological fundamental of capitalist society.

Marx had already explained how, in the circulation process, others are, for each single individual, a means, somebody they need to pass through in order to reach their goal (Marx 1993, 239 ff.). The instrumental nature of others and the universal interconnection of all exchange individuals is the essence of the circulation process, but its appearance is the opposite: everyone is autonomous, equal, and free, a person. With crepuscular capitalism, there is an essential passage: others, since the conditions to treat them as persons don't exist, can become an immediate instrument. From a formal, but apparently nonfactual instrumentalization, they pass to a factual consideration of others as non-person. This opens the door to the disappearance of the universal concept of human being and to treat humans as instruments, the most sophisticated vocal one: a slave.[10] Not a wage-worker, a factual but formally free slave, but an actual slave, that is someone that is formally not free and equal.

(5) Inasmuch as others are not anymore a person, they can be targets of uncontrolled violence. The ferocity of the 20th century is not so different from the current "extreme" one. It is the result of the undoing of the concept of person, due to the crepuscular development of capitalism. If personality can be practiced only by denying personality, the concept loses its universal character: not everybody can be a person. To be part of the "person"-élite is for few, it's a war. But *à la guerre comme à la guerre*: in order to be part of the person-paradise, one can be in favor of the introduction of selection criteria that are not universal, or that are "sub-universal," such as race, class, nationality, religion, origin, or "roots." It might be possible to put two or three of these together so that we have a more comprehensive and developed worldview. There will

be "others" that not only can but also have to be excluded; otherwise there is a risk of losing "our" own freedom and equality, the capacity of self-realization. As a part of the personal élite, one is still subjugated to capital exploitation, but exclusion means slavery or death. This is the practical and conceptual background of fascism, or whatever other ideology that promotes a "reduced universality"; these structural changes explain how such an ideology is already *factually practiced before it becomes hegemonic.*

(6) A further point is the relationship between the so-called developed and underdeveloped world. The denial of personality is new in the context of the Western élites; those, who used to promote personality at home, didn't exhitate to deny it in their colonies, where they practiced the cruelest brutality. Similarly, the slavery niches at home regarded those that they considered "inferior" such as "nigers" or other imported "vocal animals." What sounds as a scandal is the introduction of a reduced universality among Westerns themselves: this was the big challenge of fascism and nazism. Those other worlds, inhabited by nonpersons that never experienced the progressive phase of capitalist development during which the universal value of personality was a radical democratic ideology, because of the crepuscular stage of capitalism, won't even have the perspective of such a progress. They have never been and won't ever be a "person."

Subjects can then be articulated on three general levels: (1) those who are "person" (most of them are wage-workers, then factual slave although formally free), (2) the excluded ones in the Western world; these first two groups inhabit the Western community; (3) those who live at the margins and have never been and never will be a part of that system as a "person." If we theoretically and politically deal with this issue in the perspective of personal rights, there is no way out: being person or nonperson is the capitalist ideology of personality; the actual historical subjects—functional classes—are cut out. The dialectics of personality and its denial/revendication set a conflict within capitalist society between bourgeois universalism on the one hand and fascism on the other. Those three groups, that functionally are potentially anti-capitalist, are so divided into different antagonistic subjects. They can't be easily put together as a unified anti-capitalistic subject on the basis of the revendication of personality. At the same time, even if universal personality is reached, this doesn't bring us beyond capitalist exploitation.

(7) The practical and theoretical legitimation of individual violence, consequence of the crisis of personality, is a necessary premise to organized, collective violence, and of an imperialist attitude among groups one

and two against group three. The valorization crisis of crepuscular capitalism paves the way to raid capitalism; this is not anymore based on actual capitalist accumulation but stealing resources from others; these can be partly redistributed by capitalists with their workers. This makes possible a consensus to the organization of trusts, also with nationalistic features, which help one's country to obtain more wealth in the competition against other nations. We know that this has already happened: the national wage-workers will take advantage of effective imperialistic policies, if the ruling classes are intelligent enough to share part of the cake with them. The local, exploited wage-workers become supportive of their bosses. External violence and domination goes together with the internal reduced personality.

(8) The atomization and dislocation all over the world of productive processes determine the maximum of integration and, at the same time, the maximum of individualization of the activity of each worker. Their contribution is a grain of sand in a gigantic productive process; but that grain is often produced by themselves in their office, remotely, from home, call centers, and so on. The socialization of their part of the product in the final result takes place thanks to simpler or more complex machines or automatic procedures. They don't perceive other workers as part of their same productive process. They perceive themselves just as individuals, like those unemployed or insecure workers. On the other hand, the nonparticipation of a growing part of the workers to production creates a mass of inactive or partially inactive people who live thanks to expedients, or state assistance, or criminality, and so on. They mainly practice the social figures of the circulation process; they will be a person without being a worker, or being collective workers but perceiving themselves as individuals. The social character of work and society exists in front of them and they interact with it as an external something, not as something related to their own existence.

Radical individualism is the other side of the absolute socialization of the reproduction process (globalization). These actors will think that they are not denied as workers, but persons; their alienation will be experienced more in relation to their pre-social individuality than as a lack of collective control of the global process. Their revendication will be anarcoid, libertarian, and hedonistic, and will easily be attracted by different kinds of individualistic bourgeois philosophies or ways of thinking. They won't perceive themselves as class members. Alternatively, looking at themselves as generic pre-social totality, they will be attracted by abstractly total projects where their universal individuality merges into the abstract one of "their people" (fascism).

(9) Precautions. One might ask if these categories can be applied just to crepuscular capitalism or work more widely; in other terms: it could be just a phase of a cyclical process (one of the long waves of capitalism) instead of being a stable, stagnant condition. Under several regards, a similar situation developed in the 1920s and 1930s, when various forms of fascism tried to cancel universal rights, and introduced a reduced social welfare adapting capitalism to a new situation. The way out from that situation in the postwar period saw a constant and consistent growth for thirty years. Was this possible because of strict economic dynamics or dramatic political events (preparation to, reconstruction after a world war)? War and postwar reconstruction seem to have been the actual reasons for that impressive long period growth. However, given the current mass destruction weapons, a world war can't be a solution, or at the risk of destroying the same human species and the world as such. If just "the economy" is not in the condition to overcome permanent stagnation, it might be plausible to talk about a peculiar, "crepuscular" stage of capitalism. Its ideological self-consciousness implies the crisis of the concept of "person," together with the loss of universal freedom and equality. For this reason, the revendication of personality (freedom and equality) currently appears as a progressive political agenda: the bourgeois world is denying it. But we need to understand that there are structural preconditions to this ideological trend on the one hand, and, on the other hand, that this kind of revindication, even if it might be successful, doesn't bring us beyond capitalism, but into the middle of its exploitation dynamics, and more radical ideology: humans as persons.

(10) Palliatives. Massive wealth redistribution. This brings back many people to the condition of "person," but doesn't affect the structural causes of the trend. It is a social-democratic policy and can be effective as anti-fascist practice.

(11) The current historical "figures" (both empirically and logically historically determined actors) of the "forms" (functional, nonempirical subjects as determined by the logic of the system as such) include different potential subjects: all wage-workers, non just factory-workers, inclusive of all apparent, masked individual self-employed; but not just them; the mass of unemployed: their position is functionally determined by the same mechanisms of capital accumulation. The "conflicting" interest of included and excluded people is another way to mask that they are not enemies but stay on the same side of the barricade.

(12) The current valorization possibilities are linked to a more intense exploitation of labour-power but also by the absorption of the "historical" or indirect wage. The historical wage is the wealth accumulated by

workers with their savings, which is taken back by capital both through their inclusion into the financial speculative system and because of the need of maintenance of the newer generations that, either unemployed or with insecure jobs, can survive, just thanks to the help of their relatives. The wage integration takes place, thanks to the historical accumulated wage of their parents. The reduction or cancellation of the welfare state proceeds according to the same logic: the smaller the surplus value, the smaller the part that can go to indirect or deferred wage.

(13) The same happens with the trend to invest in primary goods, those that somehow people need to buy: food, water, gas, electric power, and so forth. This is, however, profit upon alienation, legal robbery, where part of social wealth passes from one pocket to another: a plus on the one hand corresponds to a minus on the other, there is no actual capital valorization, even if companies realize huge profits. There is of course nothing new in this but the connection of such a trend to the contradictory dynamics of crepuscular capitalism.

(14) The expulsion of labour-power out of the production process reduces the share for salaries; the employment of more workers with a reduction of working hours (mini-jobs) just masks reality. Further automation and mechanization increase investments in constant capital over variable capital; a trend toward production of constant capital by means of constant capital. If less and less investments go toward wages for the combined effect of automation and crisis of valorization, how will humans survive (in spite of massive wealth and unutilized productivity being available)? A "humanitarian" answer is the introduction of a universal basic income; it doesn't change anything to the structural dynamics but stops or puts under relative control possible social unrest. Alternatively, since there are too many, absolutely interchangeable people, just kill them or use them as slaves until they die, distinguishing a mass of "under-humans" and a few privileged individuals and their dream of being a "person." But they are dancing on a razor blade, and can be transformed into the next nonperson in every moment, because of a system that is paradoxically rich and bloodless.

CONCLUSION

Crepuscular capitalism seems to emerge as a stage of capitalism development where real capital valorization has become difficult. Instead of a break-down of the system, this can determine a stagnant condition, with peculiar economic and ideological features. The general law of capitalist accumulation tends to create a growing mass of unemployed that can't be reabsorbed. The corresponding praxis and ideology is not anymore universal personality, but its formal denial, and a trend toward the development of an exploitation system that combines capitalist and actualized pre-capitalist practices in a new peculiar synthesis.

NOTES

1. "Hypostatization" is the category used by Galvano della Volpe to describe this kind of incorrect abstraction; see his famous study *Logica come scienza storica* (Della Volpe 1969, passim). It had been previously introduced by della Volpe himself as translation of the German *Verselbstständigung* in his Italian edition of Marx's *Contribution to the Critique of Hegel's Philosophy of Law* (Marx 1981), particularly with reference to the concept of "abstraction."

2. This seems to me, in spite of many good points, the methodological limit, and one of the fundamental problems in several investigations on violence, such as Agamben (1975), Arendt (1970), Foucault (1975), and more recently Balibar (2015).

3. Here, we have the echo of the critique of the category of "person" by della Volpe in the first part of *Marx e Rousseau* (Della Volpe, 1957), taken up later in Mazzone (1981).

4. Marx makes this point in several passages, but in particular in Marx (1993, 239 ff.) and Marx (1990, 178 ff.). The Hegelian background of argument and wording is evident (cfr. Hegel 2010, 415 ff).

5. This terminology is used in a known essay by G. M. Cazzaniga (1981) and is based on the idea that we have organic totalities within which individuals get defined by their functional role. Social substance defines individuals and not vice versa. It is the classic theme of the relationship of the all with its parts, connection, and connected ones. The closest classic example is the Hegelian theory of Objective spirit and, of course, Marx's theory of the capitalist mode of production.

6. Those interpretations of Marx's theory that, instead of classes, focus on abstract humans and their alienated essence, in my opinion, fall into the bourgois perspective of afunctional substantial individuals; a perspective that Marx shared before he developed a more structured theory of capital, as long as he was trapped by Feuerbach's concept of *Gattungswesen*, which ends up identifying abstract individual and bourgois personality.

7. This is in my opinion the problem also with interesting and stimulating analysis of violence such as Benjamin's (1999): it is disconnected from the system dynamics of production relationships. The same applies to the so-called autonomy of politics of the workerist tradition—Tronti (1966) and Negri (1979)—where the decisive "voluntarist" moment is in the end independent from the actual trends of the model, which is taken into account just to define the fundamental opposition of capital and worker, while their theory of action—with either the help of Smith or Lenin—is conceived outside an actual consideration of the whole.

8. For an overview, see Bellofiore and Fineschi 2009.

9. For the distinction between forms and figures, see Fineschi (2008, ch. 3). For the more general issue of the levels of abstraction of Marx's theory of capital, see Fineschi (2013).

10. Varrone (1846): 495: "Quas res alii dividunt in duas partes, in homines et adminicula hominum, sine quibus rebus colere non possunt; alii in tres partes, instrumenti genus vocale et semivocale et mutum, vocale, in quo sunt servi, semivocale, in quo sunt boves, mutum, in quo sunt plaustra."

BIBLIOGRAPHY

Adorno, Theodor W. ed. 1969. *Spätkapitalismus oder Industriegesellschaft? Verhandlungen des 16. Deutschen Soziologentages*. Stuttgart: Enke.

Agamben, Giorgio. 1970. "Sui limiti della violenza." *Nuovi argomenti*, 17, 154–174.

Arendt, Anna. 1970. *On Violence*. San Diego/New York/London: Hacourt Brace Jovanovich.

Balibar, Étienne. 2015. *Violence and civility. On the Limits of Political Philosophy*. New York: Columbia University Press.

Benjamin, Walter. 1999. *Zur Kritik der Gewalt*. In *Gesammelte Schriften*, vol. II.1, edited by R. Tiedemann e H. Schweppenhäuser, 179–204. Frankfurt a.M.: Suhrkamp.

Bellofiore, Riccardo and Roberto Fineschi. ed. 2009. *Re-reading Marx*. Basingstoke: Palgrave.

Cazzaniga, Gian Mario. 1981. *Funzione e conflitto. Forme e classi nella teoria marxiana dello sviluppo*. Napoli: Liguori.

Colletti, Claudio, ed. 1975. *Il marxismo e il "crollo" del capitalismo*. Roma-Bari: Laterza.

Della Volpe, Galvano. 1957. *Marx e Rousseau*. Roma: Editori Riuniti.

Della Volpe, Galvano. 1969. *Logica come scienza storica*. Roma: Editori Riuniti.

Fineschi, Roberto. 2008. *Un nuovo Marx. Filologia e interpretazione dopo la nuova edizione storico-critica*. Roma: Carocci.

Fineschi, Roberto. 2013. The Four Levels of Abstraction of Marx's Concept of 'Capital'. Or, Can We Consider the Grundrisse the Most Advanced Version of Marx's Theory of Capital?. In *In Marx's Laboratory. Critical Interpretations of the* Grundrisse, edited by Riccardo Bellofiore, Guido Starosta, and Peter D. Thomas, 71–98. Leiden: Brill.

Foucault, Michel. 1975. *Surveiller et punir*. Paris: Gallimard.

Grossmann, Henryk. 1929. *Das Akkumulations- und Zusammenbruchsgesetz des kapitalistischen Systems. (Zugleich eine Krisentheorie)*. Leipzig: C. L. Hirschfeld.

Habermas, Jürgen. 1973. *Legitimationsprobleme im Spätkapitalismus*, Frankfurt a.M.: Suhrkamp.

Hegel, Georg Wilhelm Friedrich. 2010. *The Science of Logic*. Cambridge: Cambridge University Press.

Mandel, Ernest. 1972. *Der Spätkapitalismus. Versuch einer marxistischen Erklärung*, Frankfurt a. M.: Suhrkamp.

Marx, Karl. 1981. *Zur Kritik der Hegelschen Rechtsphilosophie*. In *Marx-Engels-Werke,* vol. 1: 1839–1844, p. 201–333. Berlin: Dietz.
Marx, Karl. 1990. *Capital. A critique of Political Economy. Volume One*. London: Penguin.
Marx, Karl. 1991. *Capital. A critique of Political Economy. Volume Three*. London: Penguin.
Marx, Karl. 1993. *Grundrisse*. London: Penguin.
Mazzone, Alessandro. 1981. *Questioni di teoria dell'ideologia*. Messina: La libbra.
Negri, Antonio. 1991. *Marx Beyond Marx: Lessons on the Grundrisse*. New York: Autonomedia.
Tronti, Mario. 1966. *Operai e capitale*. Torino, Einaudi.
Varrone, Marco Terenzio. 1846. *De Re Rustica*. In *Opere* p. 441–734. Venezia: Antonelli.

Chapter 3

The General Law of Capitalist Accumulation and a Theory of Labour-Shortage Business Cycles

Sergio Cámara Izquierdo

Marx developed the *general law of capitalist accumulation* in the lengthy chapter 25 of volume I of *Capital*, titled by the same name, of part 7 dedicated to "The Process of Capitalist Accumulation" (Marx 1867, 762–870).[1] As explicitly stated by Marx, the purpose of chapter 25 is to "consider the influence of the growth of capital on the fate of the working class" (Marx 1867, 762). To this aim, Marx divides the chapter into five sections. The first section analyzes the growing demand for labour-power in the course of accumulation. The second section deals with the repulsion of labour force due to the technical change accompanying accumulation. The third section analyzes the production and reproduction of an industrial reserve army, and the fourth section describes its forms. Lastly, the long fifth section illustrates the law through diverse historical and empirical explorations.

The general law of capitalist accumulation is an indispensable theoretical foundation for the analysis of the macrodynamics of capitalist accumulation in Marxist economic theory.[2] A fundamental postulate of this law is that the availability of labour-power does not imply a limit to capital accumulation, given the existence and reproduction of an industrial reserve army available to join the ranks of the exploited labour force. In this respect, the concept of industrial reserve army relates to, and contrasts with, the neoclassical concept of full employment. While aggregate supply is postulated to be rigid in the vicinity of full employment by neoclassical economics, the level of employment is not hypothesized as a limit to capital accumulation in Marxian theory and the rigidities in the aggregate supply arise from different economic factors.

Nonetheless, chapter 25 has been widely used by several strands within Marxist literature, reviewed in the first section of this chapter, to conceptualize and model the short-term macrodynamics, linking the recurrence of cyclical crises with the relative exhaustion of the available labour force. The apparent contradiction between this literature and the fundamental postulate of the general law is analyzed in the second section; it is argued that a theory of labour-shortage business cycles cannot be straightforwardly derived from chapter 25, let alone from its first section. Even so, the third section of the present chapter supports the case for a theory of labour-shortage business cycles by reviewing the main empirical advancements in their identification in the post–World War II United States, using previous investigations (Cámara 2012, 2013, 2020). Given the empirical support, the fourth section argues that section 4 of chapter 25 can be used to build this theory, with no contradiction with the fundamental postulate if the different time frames in which capital accumulation unfolds are incorporated into the analysis. Lastly, conclusions are drawn.

LABOUR-SHORTAGE BUSINESS CYCLES IN THE MARXIST LITERATURE

This section presents in chronological order a critical review of relevant examples in the literature of mathematical models, theoretical and analytical frameworks, and empirical analyses of business cycles related to the availability of the labour force. A significant aspect of the postulation of Marxist labour-shortage business cycles in the literature is that their existence is essentially supported by textual evidence that comes mostly from chapter 25, "The General Law of Capitalist Accumulation," and, to a great extent, from the first section of this chapter. We will show in the next section that this textual support is problematic.

The Goodwin model that served as pioneer in the field represents an imperfect example of this situation. Although the model is said to be presented in a Marxian form (Goodwin 1967, 55, 58), there is no reference to Marx's work, not to mention chapter 25 of *Capital*, volume I.[3] Goodwin elaborates an economic version of the Lotka-Volterra prey-predator system of two first-order nonlinear differential equations, in which profits are the prey and wages are the predator. Although the model behaves identically independently of the initial situation, for the sake of argument, we can start assuming a high level of profitability, which translates into a high level of investment and, consequently, an employment growth above the constant rate of growth of the working population, thus reducing unemployment and pushing up the real wage rate. The consequent reduction in profits and then investment, under the assumption of a constant investment rate, gives pace to a cyclical crisis characterized by a lower rate of employment growth (even stagnant or negative), below the growth of the working population, which reduces, in turn, the real wage growth. The continuity of this process results in an uninterrupted endogenously generated cyclical growth.

In contrast to Goodwin (1967), Eagly (1972) represents a clearer example of the exegetic use of chapter 25. He proposes a more elaborated "model of Marx's macroeconomy" that analyzes "an equilibrium solution that determines the unemployment level" and "the dynamic cyclical pattern of the system," that is, "the Marxist business cycle" (Eagly 1972, 523). Also, in contrast with Goodwin (1967), Eagly (1972) endogenizes technical change and the investment rate beyond the real wage. It is precisely to substantiate the endogenization of the investment rate when Eagly quotes a relevant passage of Marx's first section of chapter 25:

> The relation between capital accumulation and the rate of wages is nothing other than the relation between the unpaid labour which has been transformed into capital and the additional paid labour necessary to set in motion this additional capital. . . . If the quantity of unpaid labour supplied by the working class and accumulated by the capitalist class increases so rapidly that its transformation into capital requires an extraordinary addition of paid labour, then wages rise and, all other circumstances remaining equal, the unpaid labour diminishes in proportion. But as soon as this diminution touches the point at which the surplus labour that nourishes capital is no longer supplied in normal quantity, a reaction sets in: a smaller part of revenue is capitalized, accumulation slows down, and the rising movement of wages comes up against an obstacle. The rise of wages is therefore confined within limits that not only leave intact the foundations of the capitalist system, but also secure its reproduction on an increasing scale. (Marx 1867, 771)[4]

In accordance with the previous paragraph, Eagly (1972, 533–36) posits an investment rate equal to the unity (capitalists invest all the surplus value) during the expansive phase of the cycle, when the rate of profit is high and the unemployment rate is decreasing, pushing real wages up. This investment rate switches to zero when the rate of profit, squeezed by the increasing real wages, reaches a minimum acceptable profit rate. During the consequent contractive phase of the cycle, with null net investment, technological change due to the replacement of capital decreases the demand of labour and increases the rate of unemployment until it reaches a maximum point in which the investment rate switches to unity again and a new expansive phase of the cycle initiates, completing the business cycle.[5]

The rest of the textual evidence from chapter 25 provided by Eagly (1972, 526*n*) comes from two passages of section 3 and is used to support the finding that the "determinant of labor's bargain position is the unemployment level"

(Eagly 1972, 526). In these paragraphs, Marx (1867, 790, 792) establishes that the fluctuation of wages along the business cycle, that is, the recurrence of periods of stagnation and average prosperity, is mediated by the magnitude of the industrial reserve army. Two observations are to be made. First, Marx's reference to cyclical fluctuations can be found repeatedly in section 3 of chapter 25. Second, the referenced text does not mention explicitly labor shortages, but labor's relative availability as the determinant of wage cyclical fluctuations. Both elements will be discussed further in the next sections.

Boddy and Crotty (1975) aim to develop a theory of the class conflict behind the formulation of macroeconomic policies and to test it empirically for the U.S. state during the post–World War II period. Their line of argument resembles Goodwin's and Eagly's regarding the relation of the bargaining power of the working class with the unemployment level:

> During economic expansions, the reduction of the reserve army of the unemployed strengthens the bargaining position of the working class in its labor market confrontation with capital. Workers can then struggle successfully for higher real wages and a greater share of the rising national income. Correspondingly, profits are squeezed toward the top of the boom. Relaxation of this profit squeeze requires the termination of the expansionary phase of the cycle and the rebuilding of the reserve army. (Boddy and Crotty 1975, 2)

In order to substantiate this argument, Boddy and Crotty (1975, 2) choose to quote the aforementioned relevant passage of Marx's first section of chapter 25, except for omitting the first sentence, instead of passages from section 3 as Eagly does. However, their argument is not centered in an explosive investment rate as the trigger of the crisis. In its place, Laibman (1978) replicates Eagly's exegetic exercise; he quotes the same first section passage (Laibman 1978, 123*n*), except for the additional omission of the last sentence, as a reference for modeling accumulation and he references the whole chapter 25 to support the direct relation between unemployment and the exploitation rate, equivalent to the inverse relation between the unemployment rate and real wages described in previous cases due to the working class's bargaining power. Similarly to Eagly, Laibman (1978, 122–24) proposes a nonlinear investment function, which takes a positive constant rate if the unemployment rate is decreasing or is stagnant after an increasing period and zero if the unemployment rate is increasing or is stagnant after a decreasing period.

A last example of the exegetic use of chapter 25 in the prolific 1970s is found in the works of Weisskopf (1978, 1979), though more nuanced, given that there are no textual quotes. In both works, Weisskopf developed a formal analytical framework "to evaluate the current relevance of various Marxian theories of capitalist economic crisis" (Weisskopf 1979, 341) by analyzing the driving forces of the cyclical fluctuations of the profit rate throughout the business cycle (Weisskopf 1979, 342). One of these theories of crisis is the rising strength of labor (RSL) variant, explained by the decline of the profit rate caused by a shrinking profit share (Weisskopf 1978, 244–45, 247–50; 1979, 344–46, 354–57). According to Weisskopf, "This variant has been developed in recent years by several Marxian political economists pursuing a line of argument presented by Marx (in *Capital*, volume I, chapter 25)" (Weisskopf 1979, 345; see also Weisskopf 1978, 258*n*). Although Weisskopf does not support his framework in chapter 25 directly, but with an indirect reference to the literature, he certainly confirms the hypothesis advanced in this section. His line of argument is alike the previous works reviewed:

> As a cyclical expansion, develops the demand for labor grows more rapidly than the supply, the reserve army is depleted, and labor markets tighten. The growing scarcity of labor is then hypothesized to increase its political-economic power and improve the bargaining position of workers vis-a-vis capitalists. (Weisskopf 1979, 345)

To be sure, there is an ample literature in the Marxist domain that has developed the analysis of labor-shortage business cycles since the fruitful 1970s. The main characteristic of this literature is that emphasis has been placed on empirical assessments rather than on theoretical analyses and developments. Consequently, these works have as their theoretical references mainly the works published in the 1960s and 1970s, and have not developed further the foundation of their analysis in Marx's work, with insignificant explicit mentions to chapter 25 of volume I. Therefore, they share an acritical stance toward the exegetic foundation of the theoretical framework in Marx's work. Additionally, the studies have been overwhelmingly based on Weisskopf's framework and centered in the United States (Henley 1986; Goldstein 1996, 1999; Bakir 2006; Bakir and Campbell 2006, 2009; Cámara 2012, 2013; Goodfellow 2016), though a virtuous exception can be found in the recent work of Martins and Rugitsky (2021), who analyze the Brazilian economy.

An abundant literature has also developed an empirical application of Goodwin's model; a profuse review of this literature can be found in Grasselli and Maheshwari (2018). Two works should be highlighted. Desai (1984) is a breakthrough contribution, "where the foundation on how to estimate such dynamic models was laid" (Grasselli and Maheshwari 2018, 620). Harvie (2000) was the first continuation of this empirical approach, extended to 10 Organisation for Economic Co-operation and Development (OECD) countries; nevertheless, "there were several problems with the data construction in this paper, in addition to the mistake described in detail in Section 2.2, that compromised the validity of most of its results" (Grasselli and Maheshwari 2018, 620).[6] Two additional works not encompassed in the previous literature review should be mentioned; Marquetti and Miebach (2015) and Mendoza (2015) empirically test Goodwin's cycles in Brazil and in a sample of 82 countries, respectively. Lastly, Tapia's (2017) stimulating analysis of the U.S. economy cannot be placed in any of the previous two frameworks.

A notable exception to the previous characterization is the work of Sherman (1991).[7] The exception is twofold. First, Sherman develops an insightful theoretical analysis of business cycles, including those related to labor-shortage triggers, which is based on a profound discussion of the global works of Marx, Mitchel, Keynes, and Kalecki. Second, while Sherman (1991, 223) also quotes the aforementioned recurring passage from section 1 of chapter 25, yet cutting another sentence in relation to Laibman (1978), he is skeptical of the possibilities of grounding a theory of labor-shortage business cycles in Marx's work. This is the topic of the next section, where Sherman's line of argument would be further elaborated.

LABOR-SHORTAGE BUSINESS CYCLES IN CHAPTER 25 OF *CAPITAL*?

This section analyzes the first three sections of chapter 25 of volume I of *Capital* to conclude that it does not offer a theory of labor-shortage business cycles. This conclusion might appear rather critical of the literature reviewed in the previous section; nevertheless, we support empirically the case for theory of labor-shortage business cycles in the next section. Therefore, the matter relates more to an accurate exegetical reading to ground the theory than to the pertinence of the theory itself. In this respect, we definitely share the position manifested by Reuten:

> Marx does not introduce a "labour-shortage" theory of the cycle. In fact he does not present a theory of the cycle at all: in Capital I cyclical accumulation is introduced by way of an empirical reference. (I do not argue that the later Marxian theory of cyclical labour-shortage makes no sense; I argue that Marx does not introduce it in this book . . .). (Reuten 2004, 274)

Despite being a part of the completed and published work of Marx, and having been redrafted by Marx himself for the third and fourth editions of *Capital*, chapter 25 about the general law of capital accumulation is not straightforward to grasp.[8] A first major difficulty arises from the structure of the presentation of the law in the first three sections of the chapter. Marx introduces the chapter with the following hint: "The most important factor in this investigation is the composition of capital, and the changes it undergoes in the course of the process of accumulation" (Marx 1867, 762). Nonetheless, the first section of the chapter sets out that "a growing demand for labour-power accompanies accumulation if the composition of capital remains the same" (Marx 1867, 762). If the analysis of the section 1 of the chapter disregards the *most important factor in the investigation*, which is then its status and role in the chapter? The question is of most importance for our purposes, given that this section has been widely used exegetically for grounding a theory of labor-shortage business cycles in the literature as shown in the previous section.

Two possible interpretations of the role of section 1 can be examined and confronted. The first one refers to a historical interpretation, where the section corresponds to the historical stage of capital accumulation relating to the formal subsumption to capital. In chapter 6, "Results of the Direct Production Process," Marx (1864, 424–28, 430–38) defines formal subsumption as the historical development by which precapitalist production processes are converted into capitalist ones, where the labor process is intensified and prolonged, but no other change in the material real process, that is, in the composition of capital, takes place. Once the labor processes are formally subsumed to capital, the real subsumption is the consequent historical development that consists in the revolutionizing of its material content by way of the application of science and machinery, changing the composition of capital (Marx 1864, 428–30, 438–42).[9] Consequently, section 2 of chapter 25 would be interpreted as corresponding to the historical stage of the real subsumption to capital.[10]

Sherman's rejection of a theory of labor-shortage business cycles based on chapter 25 is related to this historical interpretation. According to him, the validity of Marx's arguments in section 1 is limited to "some extraordinary historical episodes in very rapid capitalist expansions that may lead to a depletion of the reserve army and a shortage of labor, resulting in higher wages." He continues that such "unusual periods, such as the late nineteenth century railway building boom in the United States," are to be understood "in the context of long-run changes resulting in a very unusual situation, but some Marxists have interpreted it as support for a short-run theory alleging higher wages in every expansion" (Sherman 1991, 223). Therefore, Sherman concludes that such anomalous structural situations cannot be extended to a recurrent cyclical phenomenon. A circumspect reading of chapter 25 seems to support Sherman's position. For instance, the most explicit reference to labor shortages in section 1 is accompanied with a historical reference:

> The requirements of accumulating capital may exceed the growth in labour-power or in the number of workers; the demand for workers may outstrip the

> supply, and thus wages may rise. This must indeed ultimately be the case if the conditions assumed above continue to prevail. For since in each year more workers are employed than in the preceding year, sooner or later a point must be reached at which the requirements of accumulation begin to outgrow the customary supply of labour, and a rise of wages therefore takes place. Complaints were to be heard about this in England during the whole of the fifteenth century, and the first half of the eighteenth. (Marx 1867, 763)

Two other passages from chapter 25 can be highlighted in support of this historical interpretation. First, Marx introduces section 2 with the following caveat:

> So far, we have considered only one special *phase* of this process, that in which the increase of capital occurs while the technical composition of capital remains constant. But the process goes beyond this *phase*. Given the general basis of the capitalist system, *a point is reached in the course of accumulation* at which the development of the productivity of social labour becomes the most powerful lever of accumulation. (Marx 1867, 772, emphasis added)

Although the reference to *phase* cannot be unambiguously interpreted as a historical period, the last sentence decidedly establishes a historical timeline in the process of capital accumulation. Second, in section 3, Marx retakes the line of reasoning of section 1 with another explicit reference to labor shortages historically delimited to the advent of capitalism:

> This peculiar cyclical path of modern industry, which occurs in no earlier period of human history, was also impossible when capitalist production was in its infancy. The composition of capital at that time underwent only very gradual changes. By and large, therefore, the proportional growth in the demand for labour has corresponded to the accumulation of capital. Even though the advance of accumulation was slow in comparison with that of the modern epoch, it came up against a natural barrier in the shape of the exploitable working population. (Marx 1867, 785)

In conclusion, the content of section 1 could not be devoted to positing a theory of labor-shortage business cycles in contemporary capitalism from the perspective of the historical interpretation, given that the description of labor shortages is historically delimited to the specific phase of the early days of capitalism.

The second possible interpretation of section 1 is a logical one. Marx might have used in chapter 25 his method of departing from abstract-simple categories in order to arrive to more concrete-complex categories by means of dialectical logic. In this process, the unity of the simple-abstract categories is found to be contradictory, then deriving new more concrete-complex categories that supersede the contradiction; therefore, categories acquire a mediated existence through conflicting relations. This dialectical progression can be represented by the dialectical triad of thesis, antithesis, and synthesis, which can be argued to shape chapter 25. Thus, section 1 would represent the thesis of an increasing demand for labor-power accompanying accumulation, section 2 would represent the antithesis of a relatively diminishing demand for labor-power as a consequence of technical change, and section 3 would represent the synthesis of the generation and reproduction of industrial reserve army, given the joint action of the thesis and the antithesis.

A simpler version of the logical interpretation would be that Marx analyzes separately the two effects affecting the working class in the process of capital accumulation—the attraction of labor-power (section 1) and the repulsion of labor-power (section 2)—before examining their joint action (section 3). Anyhow, whatever logic (formal or dialectical) is behind the structure of chapter 25,[11] the arguments drawn from section 1 cannot be considered as a definitive account of capitalist macrodynamics, but a rather partial account based on a counterfactual assumption: the absence of technical change. Consequently, the content of section 1 cannot be exegetically used to substantiate a theory of labor-shortage business cycles from the perspective of the logical interpretation of chapter 25.

After the introduction of technical change and the consequent changes in the composition of capital in the course of accumulation in section 2, along with the acceleration of this process through the centralization of capital, section 3 is dedicated to the production of industrial reserve army: "it is capitalist accumulation itself that constantly produces . . . a relatively redundant working population, i.e. a population which is superfluous to capital's average requirements for its own valorization, and is therefore a surplus population" (Marx 1867, 782). Instead of labor shortages, capitalism creates a surplus working population that "becomes, conversely, the lever of capitalist accumulation, indeed it becomes a condition for the existence of the capitalist mode of production" (Marx 1867, 782). In spite of this, the references to industrial cycles in section 3 are numerous.[12] Do these references constitute a theory of business cycles? For Marx, capital accumulation and the formation and reproduction of the industrial reserve army take the form of an industrial cycle:

> The path characteristically described by modern industry, which takes the form of a decennial cycle (interrupted by smaller oscillations) of periods of average activity, production at high pressure, crisis, and stagnation, *depends on* the constant formation, the greater or less absorption, and the re-formation of the

industrial reserve army or surplus population. *In their turn*, the varying phases of the industrial cycle recruit the surplus population, and become one of the most energetic agencies for its reproduction. (Marx 1867, 785, emphasis added)

However, Marx does not establish a causal link between the availability of surplus population and the fluctuations of capital accumulation; quite the contrary, Marx emphasizes the inverse causal relationship, that is, the needs of the process of accumulation determine the fluctuations in the industrial reserve army. This is evident in two of the most cited passages of section 3:

> Taking them as a whole, the general movements of wages are exclusively regulated by the expansion and contraction of the industrial reserve army, and this in turn corresponds to the periodic alternations of the industrial cycle. . . . The appropriate law for modern industry, with its decennial cycles and periodic phases . . . is the law of the regulation of the demand and supply of labour by the alternate expansion and contraction of capital, i.e. by the level of capital's valorization requirements at the relevant moment, the labour-market sometimes appearing relatively under-supplied because capital is expanding, and sometimes relatively over-supplied because it is contracting. (Marx 1867, 790)

> The industrial reserve army, during the periods of stagnation and average prosperity, weighs down the active army of workers; during the periods of overproduction and feverish activity, it puts a curb on their pretensions. The relative surplus population is therefore the background against which the law of the demand and supply of labour does its work. It confines the field of action of this law to the limits absolutely convenient to capital's drive to exploit and dominate the workers. (Marx 1867, 792)

Reuten stresses the lack of such casual links; first, he asserts that Marx "does not explain cyclical turning points" (Reuten 2004, 292*n*); second, in his analysis of the previous paragraphs, he states that "Marx does not posit the wage rate mechanism to *explain* the cycle; the wage movements correspond to it (and if, instead, he believed wage movements to be causative he would certainly have said so)" (Reuten 2004, 293). According to Reuten, Marx's references to the cycle are rather empirical than theoretical: "in fact Marx appends an empirical phenomenon to the theory without explaining it, i.e. without theory" (Reuten 2004, 292). In the same vein, Reuten asserts that "Marx knows that empirically the development is cyclical. Thus his theory is incomplete. . . . This theoretical problem might have been overcome by combining his theory with, what was later called, a 'labour-shortage' theory of the cycle. He seems to have the material before him to posit such a theory, but he does not do it. Instead he makes an empirical reference to the cycle" (Reuten

2004: 294–95) For Reuten, Marx's choice is justified: "a theory of the cycle cannot be developed at this level of abstraction" (Reuten 2004, 296).

THE EMPIRICAL CASE FOR A THEORY OF LABOR-SHORTAGE BUSINESS CYCLES

In the previous section, we concluded that a theory of labor-shortage business cycles cannot be substantiated in an exegetic reading of chapter 25 of volume I of *Capital*, neither from a historical nor from a logical interpretation. Nevertheless, this conclusion does not preclude the pertinence of such a theory. In the next section, we will extract elements from the fourth section of chapter 25 that are helpful to build a theory of labor-shortage business cycles. Erstwhile, the present section reviews some empirical advancements in the identification of labor-shortage business cycles in post–World War II United States. For reasons of space, the section limits to the exposition of main results of our previous investigations; nonetheless, the majority of the empirical research reviewed in the first section reaches similar conclusions.

From 1947 to 2018, the U.S. economy completed 10 business cycles. Cámara (2012, 2013, 2020) applied the methodology developed by Weisskopf (1978, 1979) to analyze the role of cyclical declines in the profit rate as the cause of crises. The analysis shows that a cyclical decline of the rate of profit in the last part of the expansion prior to the onset of the crisis took place in 9 out of the 10 business cycles; the only exception is the short expansion phase (from the third quarter of 1981 to the fourth quarter of 1982) that followed the crisis of 1980. This finding was first signaled by Boddy and Crotty (1975, 1, 5), who observed that the "labor share typically rises in the latter half of an expansion," and was retaken by Weiskopf (1979, 351) to propose an analytical division of the expansion phase of the cycle between an early stage when both the profit rate and the product grow, and a late stage when the profit rate starts to decline while the product still grows. Our analysis shows that, on average, almost two-thirds of the cyclical decline of the rate of profit takes place in the late expansion phase, while the decline is completed during the cyclical contraction.

The previous finding is robust enough to postulate that a cyclical decline of the profit rate may trigger cyclical crises and thus shape the business cycles. However, the casual relationship between the cyclical behavior of the profit rate and the business cycles must be carefully established. We have argued that this causality rests on both a temporal lag and the absolute intensity of the profit rate decline prior to the contraction. The fulfillment of the two previous strong criteria led us to discard the cyclical decline of the profit rate as the cause of crisis in three additional business cycles. In two of these cycles, the cyclical decline is short-lived and not too deep, while in another cycle, the cyclical decline is negligible. Nevertheless, there is strong evidence of 6 out of 10 postwar cyclical crises to be caused by a cyclical decline of the rate of profit.

In order to evaluate the causes of the cyclical declines in the profit rate prior to the output contraction, the profit rate is decomposed among the potential productivity of capital, the profit share, and the capacity utilization rate; the cyclical decline of each of the previous determinants generates, respectively, the rising organic composition of capital (ROC), the rising strength of labor (RSL), and the realization failure (RF) types of cyclical crisis. The evidence shows that more than three quarters of the decline in the profit rate, on average, is explained by the decline in the profit share. The profit share is the main contributor to the profitability drop in all the cycles, while the capacity utilization rate contribution is only meaningful, though certainly minor, in three cycles. In conclusion, the empirical evidence suggests that 6 out of 10 cyclical crises in the U.S. post–World War II period are caused by a cyclical decline of the profit rate caused by the dynamics of the profit share.

Lastly, in four of the six previously identified labor-shortage business cycles, the declines in the profit share in the late expansion phases are mainly explained by positive increases in real wages above the increases in productivity; in one additional cycle, the late expansion phase took place in a period of high inflation and the decline of the profit share is explained by a real-wage decline but with a deeper productivity drop. This situation has been identified as the offensive rising strength of labor variant of crisis, when workers exert their increased power as a consequence of a decline of the unemployment rate to obtain higher real-wage gains. In the other cycle, the cyclical decline in the profit share in the late expansion phase is explained by an increase of the relative price of wage goods and output. This situation has been identified as the defensive rising strength of labor variant of crisis, in which the workers are able to transfer to the capitalist class the effects of an adverse relative price change.

To sum up, a significant decline in the profit rate prior to the cyclical contraction cannot be postulated as a stylized fact of business cycles in post–World War II United States, but it is an event happening in most of the business cycles, 6 out of 10. In all these six cycles, the cyclical decline of the profit rate is explained by a cyclical decline in the profit share, giving rise to the possibility of business cycles driven by labor-shortage pressures. As a matter of fact, there is evidence for an offensive rising strength of labor in five of the cycles and for a defensive rising strength of labor in the other cycle, that is, the most common case is that workers are able to obtain real-wage increases above productivity growth in the late expansion phase of the business cycle. In conclusion, there is enough empirical evidence to substantiate the recurrence of labor-shortage business cycles in the post–World War II United States; a further scrutiny of chapter 25 of volume I of *Capital* to identify foundations to build a theory of labor-shortage business cycles is worth.

A REREADING OF SECTION 4 OF CHAPTER 25 INCORPORATING TIME FRAMES

As stated earlier, chapter 25 cannot be used to exegetically ground a theory of labor-shortage business cycles. However, the chapter offers propositions that are helpful to develop such a theory. The literature reviewed in the first section has mainly hinged on the first three sections of the chapter; instead, we contend that section 4 of chapter 25 provides relevant insights to cope with the apparent contradiction between the fundamental postulate of the general law of capitalist accumulation and postulation of labor-shortage business cycles remarked in the introduction. For this, we propose a rereading of this section introducing the role of the different time frames in which the process of capital accumulation takes place. Concretely, we argue that short-term labor shortages do not contradict the fact that the availability of labor-power does not imply a limit to capital accumulation, given the existence and reproduction of an industrial reserve army available in a longer term.

Section 4 of chapter 25 of volume I of *Capital* has been profoundly neglected in the literature on labor-shortage business cycles. Although in most cases it is simply ignored, Reuten (2004, 294) explicitly states that "the final two sections of Chapter 25 contain no new theoretical analysis. Section 4 begins with a number of 'surplus population' distinctions (floating, latent and stagnant). Then Marx summarizes the 'general law.' " On the contrary, we consider that these distinctions of the surplus population are useful to elaborate a theory of labor-shortage short-term cycles. Most probably, Reuten's disregard of the theoretical contribution of these distinctions is related with a narrow conceptualization of the industrial reserve army:

> Readers of *Capital* may wonder why Marx when addressing "unemployment" apparently uses such bombastic terminology: "reserve army of labour," "surplus population," or "redundant working population." He may have had his reasons for the particular choice, but the simple point is that in his day the term "unemployment" (or its German equivalent) just did not exist. (Reuten 2004, 290)

However, a careful reading of the different forms of the industrial reserve army will let us conclude that the industrial reserve army available to be exploited by capital is not necessarily unemployed; the Marxian concept of industrial reserve army is richer than that of unemployment. Despite this, this narrow conceptualization of surplus population as unemployment is extended in the literature on labor-shortage business cycles. For instance, Eagly (1972, 523), Boddy and Crotty (1975, 2, 8), and Laibman (1978, 122) refer to the "reserve army of (the) unemployed."

The Marxist analysis of capitalist accumulation has usually distinguished between the different time frames involved in the process. Following the traditional approaches in economic modeling, a distinction is made between fast and slow variables that give rise to the short-term and long-term time frames in the process of capital accumulation. This is certainly the case with the macroeconomic models of capital accumulation developed by Shaikh (1989) and Duménil and Lévy (1999):

> An important aspect of the approach is the distinction between fast and slow variables. Slow variables are assumed to have decision periods longer than those of corresponding faster variables (e.g., years instead of months), so slow decisions are effectively cast in terms of moving averages of the faster variables. Although one can conceive of many different sets of variables with each set operating at its own intrinsic speed, the present analysis is confined to just two speeds. The basic fast variable will be . . . the rate of accumulation in circulating capital, and it regulates the relation between supply and demand. The corresponding slow variable will be the rate of accumulation in fixed capital, which regulates the relation between supply and capacity. (Shaikh 1989, 72)

> We discuss the relationship between Keynesian and classical equilibria emphasizing the distinction between two time frames, short term and long term. . . . The convergence to a classical equilibrium follows from specific assumptions concerning the dynamics of a number of variables (capital stocks, prices etc.), called long-term variables. These variables are treated as constant parameters within short-term equilibria, and are slowly modified between two short-term equilibria. (Duménil and Lévy 1989, 684–85, 686)

In section 4 of chapter 25, Marx states that "the relative surplus population exists in all kinds of forms. . . . We can identify three forms which it always possesses: the floating, the latent, and the stagnant" (Marx 1867, 794). These different forms or components of the industrial reserve army can be analyzed and classified in terms of the different time frames of capital accumulation, distinguishing between the fast components that give rise to short-term fluctuations and the slow components that give rise to long-term tendencies. Such an approach would be helpful to distinguish the fragment of the industrial reserve army that determines business cycle fluctuations and the fragment of the industrial reserve army that is available to join the ranks of the exploited labor force in a longer term.[13]

Marx describes the floating surplus population as "the workers . . . sometimes repelled, sometimes attracted again in greater masses . . . in the centres of modern industry—factories, workshops, ironworks, mines, etc." (Marx 1867, 794). Therefore, this component of the industrial reserve army is characterized by its fast adjustment along with the business cycle. It is also the component of the industrial reserve army that is mostly unemployed, though it can also be also under-employed, especially if workers can enjoy unemployment benefits for a long enough period to reproduce themselves until they are hired again, probably in a new cyclical expansion. This situation is common in developed or central countries, but it is not the standard case in developing or peripheral countries. On the other extreme, Marx defines the latent surplus population:

> Part of the agricultural population is therefore constantly on the point of passing over into an urban or manufacturing proletariat. . . . There is thus a constant flow from this source of the relative surplus population. But the constant movement towards the towns presupposes, in the countryside itself, a constant latent surplus population. (Marx 1867, 796)

Thus, the latent component of the industrial reserve army can be considered to adjust slowly along the long-term tendencies. Marx confines this component to the rural population, but the latent surplus population is nowadays also composed by urban population. It is formed by self-employed workers, who own the means of production, and their subordinated employees in processes of production that employ below-average technological capabilities, normally in small establishments; they conform a non-capitalist sphere within the capitalist mode of production. Consequently, the velocity of adjustment of the latent population depends heavily on the gap between the average technological capabilities and the particular ones that they employ. The narrower the gap, the slower they are forced (or eager) to be employed capitalistically, and vice versa. This component of the industrial reserve army tends to be more quantitatively relevant in developing or peripheral countries, where the informal part of this surplus population dominates.[14] Additionally, most of the immigrant flows can also be considered part of the latent surplus population. The third component of the industrial reserve army is also the hardest to assess in terms of the short and long-term time frames. Marx defines:

> The stagnant population [as] a part of the active labour army, but with extremely irregular employment. . . . Its conditions of life sink below the average normal level of the working class, and it is precisely this which makes it a broad foundation for special branches of capitalist exploitation. It is characterized by a maximum of working time and a minimum of wages. (Marx 1867, 796)

Given this description, the stagnant surplus population can be classified into both the fast and the slow adjustment surplus populations. The population that is employed in longer than usual workdays in a regular basis, even if obtaining a below average remuneration, would be less (or more slowly) compelled to be employed under normal capitalist conditions. In contrast, the population that is irregularly employed or that is underemployed in a normal basis, given that it is unable to enjoy even the below average life conditions, would be more (or more rapidly) compelled to be employed under normal capitalist conditions. This would be especially true if the short-term needs for labor-power cannot be adequately met with the floating surplus population. Hence, the stagnant population adjusts not so fast as the floating population and not so slowly than the latent population. Nonetheless, for the simplicity of modeling, it can be split into the short-term and the long-term time frames.

The previous characterization of the industrial reserve army is rather simplistic. An empirical application to a concrete economy would require a deeper analysis of the inactive, active, employed, under-employed, unemployed, and other working population. Nonetheless, it is satisfactory for the purpose of the present chapter to distinguish between the fraction of the industrial reserve army that determines the short-term fluctuations (the floating and part of the stagnant surplus population) and the fraction of the industrial reserve army that is available to be employed capitalistically in a longer term (the latent and another part of the stagnant surplus population). Significantly, the previous classification of the industrial reserve army into a short-term fraction and a long-term fraction is highly relevant for a reconceptualization of a theory of labor-shortage business cycles in capitalism.

Particularly, labor shortages should be confined to the short-term fraction of the surplus population, while the long-term fraction of the surplus population is continually reproduced to provide a slower source of labor force supply for capital accumulation. Contrary to Sherman's (1991, 223) previously referred assertion, labor shortages cannot be conceptualized as a long-term phenomenon, but as a potential short-term occurrence that might shape capitalist macrodynamics. Potential labor-shortages might trigger a cyclical crisis, activating the cyclical mechanisms that replenish the short-term fraction of the surplus population; additionally, the generation, reproduction, and use of the long-term fraction of the industrial reserve army is also reinforced by these potential cyclical episodes. Therefore, a theory of labor-shortage cycles does not contradict the fundamental postulate of the general law of capitalist accumulation: short-term labor shortages are perfectly compatible with the reproduction of an ever-greater industrial reserve army; in Marx's words:

> The greater the social wealth, the functioning capital, the extent and energy of its growth, and therefore also the greater the absolute mass of the proletariat and

the productivity of its labour, the greater is the industrial reserve army. (Marx 1867, 798)

CONCLUSION

This chapter has contributed to develop a theory of labor-shortage business cycles from a Marxian perspective. First, it provides an exegetic reading of chapter 25 of volume I of *Capital* to identify insights to ground this theory. In a first step, it is concluded that Marx does not provide a theory of labor-shortage business cycles in this chapter. The Marxist literature proposals of such a theory based on exegetic readings of chapter 25 are ill-founded. Either from a historical or logical interpretation, the presence of a theory of labor-shortage business cycles in chapter 25 can be discarded. This conclusion does not preclude that such a theory can be built on insights found in this same chapter. In a second step, we have identified these insights in the normally neglected section 4 of chapter 25. Concretely, Marx's analysis of the forms of the surplus population was helpful to derive a short-term fraction and a long-term fraction of the industrial reserve army. Second, when this differentiation is applied to the development of a theory of labor-shortage business cycles, the apparent contradiction between this theory and the fundamental postulate of the general law of capitalist accumulation vanishes.

The present chapter can serve as the basis to develop further theoretical expansions of a theory of labor-shortage business cycles. Specifically, the theoretical models and frameworks of labor-shortage business cycles can be enlightened by the distinction between the short-term and long-term fractions of the surplus population. Additionally, the chapter can be helpful to develop a further-reaching theory of business cycles that encompasses labor shortages only as one of the potential causes of cyclical crises. Finally, the chapter can also be illuminating for the empirical applications of the theoretical models and frameworks of labor-shortage business cycles; empirical estimations of the short-term and long-term fractions of the surplus population would be useful to adequately test the theory in concrete cases.

NOTES

1. Chapter 25 of the English edition corresponds to chapter 23 of the German edition of *Capital*.
2. Reuten observes that in Part Seven of *Capital*, "the analysis leans, and sometimes explicitly, towards a macroeconomic treatment" (Reuten 2004, 276–77).
3. Actually, there is not a single reference in the 6-page chapter.

4. While Eagly (1972) employs New York's Modern Library edition of *Capital*, we use hereafter the Penguin edition.

5. Laibman (1978), which is reviewed below, is critical of Eagly's (1972, 532, 534) explicit assumption of the fulfillment of Say's Law; according to him, "this strict Say's Law position makes it impossible to explain the crucial turning points in the cycle" (Laibman 1978, 119).

6. Harvie (2000, 351–52) presents a brief digression on the "Marxian basis of Goodwin's model" referring to "a simple model Marx presents in the first section of Chapter 25."

7. This book contains parts of works previously published by the author in the 1970s and 1980s.

8. The present chapter analyses this latter version of chapter 25 of volume I of *Capital* and abstracts from its differences with previous versions.

9. The logical definitions of formal and real subsumption to capital complement these historical definitions. Unlike other concepts in Marx's work, the historical and logical definitions of formal and real subsumption to capital are coincident. On the contrary, in chapter 6, Marx (1864, 427–28) exemplifies the formal subsumption of labor to capital by analyzing usurers' capital and merchants' capital, whose historical existence precede their formal development.

10. This historical interpretation of chapter 25 does not necessarily endorse Engels's interpretation of Marx's method as a logical-historical one, which has been widely rejected in the literature. As a matter of fact, historical parts in the analysis of *Capital* are well delineated and the historical and logical analyses are not interspersed. For instance, in chapter 25, the historical analysis is clearly delimited in section 5. Also, the historical analysis of capital accumulation is delimited in part 8 in the English edition of *Capital*, corresponding to chapters 24 and 25 of part 7 in the original German edition, given that Engels broke up part 7 into two subparts, and the seven sections of chapter 24 were converted into 7 chapters, from 26 to 32, while chapter 25 passed to be chapter 33.

11. A more substantial methodological reading of *Capital* and, in particular, chapter 25 is beyond the scope of the present chapter; it is neither needed to develop the arguments presented. The interested reader is referred to the vast and diverse literature on Marx's method of political economy.

12. Prior to section 3, there is only one reference to the industrial cycle in section 1, which is not significative for the line of argument of the section (Marx 1867, 770–71). In the present chapter, Marx's industrial or decennial cycle is deemed synonymous with business cycle.

13. This analysis is enlightened by my academic exchange with Abelardo Mariña. He has researched about both the time frames in capital accumulation (e.g., see Mariña 2020) and the components of the industrial reserve army (e.g., see Legaria, Barrios, and Mariña 2004). The remaining errors and omissions, needless to say, are mine.

14. One may wonder if the narrow definition of the industrial reserve army exposed given earlier is related to a Western-centric analysis of the labor market. In developed or central countries, the unemployed composition of the industrial reserve

army is surely relatively higher than in developing or peripheral countries, where the presence of self-employed with below-average technological conditions of production is extended. In any case, we either do not find the narrow definition of the industrial reserve army to be useful for developed or central countries.

BIBLIOGRAPHY

Bakir, Erdogan. 2006. "The Post WWII Nonfinancial Corporate Rate of Profit in the US: Cycles, Trends, and the Effects of Financialization." PhD diss., The University of Utah.

Bakir, Erdogan, and Al Campbell. 2006. "The Effect of Neoliberalism on the Fall in the Rate of Profit in Business Cycles.," *Review of Radical Political Economics* 38, no. 3 (Summer): 365–73. https://doi.org/10.1177/0486613406290901.

——— 2009. "The Bush Business Cycle Profit Rate: Support in a Theoretical Debate and Implications for the Future." *Review of Radical Political Economics* 41, no. 3 (September): 335–42. https://doi.org/10.1177/0486613409336346.

Boddy, Rafford, and James Crotty. 1975. "Class Conflict and Macro-Policy: The Political Business Cycle." *Review of Radical Political Economics* 7, no. 1 (April): 1–19. https://doi.org/10.1177/048661347500700101.

Cámara, Sergio. 2012. "La dinámica coyuntural de la tasa de ganancia en Estados Unidos (1947–2010)." In *Estudios sobre México en la crisis mundial: Escenario nacional tras dos décadas de apertura y desregulación*, edited by Beatriz García, 183–232. Mexico City: Universidad Autónoma Metropolitana-Azcapotzalco.

——— 2013. "The Cyclical Decline of the Profit Rate as the Cause of Crises in the United States (1947–2011)." *Review of Radical Political Economics* 45, no. 4 (December): 459–67. https://doi.org/10.1177/0486613412475186.

__________ 2020. "Elementos teóricos y empíricos para una taxonomía de la crisis capitalista en la teoría económica marxista." In *La naturaleza contradictoria del capitalismo contemporáneo. Ensayos de economía política*, edited by Sergio Cámara, 61–102. Mexico City: Universidad Autónoma Metropolitana-Azcapotzalco.

Desai, Meghnad. 1984. "An Econometric Model of the Share of Wages in National Income: UK 1855–1965." In *Nonlinear Models of Fluctuating Growth: An International Symposium Siena, Italy, March 24–27, 1983*, edited by Richard M. Goodwin, Michael Krüger, and Alessandro Vercelli, 253–77. Berlin, Heidelberg: Springer.

Duménil, Gérard, and Dominique Lévy. 1999. "Being Keynesian in the Short Term and Classical in the Long Term: The Traverse to Classical Long-Term Equilibrium." *The Manchester School* 67, no. 6 (December): 684–716. https://doi.org/10.1111/1467-9957.00175.

Eagly, Robert. 1972. "A Macro Model of the Endogenous Business Cycle in Marxist Analysis." *Journal of Political Economy* 80, no. 3, Part I (May–June): 523–39. https://doi.org/10.1086/259903.

Goldstein, Jonathan. 1996. "The Empirical Relevance of the Cyclical Profit Squeeze: A Reassertion." *Review of Radical Political Economics* 28, no. 4 (December): 55–92. https://doi.org/10.1177/048661349602800403.

——— 1999. "The Simple Analytics and Empirics of the Cyclical Profit Squeeze and Cyclical Underconsumption Theories: Clearing the Air." *Review of Radical Political Economics* 31, no. 2 (Spring): 74–88. https://doi.org/10.1177/048661349903100205.

Goodfellow, Robin. 2016. *Le cycle des crises aux États-Unis depuis 1929: essai de systématisation de la conjuncture.* Paris: L'Harmattan.

Goodwin, Richard. 1967. "A Growth Cycle." In *Socialism, Capitalism, and Economic Growth. Essays Presented to Maurice Dobb*, edited by Charles Feinstein, 54–9. Cambridge: Cambridge University Press.

Grasselli, Matheus R., and Aditya Maheshwari. 2018. "Testing a Goodwin Model with General Capital Accumulation Rate." *Metroeconomica* 69, no. 3 (July): 619–43. https://doi.org/10.1111/meca.12204.

Harvie, David. 2000. "Testing Goodwin: Growth Cycles in Ten OECD Countries." *Cambridge Journal of Economics* 24, no. 3 (May): 349–76. https://doi.org/10.1093/cje/24.3.349.

Henley, Andrew. 1987. "Labour's Shares and Profitability Crisis in the US: Recent Experience and Post-War Trends." *Cambridge Journal of Economics* 11, no. 4 (December): 315–30. https://doi.org/10.1093/oxfordjournals.cje.a035034.

Laibman, David. 1978. "The Marxian Profit Cycle: A Macromodel." *Eastern Economic Journal* 4, no. 2 (Spring): 119–28. https://www.jstor.org/stable/20642312.

Legaria, Loth, Miguel Ángel Barrios, and Abelardo Mariña. 2004. "El ejército industrial de reserva en México en el contexto del imperialismo contemporáneo." In *Imperialismo, crisis de las instituciones y resistencia social*, edited by Ana Alicia Solís, Max Ortega, Abelardo Mariña, and Nina Torres, 95–121. Mexico City: Itaca.

Mariña, Abelardo. 2020. "Tendencias de largo plazo de la acumulación de capital y crisis estructurales: una perspectiva marxista de las ondas largas." In *La naturaleza contradictoria del capitalismo contemporáneo. Ensayos de economía política*, edited by Sergio Cámara, 19–60. Mexico City: Universidad Autónoma Metropolitana-Azcapotzalco.

Marquetti, Adalmir A., and Alessandro D. Miebach. 2015. "Distribución del ingreso y nivel de actividad. El ciclo de Goodwin en la economía brasileña." In *Tendencia y ciclo en economía: Teoría y evidencia empírica*, edited by Gabriel Mendoza, 177–204. Mexico City: Facultad de Economía, Universidad Nacional Autónoma de México.

Martins, Guilherme K., and Fernando Rugitsky. 2021, "The Long Expansion and the Profit Squeeze: Output and Profit Cycles in Brazil (1996–2016)." *Review of Radical Political Economics* 53, no. 3 (September): 373–97. https://doi.org/10.1177/0486613420982083.

Marx, Karl. 1864. "Chapter Six. Results of the Direct Production Process." In *Marx & Engels Collected Works*, Vol. 34, 1861–1864, 2020, edited by Karl Marx and Frederick Engels, 355–471. London: Lawrence & Wishart.

——— 1867[1890]. *Capital, A Critique of Political Economy*, Volume 1, 1976. Harmondsworth: Penguin.

Mendoza, Gabriel A. 2015. "Una aplicación empírica de la dinámica entre salarios y empleo formulada por Goodwin." In *Tendencia y ciclo en economía: Teoría y evidencia empírica*, edited by Gabriel Mendoza, 223–58. Mexico City: Facultad de Economía, Universidad Nacional Autónoma de México.

Reuten, Geert. 2004. "The Inner Mechanism of the Accumulation of Capital: The Acceleration Triple. A Methodological Appraisal of 'Part Seven' of Marx's *Capital I*." In *The Constitution of Capital. Essays on Volume I of Marx's* Capital, edited by Riccardo Bellofiore and Nicola Taylor, 274–98. Houndmills, Basingstoke, Hampshire: Palgrave Macmillan.

Shaikh, Anwar. 1989. "Accumulation, Finance, and Effective Demand in Marx, Keynes, and Kalecki." In *Financial Dynamics and Business Cycles: New Prospects*, edited by Willi Semmler, 65–86. Armonk, New York: M.E. Sharpe.

Sherman, Howard J. 1991. *The Business Cycle: Growth and Crisis Under Capitalism.* Oxford: Princeton University Press.

Tapia, José A. 2017. *Rentabilidad, inversión y crisis. Teorías económicas y datos empíricos*. Madrid: Maia.

Weisskopf, Thomas E. 1978. "Marxist Perspectives on Cyclical Crises." In *U.S. Capitalism in Crisis*, edited by Union for Radical Political Economics, 241–60. New York: Union for Radical Political Economics.

——— 1979. "Marxian Crisis Theory and the Rate of Profit in the Postwar U.S. Economy." *Cambridge Journal of Economics* 3, no. 4 (December): 341–78. https://doi.org/10.1093/oxfordjournals.cje.a035429.

Chapter 4

The Determination of Wages in the Framework of Capital Accumulation

The Industrial Reserve Army and the Value of Labor-Power

Abelardo Mariña Flores

INTRODUCTION

Even on the more superficial level, wages express in a concentrated way the contradictory nature of the operation of capitalism. On the one hand, wages constitute purchasing power for wage workers who acquire with it commodities that satisfy their needs through final consumption. For employees, it is vital to maximize their wages to expand the possibility of fulfilling their needs. On the other hand, wages are a cost of production for capitalists who, therefore, need to minimize their amount to strengthen their profitability. An irreconcilable contradiction is thus manifested between the individual economic agents that concur as suppliers (sellers) and demanders (buyers) in the labor markets. Socially, total wages are one of the components of aggregate effective demand, on which volume and structure of the general and sectoral conditions of realization and, therefore, of valorization, directly depend, and, indirectly, therefore, also the conditions of reproduction and accumulation. A reduction of wages that is functional for individual capitals can be dysfunctional for social capital by making more difficult the general conditions for the realization of commodities and for the valorization of capital. Hence, another contradiction manifests itself between the interests of individual capitals and global capital, which under certain conditions is also irreconcilable.

On the essential plane of capitalism, wages express the basic contradiction of the system. Capitalism is based on the exploitation of wage labor derived from the fact that the new value in which the living labor of producers is objectified is divided in two parts: wages paid to producers, and surplus value which is appropriated by the nonproducers who monopolize the ownership of the means of production. However, although the process of capital accumulation tends to incessantly increase the production of surplus value and the rate of exploitation (the ratio of surplus value to wages), which strengthens profitability, at the same time, it increases the composition of capital, which weakens the rate of profit. Fluctuations in profitability are the cause of recurring capitalist crises. Periodical decreases in profit margins generate cyclical conjunctural crisis. The tendential fall of the general rate of profit has been the cause of structural profitability crises such as the one that took place since the late 1960s and early 1970s.

Therefore, the analysis of wage determinations has been a fundamental task for the different economic theories. Generally, apart from the Marxist perspective, they analyze wage determinations on the superficial plane of operation of the capitalist system, avoiding the essential plane. In doing so, they evade the essential contradiction of capitalism, the exploitation of labor, and therefore have difficulties dealing with the general contradictory nature of wages.

In this chapter, the more general determinations of wages are analyzed from a Marxist viewpoint. Recognizing that there is no consensus among Marxists regarding some issues involved, nevertheless the common foundations of such perspective are considered to be the following:

(i) The exploitation of wage labor is the basis of the conditions of production, distribution, circulation, and consumption, as well as of their articulations, in the process of capitalist reproduction.
(ii) The price system that regulates exchanges is determined by the socially necessary quantities of abstract wage labor objectified in each commodity.
(iii) The fluctuations of profitability, capital accumulation, and the consequential recurring economic crises are immanent to the operation of the system.

This analysis, for simplifying purposes, abstracts from several elements considered nonessential for the explanation of wages. First, as a more general assumption, it does not consider the determination of incomes received by non-wage-earning workers that always exist in a capitalist social formation along with noncapitalist forms of production. Second, as an intermediate assumption, only the determinations of direct wages paid by capitalist firms are studied and not those of indirect wages, such as social benefits, nor those of the social expenditure of reproductive labor. Third, as a more specific assumption, the determinations of wage differences among companies in the same sector, different sectors of the economy, different countries, different types of work, and workers who do the same type of work, whether for reasons of gender, age, ethnicity or otherwise, are not studied.

Therefore, the investigation is limited to examining the determinations of the economy's average nominal wage and its relations with the average real wage and with the value of labor-power. This is done in a framework that contemplates the effects on the operation of the labor markets of cyclical fluctuations and long-term trends of capital accumulation. The simplifying assumptions made may be raised in future research works, based on the results expounded here, which would allow incorporating more specific determinations of wages and other phenomena to advance a more concrete understanding of the operation of labor markets in capitalism.

This work consists of five sections. After this Introduction, section "General Determinations of Wages in a Marxist Perspective" analyzes the general determinations of wages. Next Section "Labor Markets, Capital Accumulation, and the Industrial Reserve Army" examines, firstly, the operation of labor markets and upon it, the creation by capital of an Industrial Reserve Army (IRA). In its next section "Different Forms of the Industrial Reserve Army, Accumulation, and Regulation of Labor," the role of the different forms of existence of the IRA in the regulation of employment and of the conditions of productive consumption, buying and selling of labor-power, and reproduction of the labor force are studied. In last section, some synthetical final considerations are presented.

GENERAL DETERMINATIONS OF WAGES IN A MARXIST PERSPECTIVE

In a Marxist theoretical perspective, the determination of wages shows several peculiarities.

(i) Wage is the price, not of the work executed by workers, but of their labor-power. The distinction between work and labor-power, not considered by other theoretical perspectives, is fundamental in understanding the exploitation of wage labor. Workers are not paid neither for their work nor for the result of their work. If this were the case, the wage received by workers would be equal to the value they add in production with their living labor and, therefore, there would be no profit.[1] What the worker sells and what the capitalist buys is the working capacity of the former for a specified time, that is, during a working day.

(ii) The difference between the value added by workers with their living labor in production during the working day and the price of their labor-power is the surplus value, appropriated without any payment by the capitalist class. The relation between total surplus value and total wages paid is the general rate of surplus value, which expresses the degree of exploitation of wage workers by capitalists. The relation between total surplus value and the value of total capital advanced by capitalists is the general rate of profit, which expresses the degree of valorization of capital.

(iii) Labor-power is a commodity that workers sell to capitalists because they lack the means of production to objectify their own work in the production of use-values to satisfy their needs. The existence of labor-power as a commodity presupposes that those producers (wage earners) have been expropriated of their means of production by nonproducers (capitalists). It implies, also, that wage earners legally are free people who can establish commercial contracts for the sale of their labor-power and for the purchase of commodities that they consume to satisfy their needs. Formally, the buying and selling of the labor-power commodity appears, similarly to that of the rest of commodities, as a voluntary and symmetric (equivalent) transaction. Nevertheless, its content is essentially coercive and asymmetric.

Industrial capitals, to valorize, need to buy means of production and labor-power so that, under their direction, production of commodities can take place. Wage workers require selling their labor-power to capitalists to earn a salary with which they can satisfy their needs in consumption. There certainly is a relationship of interdependence between the two poles of the buying and selling of labor-power. However, if capitalists do not buy labor-power, they could survive by working themselves, consuming means of production and producing use-values that satisfy their needs in consumption, although they would certainly cease to be capitalists. In contrast, if wage workers do not sell their labor-power, lacking the means to buy the products that satisfy their needs in consumption, they put at risk their own survival. The coercive nature of the relationship is, therefore, evident. The appearance of symmetry in the exchange between capital and wage labor collapses when considering that such exchange, being the source of the appropriation by capital of a part of the product of wage labor, is in its essential content a nonequivalent exchange.

Although labor-power and means of production are commodities whose purchase is indispensable for the process of production, the role of each one is qualitatively different. Labor-power realizes in production as living labor that productively consumes means of production in the manufacturing of commodities. Living labor is the *active* subjective factor of the process, while means of production are the *passive* objective factor of it. For this reason, labor and means of production cannot be standardized as analogous "factors" that participate in general alike terms, although in different specific ways and proportions, in the production of commodities and of value.

(iv) Like all commodities, labor-power has a use-value which evidences in its consumption. This use-vale is its realization as living labor that produces other use-values (wealth), value (price of commodities), and surplus value (profit). Like all commodities, labor-power has a price, expressed in the nominal wage per worker per working day. However, unlike other commodities, labor-power is not produced in the sphere of production by capitalist companies, so it is not a carrier of surplus value.

The productive consumption of labor-power and the consequent destruction of its use-value and its value is the process of productive consumption of the means of production that workers realize with their work. This process, in which workers produce new commodities, in addition to preserving the value of the means of production consumed, aggregates new value. And, a part of this new value is appropriated by capital as surplus value, which is the source of various forms in which this value itself is distributed (ground rent, profit of enterprise—industrial and commercial—interest, speculative profit).

(v) Formally, wage, like any price, in this case of the labor-power commodity, is the monetary expression of the value of labor-power and this, like the value of all commodities, is determined by the quantity of abstract labor socially necessary for its production and reproduction. However, unlike other commodities, the production and reproduction of labor-power does not take place in the sphere of production but in the sphere of final consumption. As during its production and reproduction no work is objectified, the amount of abstract labor socially necessary for its production and reproduction does not have a direct technical-economic determination.

The production and reproduction of labor-power is carried out not only through the final consumption of wage-commodities by workers to replenish their work capacity but also by their families, which allows for the reproduction of the social labor force over time.[2] Therefore, the value of labor-power has an indirect determination that corresponds to the value of the basket of wage-commodities necessary for the reproduction of the working capacity of wage earners and of the labor force as a whole; that is, to the amount of socially necessary abstract labor objectified in the wage-commodities that make up that basket.

Although the size and composition of the wage basket necessary for the reproduction of labor-power certainly has physiological grounds, it does not have a technical-biological determination. This contrasts with the case of other living beings, animals, or plants, that are produced and sold as commodities for final and productive consumption and whose value is determined by the amounts of abstract labor socially necessary to produce the nutrients required by the technical-biological conditions of their production and reproduction.[3]

The determination of the amount of abstract labor socially necessary for the production and reproduction of labor-power does not have an objective character, neither direct nor indirect, because labor-power is an attribute of formally free human beings who do not participate in production as objects (as means of production), but as subjects, even if subsumed, of such production. In contrast, the value and price of a slave is objectively determined as the case is for other living beings that are consumed as means of production. Therefore, the determination of the value of labor-power has a subjective nature. It depends on the confrontation between two irreducibly antagonistic social classes: the nonproducers who own the means of production, that is the capitalist class; the producers who must sell their labor-power, that is the wage-earning class. These two fundamental social subjects of the capitalist mode of production are systematically confronted during the different moments of the social process of reproduction: in production, around the conditions of the productive consumption of labor-power; in distribution, over the distribution of social product; in exchange, regarding the conditions of buying and selling of labor-power and wage-commodities; in consumption, with respect to the direct and indirect requirements socially recognized as necessary for the reproduction of the labor-power. The results of the confrontation in each of these moments depend on economic, social, political, cultural, and ideological correlation of forces that are historically and geographically determined.

The size and composition of the commodity-wage basket accepted as socially necessary for the reproduction of labor-power depends on the one hand on the normal price of labor-power (the average nominal wage) and, on the other, on the normal price (and value) of wage-commodities. The higher (lower) the level of the average nominal wage, the higher (lower) is the volume of wage-commodities that can be acquired with it. Simultaneously, the lower (higher) the normal price (value) of such commodities, the higher (lower) is the quantity of wage-commodities purchasable.

Thus, the value of that basket and, therefore, the value of labor-power, which is the amount of abstract labor necessary for its production, has a qualitatively different determination from that of the rest of commodities, as it depends, both on the correlation of forces between the capitalist and wage labor classes in the process of social reproduction and on the normal social conditions of production of wage-commodities.

(vi) The average nominal wage, the normal price of labor-power, is a peculiar price because labor-power is not a commodity produced and reproduced directly by labor.[4] As the normal price of other commodities, it constitutes the gravitation center of the fluctuations, in this case, in the labor markets in the sphere of circulation, of nominal market wages. But the negotiations between capitalists and wage earners regarding nominal wages in the different labor markets have broader implications than the mere determination of the price of the labor-power commodity. The overall outcome of such negotiation determines the social distribution of new value added between wages and surplus value and, therefore, the rate of exploitation. Nominal wages are, hence, determining and determined elements in both the moments of circulation and distribution of social reproduction.

The determination of the average real wage is given by the relationship between the normal price of labor-power (the average nominal wage) and the normal price (value) of wage-commodities. It expresses, given the distribution of the new value added between capital and wage labor, and given the normal social conditions of production of wage-commodities, the normal purchasing power of wage earners and their possibility to satisfy their needs through consumption. For this reason, socially, it is a determining factor of the general structure of effective demand (for final consumption and investment) and of consumption (wage-commodities, luxury commodities, and means of production). Therefore, the average real wage, relative price of average nominal wage with respect to the normal prices of wage-commodities, is simultaneously determined in all the moments of social reproduction: circulation, distribution, production, and consumption.

Then, the determination of the average nominal wage, normal price of labor-power, as well as the value of labor-power, presents a qualitative inversion in its determination with respect to that of the price and the value of the rest of commodities. The average nominal wage is not the monetary expression of the value of labor-power. Rather, since the average real wage depends on the ratio of the average nominal wage to the normal price of wage-commodities, then the value of labor-power is the expression, in quantities of abstract social labor, of the normal real wage.[5]

LABOR MARKETS, CAPITAL ACCUMULATION, AND THE INDUSTRIAL RESERVE ARMY

Since the determination of the price and value of labor-power is inverse to that of the price and value of the rest of the commodities produced directly in the sphere of production, its analysis requires (i) to initiate with the determination, in the sphere of circulation, of the fluctuations and trends of nominal wages in the operation framework of labor markets; (ii) to continue with the examination, also in the sphere of circulation, of fluctuations and trends of the price of wage-commodities, to elucidate those of real wages; (iii) to end with the determination, now in the sphere of production, of the trends in the value of wage-commodities, to derive the determination of the value of labor-power.

The analysis is framed within that of cyclical fluctuations and long-term trends of capital accumulation. First, because they determine the fluctuations and trends in the dynamics of the demand and supply of labor-power and, as will be seen, of the production and permanent reproduction of an IRA functional to the requirements of accumulation itself. Likewise, because they are determinants of fluctuations and trends of market prices of wage-commodities, as well as of the trends of their values.

Labor Markets

Labor markets are the space of concurrence and confrontation, that is, of competition between suppliers and demanders, and among suppliers and among demanders, of the labor-power commodity: wage earners and capitalists. As a result of this competition, the formation of nominal wages is carried out in different time horizons. In the short term, nominal market wages based on the fluctuations of accumulation associated with the industrial cycle[6]; in the medium term, normal average nominal wages in the framework of the normal operating conditions of accumulation; in the long term, changes in average nominal wages associated with long-term trends of accumulation.[7]

The economic rationality of suppliers and demanders of labor-power is like that of all suppliers and demanders of commodities. Sellers seek to maximize their income from sales, which implies that workers try to maximize the nominal wage they obtain. Buyers, the capitalists, seek to minimize their spending on purchases, which, in turn, implies they try to minimize the nominal wage they pay.

The dynamics of labor supply and demand are linked to the quantitative and qualitative, conjunctural and structural, dynamics of capital accumulation. The Marxist theory of the IRA explains such articulation beyond demographic factors, providing elements to understand the determination of the fluctuations, average levels, and trends of nominal wages.

To understand the determination of fluctuations and trends of real wages based on those of nominal wages, it is also necessary to analyze, within the framework of accumulation, the determination of fluctuations of wage-commodities prices and of the trends in the value of those wage-commodities. The tendencies of the value of labor-power are the result of the articulation of the trends of nominal wages, as well as of the value of wage-commodities.

Capital Accumulation and the Industrial Reserve Army

Capital accumulation unfolds simultaneously through several time horizons, each associated with different sets of variables upon which capitals make different types of investment decisions based on the respective profitability prospects.

The flow of profits in relation to the value of sales is the basis of decisions made regarding investment in inventories. When the profit margin over the value of sales weakens, a normal response is to increase the volume of inventories, while an increase in such margin tends to decrease such volume. Inventory cycles result from such fluctuations.

The flow of profits in relation to the value of production in a specific period is the basis for decisions regarding investment in circulating capital, both constant (raw materials and auxiliary substances) and variable (labor-power), and therefore of the degrees of utilization of the productive plant. With the decrease in such margins, the degree of utilization of the plant tends to decrease; with its increase, it tends to increase. Industrial cycles result from these fluctuations.

The flow of profits with respect to the value of the total capital invested, that is, the rate of profit, is a determining factor in the investment decisions relating to the different components of fixed capital (machinery and equipment and construction and facilities) and, therefore, of the size and technological characteristics of the productive plant. Long-term trends in accumulation and its inflections are associated with trends of the rate of profit.

Marx defines the IRA as a relative overpopulation that capital, in its accumulation process, produces and reproduces beyond the dynamics of the demographic determinants of the volume and structure of the working population. It is the expression of the peculiar population law that capital, in its accumulation process, creates and which is the core of the general law of capitalist accumulation.[8] What characterizes this historically determined population law is that capital tends to make the dynamics of the supply of labor relatively independent from its demographic factors and, with it, to overcome labor as a central obstacle for accumulation condemning wage workers to an absolute or relative state of misery relating to the incessant increase of capital and wealth.

DIFFERENT FORMS OF THE INDUSTRIAL RESERVE ARMY, ACCUMULATION, AND REGULATION OF LABOR

The IRA has different forms of existence that are articulated through dynamic interflows among each other.[9] The main ones are the floating, the stagnant and the latent forms of the IRA. Such forms can be related to the different time horizons in which capital accumulation unfolds. The floating form is directly linked to industrial cycles. The stagnant form is mainly associated with long-term accumulation trends. The latent form is related with both long-term trends and secular trends of accumulation.

The dynamics, fluctuations, and trends of capital accumulation shape, through the contraction and expansion of the IRA, the operation of labor markets to the extent that the fluctuations of the IRA determine quantitatively and qualitatively the conditions of articulation between the demand and supply of labor and labor-power and, therefore, the context of determination of the levels of occupation, unemployment, and underemployment, of the intensity and length of working days, as well as of nominal wages and their structure. In turn, the dynamics, fluctuations and trends of employment, intensity and length or working days, and nominal wages affect the profitability of capital and, therefore, the determining conditions of the dynamics of accumulation in the different time horizons in which it unfolds. This feedback process expresses the regulating mechanisms of the capital reproduction process that are embodied in both the general law of capitalist accumulation, which reveals how capital produces and reproduces the IRA, and the law of the tendential fall of the general rate of profit, which explains the outbreak of structural crises, but also, when it is specified in order to consider the fluctuations of profit margins over the value of production, of recurrent cyclical crises.[10]

It is important to notice that capital accumulation, understood as the creation of new capital from the surplus value previously produced or from credit, is a process that implies the reproduction on an enlarged scale of the productive plant (fixed capital) and the increase in the circulating capital required for its operation (both means of production and labor-power). But expanded reproduction necessarily presupposes simple reproduction, that is, the renewal of fixed capital commodities that are continually ending their useful life. Therefore, the accumulation process always involves simultaneously renewal of old capital and addition of new capital to the productive plant.

The accumulation process unfolds by continuously modifying the technical and organizational bases of production and work processes. Technological innovations that save living labor are the result of the competition process itself, in which a reduction in production costs is imposed as a necessity for the survival of individual capitals.[11] The consequent increase in the technical composition of capital (the ratio between the means of production used and the labor-power that productively consumes them) implies that the components of new capital increase at unequal rates. The constant part (fixed and circulating) increases in greater proportion than the variable part. Therefore, although accumulation attracts new labor-power to the productive sphere, this attraction is relatively decreasing with respect to the expansion of total capital. In addition, the increase in the technical composition of capital means that the renewal of the fixed capital that ends its useful life is carried out by repelling labor-power. In this way, capital accumulation, as expansion investment, attracts new labor-power to the productive sphere (positive effect on the demand for labor-power), but, as renewal investment, it expels previously employed labor force (positive effect on the supply of labor-power).[12]

It is in this sense that capital, in its accumulation process, not only regulates, unsurprisingly, the dynamics of the demand for labor-power, but also, startlingly, the dynamics of the supply of labor-power beyond its demographic determinants.[13] As a result of living labor-saving technological and organizational innovations, which increase the technical composition of capital, it creates a specific population law that is functional to its own expansion process.

The dynamics of the demand for labor-power is a positive function of the accumulation rate and a negative one of the increase of both the technical composition of capital (innovation biased toward fixed capital), which substitutes living labor for objectified labor, and the intensity of labor and the length of the working day, which allow capital to obtain more work without demanding more labor-power and without hiring more workers. The dynamics of the supply of labor-power relatively autonomizes from demographic factors. It is certainly a positive function of demographic growth, and it can be of certain types of changes in the population structure, but it also depends on the systematic expulsion of workers from the productive sphere derived from the incorporation of labor-saving technological and organizational innovations in renewal investment, as well as on the periodic expulsion of workers from production during the contractive phases of cycles.

In addition to its conjunctural and structural, demographic, and economic factors, the relative strength of the dynamics of demand and supply of labor-power depends on a wide set of noneconomic factors (normative and institutional) that have historical social and political determinations.

Fluctuating form of the IRA, Industrial Cycles, and Market Wages

The floating form of the IRA is constituted by workers who have already been salaried or who are preparing to do so for the first time. Its volume is continually fed by the incorporation of young proletarians seeking a waged job. It reduces and expands cyclically due to the fluctuations of capital accumulation and the concurrent changes in the dynamics of expansion investment, and attraction of labor-power to the productive sphere, relative to renewal investment, and repulsion of labor-power from production.

In the short and medium-terms, during the progress of industrial cycles, the floating form of the IRA in its relationship with the active industrial army (AIA), through its reductions and expansions, regulates the conditions of the productive consumption and price of labor-power. On the one hand, it regulates the possibilities of making more or less flexible the length and intensity of working days and, therefore, the amount of work per worker. On the other hand, it regulates the gravitation of nominal market wages, which express the concrete conditions of buying and selling of labor-power, around the average wage.

Fluctuations in demand for labor derived from changes in the degree of utilization of the productive plant can be faced, firstly, through changes in the degree of utilization of the labor force, that is, through changes in the length and intensity of the working day of hired workers. As they allow capital to obtain more or less work without modifying the demand for labor-power and the volume of employment, they attenuate fluctuations in market wages. When changes in the length and intensity of the working day are insufficient to respond to fluctuations in the demand for labor resulting not only from changes in the degree of plant utilization but also from changes of its size, such variations are faced with the oscillating absorption and repulsion of the floating form of the IRA.

(i) During the expansive phase of a cycle, the strength of accumulation stimulates the demand for labor and labor-power. The attraction of labor force to the productive sphere is vigorous due to the strong expansion investment. The increased demand for labor-power is satisfied with the hiring of workers who are part of the floating form of the IRA: those who had been dismissed in contractive phases of previous cycles, those being expelled from the productive sphere due to the increased composition of old capital in process of renewal, and those that are entering for the first time the labor markets. The net effect on employment and on the relative size of the floating form of the IRA with respect to the AIA depends on the rate of accumulation, the rate of innovation, and the extent and intensity of the expansion. The higher the accumulation rate and the longer and stronger the expansion, the floating form of the IRA tends to contract, which strengthens the bargaining power of labor-power suppliers in labor markets, which makes possible improved working conditions and a cyclical upward pressure on nominal market wages. When increases in nominal wages surpass increases in the prices of the rest of commodities, profit margins of individual capitals are negatively affected. And if they increase more than wage-commodity prices, real wages increase. This cyclical increase in the relative nominal wage (and its purchasing power) is one of the contributory factors (together with the cyclical increase in the relative prices of certain raw and auxiliary materials with relatively inelastic supply, as well as in the real rates of interest) of the termination of the expansion and of the outbreak of a conjunctural cyclical crisis.

(ii) During the contractive phase of a cycle, the decline and stagnation of the rate of accumulation slows down the dynamics of demand relative to that of the supply of labor-power. The attraction of workers to the productive sphere weakens in relation to its repulsion. As the contraction advances, and depending on its intensity and length, the dismissal of wage earners due to the decrease in the level of economic activity increases the size of the floating form of the IRA, which weakens the general negotiating capacity of workers in terms of both their working conditions and their nominal wages. In this context, a cyclical decrease in nominal market wages in relation to the price of the rest of the commodities, together with the eventual decrease in the relative price of certain raw and auxiliary materials and in real interest rates, sooner or later strengthens profit margins. The conditions for a recovery unfold, putting an end to the contraction and allowing for the beginning of a new expansive phase.

(iii) In summary, in each industrial cycle there is a reduction, first, and a reconstitution, later, of the floating form of the IRA, which, in its quantitative relation with the size of the AIA, regulates, in a form that is functional to capital accumulation, the cyclical fluctuations in employment, working conditions, and nominal and real wages.

Stagnant and Latent Forms of the IRA, Long Waves of Accumulation, Average Wages, and Value of Labor-Power

The stagnant form of the IRA is composed by workers who have been discarded by capital for having exhausted their useful lives for reasons of age, health, and other, or because capital accumulation entered a long period of contraction and stagnation.[14] Its volume is fed immediately with the definitive dismissal of active workers or, mediately, with temporary dismissals of the floating form of the IRA that, finally, cease to be floating to become permanent.

The latent form of the IRA is constituted by the population that is not integrated into the capitalist circuits of production and direct exploitation. In his time, Marx related the latent form of the IRA with the rural population that, when dispossessed of its means of production, was the basis of massive migrations to cities that constituted the source of growth of the proletariat required during the long-term periods of expansion of accumulation, as well as for the secular expansion of capitalism. In current times, specifically since the end of the 20th century, in addition to the persistence of rural latent forms of the IRA, the formation of expanding urban latent forms can be acknowledged. A part of the proletariat has been expelled from the labor force exploited by capital, because of a long-term slow accumulation. After its cyclical withdrawal from waged workforce became permanent this segment joined either the stagnant form of the IRA, or a new type of latent form. The latter constituted by former wage workers, and especially their descendants that, having acquired some precarious means of production to survive, have severed their direct links with capitalist exploitation. The resulting expanding contingents of urban population not directly exploited by capital but whose reproduction depends on the circuits of capital would constitute a "modern" type of the latent form of the IRA.[15]

This perspective likens the periodic reconstitution of the size of the floating form of the IRA associated with contractive phases of industrial cycles, with a long-term reconstitution of the latent form of the IRA associated to contractive and stagnated long-term trends of capital accumulation.

(i) Industrial cycles are generally asymmetric. A cycle is expansive when its expansive phase is relatively longer and more intensive than its contractive phase. In contrast, it is contractive when its expansive phase is of less amplitude and length than its contractive phase. There are also neutral cycles with expansive and contractive phases of similar amplitude and extent.

When there is a succession of cycles in which one of its different types predominates, whether expansive, contractive, or neutral, the process of capital accumulation, in addition to cyclical fluctuations, experiences long-term trends that historically have been of two alternate kinds: expansive and then contractive and stagnated. This implies that the dynamics of the demand and supply of labor-power also experiences long-term trends linked to those of accumulation.

(ii) A succession of expansive cycles generates a long-term expansive wave. During each expansive cycle, the balance between the initial contraction and the subsequent reconstitution of the floating form of the IRA results in its net reduction, because during the complete cycle, the attraction of workers to the productive sphere predominates over the repulsion of them. Although the renovation of the floating form of the IRA is continually fueled by the incorporation to the labor markets of new workers and by the expulsion of workers derived from the renewal investment under new technological conditions and, therefore, with increased technical composition of capital, the strength in amplitude and duration of the expansions versus the relative weakness of the contractions result in a long-term expansive trend of the dynamics of the demand for labor-power

> in relation to the dynamics of its supply. As the expansive long wave of accumulation unfolds, the negotiating capacity of wage workers regarding the conditions of productive consumption and compensation for their labor-power is strengthened. Therefore, the increase in the rate of surplus value, and therefore of profitability, by absolute means (increasing the length and intensity of the working day) and by the decrease in wages faces obstacles derived from the sustained energy of accumulation.

The floating form of the IRA is insufficient to satisfy the long-term expansion of the demand for labor-power. Capital requires incorporating more workers to the productive sphere than those provided by the floating form to limit the improvement of the bargaining position of the suppliers of labor-power and, therefore, to confront increases in labor costs. A first source of the additional supply of labor-power needed is the stagnant form of the IRA, conformed by former wage workers that had been discarded from the working force due to their age, physical deterioration, or to a chronic insufficient demand for wage workers. A second source is the latent form of the IRA, made up of population which has not previously been integrated, at least regularly, in the cycles of industrial capital accumulation, either the more traditional rural based or the more present-day urban. Thus, the long-term trends in the dynamics of the labor force supply are explained by the dynamic articulation of the floating form of the IRA with the stagnant and latent forms. This articulation, which regulates the negotiating capacity of workers during an expansive long wave, does not cancel out its tendential strengthening since wage workers who enter the productive sphere from the stagnant and latent forms of the IRA occupy new jobs, so they do not directly compete with those already employed.

The long-term response of supply of labor-power in relation to the capital needs is a determining factor in long-term tendencies of working conditions and wages. Historically, the long-term vigor of accumulation dynamics during a succession of expansive cycles and the strong dynamism of the demand for labor-power generated has resulted in the absolute and relative expansion of the labor force incorporated in the productive sphere, the active industrial army (AIA), the increase in average wages, and the improvement of working conditions. The strong dynamism of accumulation not only results in the expansion of the productive plant and the labor force but also implicates high rates of innovation, both technological and organizational. In addition to the fact that the dynamism of innovation accelerates the repulsion of the labor force associated with renewal investment, it causes a strong progress of the productive force of social labor, that is, of the social productivity of labor. The increase of the social productivity of labor in the sectors that produce wage-commodities and the means of production used for their production reduces the amount of abstract labor that is socially necessary directly and indirectly to produce the diverse wage-commodities. The decrease in the value of wage-commodities, which also implies the reduction of their average prices, has as a result that, even with a constant average nominal wage, its purchasing power (the real wage) tends to increase beyond its cyclical fluctuations. Obviously, if the nominal average wage shows an upward trend during the expansive long wave, the upward tendency of the real average wage is reinforced. And with it, the basket of wage-commodities that can normally be acquired by the nominal average wage expands and diversifies. The expansion of the average real wage does not necessarily imply an increase in the amount of abstract labor socially necessary to produce the wage-commodities that make up the basket if its growth is relatively less intense than that of the social productivity of labor in the sectors that directly and indirectly produce wage-commodities.[16] When the upward trend of the real wage unfolds together with a decrease in the value of labor-power, the rate of surplus value increases in a relative way and, with it, the general rate of profit is strengthened at the same time as the purchasing power and effective demand of workers expand.

In the context of the relative strengthening of workers bargaining power and the strong dynamism of labor productivity, relatively progressive labor regimes have historically unfolded during expansive long waves. The regulatory function of the capital-wage labor relationship of the Capitalist State, one of its two basic functions together with the regulation of the monetary-credit systems, is focused during an expansive long wave of accumulation in facilitating social capital with a supply of labor-power appropriate in quantity and quality for its vigorous accumulation needs, as well as with a volume of social effective demand sufficient for its realization necessities. The normative and institutional basis of these regimes, as well as the policies (labor, social, education, etc.) associated with them, has promoted the incorporation in the productive sphere of new wage workers with adequate levels of education, the conservation of working population´s health, job stability, and the expansion of wages and social benefits.

At the general social level, the upward trend of average real wages means that the basket of wage-commodities that is socially recognized as necessary for the reproduction of the labor force increases and diversifies. This social recognition is possible because the consumption needs of wage earners, always subsumed to the needs of capital, can be increasingly satisfied due to the fact that capital, in order to sell the growing volumes of production generated by the high rates of accumulation, requires an expansion of the general purchasing power of the population not only extensive (with the incorporation as new demanders of the new employees) but also intensive (with the increase in the individual purchasing power of all workers).

(iii) The rise in the rate of surplus value by relative means, which has a positive effect on the general rate of profit, is based on the increase in the composition of capital, which negatively affects the general rate of profit. When the positive effect of the increase of the rate of surplus value is no longer sufficient to counteract the negative effect of the rise of the capital composition, the tendential fall of the general rate of profit materializes, causing the end of the expansive long wave and the start of a structural crisis of productive over-accumulation.

The crisis is expressed, first, with the weakening of accumulation rates and the intensification of competition between capitals. For individual capitals, it becomes imperative to reduce production costs and, especially among them, wage costs. For this reason, competition between capitalists and wage workers in the labor markets also intensifies. In addition, capitals, which cannot be idle, push for forms, mechanisms, and spaces for valorization alternative to productive ones, which encourage financialization processes. They also promote the opening of new spaces for valorization, both sectoral and geographic. Complementing these counteracting factors to the fall of the general rate of profit, processes of privatization of public companies and communal properties, destruction of noncapitalist forms of production, and processes of liberalization of international capital flows historically have unfolded.

(iv) The end of an expansive long wave, which is a succession of expansive cycles, manifests itself with the beginning of a new type of succession of cycles, now of contractive and stagnated types; that is, with the progression of a contractive and stagnated long wave.

In each contractive cycle, the alternate weak reduction and strong expansion of the floating form of the IRA have as a net balance the increase in the volume of this form. During a complete contractive cycle, the attraction of labor force to the productive sphere is overpowered by its expulsion. The weakness in amplitude and duration of expansions and the relative strength of the contractions generate a contractive and stagnated tendency in the dynamics of the demand for labor-power in relation to its supply. As the contractive and stagnated long wave unfolds, the bargaining power of wage earners to sustain their previous working conditions and wages weakens, forced by the urgent need for individual capitals to reduce their production costs to survive in the heightened context of competition, and by the increased competition among workers to conserve their jobs or to get one.

Class struggle between capital and wage labor exacerbates in all its dimensions, both economic and political. The increase of the rate of surplus value to reconstitute the conditions of profitability focuses on the absolute mechanisms (intensifying and making more flexible the working days) and by means of wage reduction. Depending on the type of monetary and credit system prevailing and on the associated monetary and fiscal policies, the contraction of the real wage has historically been carried either by deflationary or inflationary means. In the first case, nominal wages tend to fall during each cycle, especially in its contractive phase. When this reduction is greater than that of the prices of the rest of the commodities, profitability margins of individual capitals cyclically strengthen, albeit moderately, and if it is greater than that of the prices of wage-commodities, real wages diminish. During the successive contractive cycles, a long-term downward and stagnated tendency of average nominal and real wages manifests. In the second case, although nominal wages do not fall in absolute terms throughout their fluctuations, the cyclical strengthening of profit margins and the decrease in real wages are the result of a more than proportional increase in the price of the rest of the commodities, including wage-commodities. During the successive contractive cycles, a long-term downward and stagnated trend of the average real wage accompanied by a long-term increasing trend of the average nominal wage is displayed.

Due to the long-term weakening of the dynamics of the demand for labor-power, not only does the absolute size of the floating form of the IRA tends to expand but also a part of the labor force is definitively expelled from the productive sphere. The stagnant form of the IRA expands directly with the incorporation of older employees with deteriorating health conditions who are fired without hope of being rehired; indirectly, with the incorporation of wage workers who, having temporarily incorporated to the floating form of the IRA, are also finally expelled from the wage labor force. Simultaneously, the latent form of the IRA tends to rebuild quantitatively and qualitatively while the duration of the contractive and stagnated long wave lengthens. Some laid-off workers can become owners of means of production, generally very precarious, to become independent private producers of goods and services. Worker families develop survival mechanisms in noncapitalist mercantile activities and even in non-mercantile activities that are relatively disconnected from the capitalist circuits of surplus production.

The long-term slow rates of accumulation during a succession of contractive and stagnated cycles and the consequent long-term weakening of the dynamics of the demand for labor and labor-power relative to the dynamics of their supply have historically resulted in a slow growth of the active industrial army (AIA), a growing precariousness of the working conditions of the employed workers, the decrease in average real wages, and the increase of all kinds of "informal" activities. The falling trend of average real wages implies a devaluation of the labor-power, which is the result, not of the decrease of the amount of abstract labor socially necessary to produce wage-commodities, but of the contraction in volume and impoverishment in content of the basket of wage-commodity socially recognized as necessary for the reproduction of the labor force. In fact, it supposes the destruction, certainly partial, of the value of variable capital (value of labor-power). At the beginning of a contractive long wave, this appears as a generalized over-exploitation of the labor force resulting from the general decrease in average real wages with respect to those that were normal during the preceding expansive long wave. But, as the contractive and stagnated long wave consolidates, the decrease of average real wages becomes the basis of a new social labor regime that, determined by the lower requirements of labor-power by capital accumulation, tends to deteriorate the normal structural conditions of the productive consumption, buying and selling, and reproduction of the labor force. The partial destruction of the value of labor-power does not imply in any way that the physiological, biological, and cultural requirements for the reproduction of the labor force diminish themselves. It simply expresses the fact that the possibility of satisfying the needs that had been socially recognized during a previous expansive long wave is constrained because of the lower requirements of labor-power for capital valorization and accumulation. The new levels of average real wages, lower than the previous one, are finally imposed as the new social norm, so the initial generalized over-exploitation of the working forces becomes the new normal. The partial destruction of the value of labor-power is generally accompanied by a reduction of the amount of abstract labor socially necessary to produce the basket of wage-commodities recognized as socially necessary for the reproduction of the labor-power. In this case, the rate of surplus value increases in the long term, not only through the absolute means of intensification and deregulation of the length of working days but also through the modification of the distribution of the new value added by living labor; not because of the decrease in the value of each wage-commodity, but because of the contraction of the average real wage.

Something similar happens with the destruction, also partial, of the value of constant capital that structural crises unleash. In addition to the generalized bankruptcies, there is a social questioning of the traditional mechanisms of exploitation of wage labor and valorization of capital, which implies the emergence of new technological and organizational paradigms that, in the end, tend to constitute as the new social foundations of valorization and accumulation.

Capital, when accumulated at slow rates, does not massively expand the volume of production, so it can face the problem of realization in the markets without the need to increase the overall purchasing power of the population in general, and even with a reduction of the individual purchasing power of workers. Slow general rates of accumulation can be accompanied by negative incentives to investment in machinery and equipment when the relative excess supply of labor-power tends to make more feasible the reduction of production costs through the deterioration of working conditions and the reduction in wages. Both trends weaken the general rate of technological innovation and the general dynamics of social labor productivity. Thus, a negative feedback loop is generated in which the absolute mechanisms of strengthening the rate of surplus value inhibit the deployment of the relative ones. This is a typical vicious circle that limits the full recovery of the general rate of profit of capital and, therefore, the possibility of massively expanding productive accumulation and production.

Historically, during contractive and stagnated long waves, characterized by the relative weakening of the bargaining position of workers and the limited dynamism of labor productivity, particularly regressive labor regimes have been established. During a contractive and stagnated long wave of accumulation, the function of the Capitalist State of regulating the relation between capital and wage labor focuses on the objective of recovering general profitability, by promoting reductions of labor costs of production through more flexible working conditions and the restraint of direct and indirect wages. The slow accumulation of productive capital makes public expenditure on education, health, and other social benefits relatively superfluous. Moreover, it does not require as a general condition for the realization of commodities and surplus value a strong expansion of total effective demand or of the individual purchasing power of workers.

(v) The end of a contractive and stagnated long wave of accumulation would require a long-term recovery of the general rate of profit, which, in turn, would involve a dynamization of the relative mechanism of increasing the rate of surplus value compared to the absolute mechanisms and to the reduction of real wages. This would potentially make possible a long-term recovery in the quantitative and qualitative tendencies of both employment and wages.

However, the recovery of such conditions is not guaranteed by the mere operation of the laws of value and accumulation, since it would need profound transformations in the structures of social and political interactions among classes, class fractions, and power groups within each national space of accumulation, in the forms of articulation among the different forms and mechanisms of valorization, as well as in international economic and political relations.

The possibility of an ever-continuing, chronic, slow accumulation long-term tendency and the consolidation of permanent precarization of labor is very real. The high levels of concentration and centralization of capital, as well as of articulation at all levels of operation of capital of productive and commercial mechanisms of valorization, on the one hand, and financial and speculative ones, on the other, make it increasingly difficult to advance in the competitive destruction of inefficient but "too big to fail" capitals, which would contribute to reinforce the recovery of the general rate of profit. The relative financial-speculative hegemony and the precarious conditions of productive consumption, buying and selling, and reproduction of the labor force feed each other. The same happens with the over-exploitation of labor and nature when extensive mechanisms for strengthening profitability compete favorably in many segments in which capitals operate against mechanisms based on technological innovation and on the enhancement of the productive force of labor.

SYNTHETICAL FINAL CONSIDERATIONS

(i) The determination of normal wages, both nominal and real, and of the value of labor-power in capitalism is a complex process that depends, on the one hand, on the correlation of forces between capitalist and wage-earning classes, and, on the other, on the normal conditions of production of wage-commodities.
(ii) The normal price and therefore the value of the labor-power commodity are determined in an inverse form than the normal price and value of other commodities. Wages are, therefore, a peculiar form of price, not being the monetary form of expression of the value of labor-power. Instead, the value of labor-power is the expression in quantities of socially necessary abstract labor of the average real wage.
(iii) The IRA and its different forms of existence, in their relationship with the active industrial army (AIA), regulate the fluctuations, average levels and tendencies of employment, wages, value of labor-power, and intensity and length of working days.

NOTES

1. Smith acknowledges that "the whole produce of labour belongs to the labourer" only when there are no capital stocks that claim profits (1776, Book I, ch. VI: 32–34). Ricardo is less clear about this issue. When he affirms that the produce of labor *and* capital is divided between wages and profits (1821, ch. XVI: position 2813), in fact he is conflating the immediate labor applied in production (which would be paid with wages) with the labor applied not-immediately on the production of means of production used (which would be paid with profit) (1821, ch. I: Section III: position 408–495).

2. The social expenditure of reproductive labor, that is, performed in the sphere of final consumption, as well as the final consumption of non-commodified products, is not analyzed here.

3. The ethical dimension of the final and intermediate consumption of living animals is a relevant current discussion that is not addressed here.

4. Also peculiar are the prices of land (capitalized ground rent) and capital (interest rate) that are commodities not produced in the sphere of production. In the analysis of the Trinity formula, Marx explains the links of the "prices" of these three peculiar commodities with the revenues perceived by the three main social classes of capitalist societies (Capital, V3, ch. 48: 953–970).

5. In the Marxist perspective, this point is controversial. The more conventional approach, in which wages are the monetary expression of the value of labor-power can be found in Fine (1998, ch. 7: 175–200) who, nevertheless, focuses on a crucial issue in the determination of wages: the requirements for the social reproduction of labor-power beyond wages. Gouverneur (2002) states that "wage does not depend on the value of labor-power: it's the value of labor-power which depends on wage" (Appendix 5: 199–201) but, in his case, because he considers that the labor-power is not a commodity.

6. According to Marx, the decennial cycle is the normal path of modern industry (Capital, V1, ch. 25: 785).

7. The short-term is conceptualized as the time horizon in which the size and technological characteristics of the productive plant are given, and the degrees of plant utilization and the volume of inventories are variable. This period is that of the fluctuations of market prices of commodities around their centers of gravitation, their respective values. The medium term is a succession of short-term periods. The size and technological characteristics of the productive plant are also given constituting, together with the average degrees of plant utilization and of inventories, the normal conditions of operation of the system. This time horizon is that of the determination of the normal prices of commodities, that is, of their values. The long run is the time horizon in which the size and technological characteristics of the productive plant are variable. In this time horizon, the value of commodities changes (Mariña 2008: 116).

8. "But in fact, it is capitalist accumulation itself that constantly produces, and produces indeed in direct relation with its own energy and extent, a relatively redundant working population, i.e., a population which is superfluous to capital's average requirements for its own valorization and is therefore a surplus population" (Capital, V1, ch. 25: 782)

9. Marx does not extend much on the conceptualization of the different forms of the IRA. Some few mentions are found in section 4 of chapter 25 (Capital, V1: 794–801).

10. Marx elaborated the law of the tendential fall of the general rate of profit in the manuscripts that Engels edited for volume III of *Capital* (V3, Part Three, chapters 13–15). The time horizon of his analysis there is the long term and the secular trends of accumulation in which the rate of profit, the ratio of profit to the value of total capital advanced, is the relevant measure of profitability. When he works on the edition of volume 1 of Capital, particularly its chapter 25, he must address not only the long-term and secular trends of accumulation but also its shorter-term fluctuations in which profitability margins, over the value of sales or the value of production, are more relevant measures of profitability.

11. Intensification and flexibilization of the length of the working day, as well as reduction of wages, are also means to reduce production costs. But, in contrast with fixed capital biased technological innovations, they have precise limits (Mariña and Rangel 2011).

12. "On the one hand, therefore, the additional capital formed in the course of further accumulation attracts fewer and fewer workers in proportion to its magnitude. On the other hand, the old capital periodically reproduced with a new composition repels more and more of the workers formerly employed by it" (Capital, V1, ch. 25: 780–781).

13. Botwinick (2017: 82–91) analyzes how the relation of Capitalist Accumulation and the IRA explain the fact that capital regulates both poles, supply and demand of labor-power, that compete in the labor markets.

14. A theoretical presentation of a Marxist approach of long waves of accumulation is done in Mariña (2020).

15. Botwinick (2017: 91–96) reviews some of the contemporary manifestations of the different forms of the IRA.

16. Marx even considers the case in which "a rise of wages in accompanied by a fall in the price of labour" (Capital, V1, ch. 25: 769).

BIBLIOGRAPHY

Botwinick, Howard (2017), *Persistent Inequalities. Wage Disparity under Capitalist Competition*, Haymarket Books, Chicago.

Fine, Ben (1998), *Labor Market Theory. A Constructive Reassessment*, Routledge, London and New York.

Gouverneur, Jacques (2002), *Comprender la Economía. Un manual para descubrir la cara oculta de la economía*, Diffusion Universitaire CIACO, Louvaine.

Mariña Flores, Abelardo (2008), "Un modelo de determinación de valores y precios normales en un horizonte temporal de medio plazo," Cámara, Ortiz and Robles (editors), *Reproducción y capital: equilibrio y desequilibrio desde una perspectiva crítica de la economía*, UAM-A/EÓN, Mexico: 107–142.

Mariña Flores, Abelardo (2020), "Tendencias de largo plazo de la acumulación de capital y crisis estructurales: una perspectiva marxista de las ondas largas," Cámara (editor), *La naturaleza contradictoria del capitalismo contemporáneo. Ensayos de Economía Política*, UAM-A, Mexico: 19–60.

Mariña Flores, Abelardo and Raúl Alberto Rangel (2011), "Diferencias salariales intrasectoriales y valorización del capital: una perspectiva marxista desde el capital individual," *Denarius*, 23, november, UAM-I, Mexico: 73–96.

Marx, Karl (1873, 2nd edition), *Capital, Volume 1*, The Pelican Marx Library, London, 1976.

Marx, Karl (1885), *Capital, Volume 2*, The Pelican Marx Library, London, 1978.

Marx, Karl (1894), *Capital, Volume 3*, The Pelican Marx Library, London, 1981.

Ricardo, David (1821), *The Principles of Political Economy and Taxation*, Dover Publications, Inc., New York, 2004.

Smith, Adam (1776), *The Wealth of Nations*, Books I-III, Penguin Books, London, 1999.

Chapter 5

Labor Precariousness as an Abstract Form of Domination

Sibyl Italia Pineda Salazar

INTRODUCTION

Labor precariousness is a phenomenon explained in the general law of capitalist accumulation developed by Marx in chapter 23 of *Capital*. This law proposes that the dynamic of capital accumulation generates a surplus population that exceeds the needs of capital, which Marx calls the "Reserve Army of Labor." This army refers to a group of people who confront labor instability and must constantly struggle to find or maintain a job. In Marxist literature, precarious conditions refer to various meanings and take different forms related to this army, but usually apply to a constant threat of losing jobs or fall into underemployment (Engels [1845] 1993) and living conditions that are degrading due to exploitation. These conditions lead workers to extreme moral and physical suffering (Morris [1887] 2013).

More recent theoretical interpretations of the general law analyze how accumulation leads to the inevitable existence of the reserve army of labor and brings about a degradation of work conditions. These interpretations consider that the technical and economic conditions alongside the domination exercised by capitalists are central to the expansion of the reserve army and, at the same time, foster the proliferation of low wages, zero-hours, temporary, or partial contracts (Foster, McChesney and Jonna 2011).

While these interpretations are fundamental to understanding the impact of accumulation on the working class and the depth of precarious conditions, they miss the fact that the general law involves not only technical and class domination elements but also a social contradiction between the production sphere and the structure of social relations configured by work and grounded on Socially Necessary Labor Time (SNLT). This contradiction refers to the fact that while capital reduces the amount of working time required in production to a minimum, it also places work at the center of social life. As a result, accumulation does not bring about a general saving in working time but instead is associated to the emergence of an unequal distribution of the working time allocated to workers. This unequal distribution of working time is related to an abstract form of domination present in the logic of capitalism subjecting workers, making it possible to expand the theoretical concept of labor precariousness.

In this sense, this chapter aims to contribute to the theoretical discussion around the phenomenon of labor precariousness based on the general law and, specifically, on the notion of abstract domination. This form of abstract domination operates as a social mechanism that subordinates the conditions under which the working class enters the productive sphere, so their precarious condition represents a concrete manifestation of an abstract structure that subjects them. The discussion is organized as follows: the second section explores theoretical and contextual elements to lay the foundations for the Marxist analysis of precariousness, specifically, the general law of capitalist accumulation, the reserve army category, and its different forms of existence. These concepts help understand that precariousness is a phenomenon immanent to capital, which confronts workers with a given labor condition and incorporates them into a process that constantly redefines their precarious situation. The third section discusses the abstract domination present in the general law. This section aims to demonstrate that labor precariousness is not only the manifestation of personal domination (i.e., domination exercised by the capitalist class over the worker), but it also represents an expression of the impersonal, abstract structure that subjects workers to an unequal labor configuration and to a time discipline that continually reasserts itself as an external and internal coercion. Lastly, a summary presents the final remarks.

LABOR PRECARIOUSNESS FROM THE MARXIST PERSPECTIVE

From the Marxist perspective, labor precariousness is neither a new phenomenon nor one exclusive to contemporary societies, but rather one immanent to capitalism related to the dynamics of capital accumulation. According to the law of accumulation, the logic behind all capitalist decisions is appropriating greater surplus value. To achieve it, capitalists seek to continually introduce more efficient production methods to increase labor productivity, improve their prices, and help them create favorable conditions to compete against other capitalists. Introducing these methods, whether by means of technology, a change in the organization of work or through the division of labor, allows capitalists to mobilize more means of production and produce more commodities. All methods result in reducing labor time required for producing commodities.

Socially, this logic translates into regular increases in the productivity of social labor and therefore in a reduction of the amount of variable capital employed in the social production process (i.e., the value of labor hired and paid by capitalists) relative to constant capital (i.e., the value of means and instruments of production). Consequently, this process creates a working population that exceeds the average needs of capital accumulation, thereby forming a Reserve Army of Labor.

The Reserve Army of Labor is a category that refers to a population of workers made superfluous by capital accumulation but from whom it can make use of and exploit when it so requires. In Marx's terms, this army represents a surplus population with diverse characteristics that may take three forms: floating, latent, and stagnant.

The floating surplus population refers to those employed at times and unemployed at other times but who remain somehow connected with the accumulation process. The floating population is "the most tumultuous layer of the reserve army" (Jonna and Foster 2015, 26) because accumulation subjects it to attraction and expulsion effects. Hence, their precarious conditions are constantly in flux. Capitalized surplus value increases capital, making it possible to reduce the floating population by employing them. However, introducing new technical methods generates an expulsion effect that enlarges the floating population. For instance, when accumulation results in expelling the floating population and the reserve army increases, this creates a double effect. First, it weakens the position of all the workers because wages fall, labor journeys intensify, and opportunities to negotiate better conditions are lost. Second, it creates acute precarious conditions for the floating population, making it harder for them to develop coping mechanisms (Mariña 2019). Consequently, the precarious existence of this layer of surplus population arises because accumulation raises the uncertainty of underemployment and fosters a constant risk of falling into unemployment.

The latent surplus population corresponds to a rural[1] or unwaged population recruited by capital as it expands (whether through the seizure of their means of production or other circumstances), that is, it incorporates them into accumulation and transforms them into waged workers. Recruiting this type of surplus population is attractive for capitalists because their poor living conditions attract them to accumulation as a group entirely willing to accept over-exploiting labor conditions and because they are also easily discarded. Lastly, the stagnant surplus population comprises a part of the active labor army whose work is entirely irregular. Whose work implies discontinuous or excessive working hours, low wages, and conditions of life that sinks below the average normal level of the working class (Marx [1981] 1991).

In this way, the Reserve Army represents a broad category. It encompasses not only itinerant workers but also those who are unemployed or have not joined the proletariat or those excluded from accumulation over long periods. On the one hand, the floating surplus population confronts the vulnerability arising from the constant threat of being expelled from accumulation, which leads them to suffer the difficulties of not being able to sell their labor force. Meanwhile, the latent and stagnant surplus population is most at risk of irregular jobs, low wages, few or zero labor guarantees, and higher levels of exploitation (Jonna and Foster 2015). Thus, from a Marxist standpoint, precariousness refers not to an immutable circumstance, instead to a process that continually redefines the precarious existence of workers.

Due to the broadness of this category, contemporary interpretations conceptualize labor precariousness primarily as an objective condition related to the contingency of employment that "reflects a fluidity and fickleness of employment relations" and involves a subjective feeling related to insecurity in work that reflects in their whole life (Choonara 2019, 7). These interpretations, however, explain the causes of precariousness from different perspectives. According to Jonna and Foster (2015), labor precariousness exacerbates because the Reserve Army broadens as capital expands globally. Global expansion of accumulation allows capital to increase the pressure on employed workers, limiting their demands for better wages and conditions.

From Autonomist Marxism's perspective, an increasing proportion of the workforce engages in irregular work due to the breakdown of Fordist accumulation and the introduction of new labor organization methods that allow greater flexibility (Choonara 2020). In their interpretation, labor precariousness relates mainly to a segment of immaterial workers who do not follow definable fixed rules relative to the labor relation, to salary and the length of the working day. Gorz's approach takes on flexibility as well to explain labor precariousness. From his perspective, flexibility alongside technical and scientific progress results in dividing waged workers into two categories, those who work permanently and those who work on part-time journeys and earn variable wages. Advanced technology and highly developed communication media enable capitalists to pressure workers and, therefore, create the ideal scenario to exacerbate precarious labor (Gorz 1997).

All these interpretations are linked to an implicit theoretical understanding that the precarious conditions suffered by the surplus population are related to the productive and technical innovations introduced by capitalists into the productive process and, therefore, result from the domination exerted by capitalists over workers. However, it is essential to consider that the general law of accumulation involves a social contradiction between the sphere of production and the structure of social relations configured by capitalist labor. This contradiction concerns that while capital tends to reduce to a minimum the working time required for the production process, it reaffirms labor as the necessary structural precondition of capitalist society (Postone 1996). Accumulation, therefore, does not result in a general saving of labor time but creates an unequal and precarious structure in which labor time unevenly distributes among all workers. Thus, it is essential to consider that this contradiction configures an impersonal, abstract structure that coerces workers and unveils a different dimension of labor precariousness.

ABSTRACT DOMINATION AND ACCUMULATION

In order to understand how abstract domination works, it is essential to remember that accumulation dynamics, which result in a continuous reduction of the amount of labor required for production, rests on abstract labor and its magnitude, Socially Necessary Labor Time (SNLT). According to Marx ([1867] 1976), SNLT represents a quantity of socially determined labor time and consists of an amount of labor-time required to produce any given use-value under normal production conditions for a given society and with an average degree of skill and intensity of labor prevalent in that society.

This magnitude is essential because by equating all products in the market, to exchange them, every product produced by private labor must be reduced to a measure of social working time, namely, a socially abstract quantity of labor. Consequently, SNLT represents an average temporal measure established by all private producers' actions and works as a measure that continually confronts them. This confrontation refers to a constant opposition and tension between individual capitalists and society (i.e., the group of all individual capitalists operating in a society); opposition in which society subsumes all the individual capitalist actions.[2]

This confrontation arises because the quantity of SNLT operates almost independently from the individual capitalists' will, previsions, or actions. Even though their private work constitutes a part of the social whole, any fluctuation of it operates as a law imposed on them.[3] Indeed, the quantity of SNLT, as a social measure subjecting capitalists, changes according to the level of social productivity, the improvements in science and technology, the social coordination of the production process, as well as any changes in natural conditions or the scale and efficiency of the means of production.

For instance, if any given capitalist carries out his or her production by hand and produces x quantity of goods in one hour of labor and a value equivalent to x, this capitalist will only receive the total value of his or her production if his or her technique is compatible with the current social abstract measure, namely if the production of this commodity in this given society is carried out by hand. Suppose another capitalist introduces a technological innovation that allows him or her to produce $2x$ goods in the same hour of work. In that case, the technical change will allow him to receive a value equivalent to *2x*, as long as the method does not become widespread. However, once the new technique becomes available to all society, a new social standard will be established so that the amount of labor time socially required to produce it will be *2x* goods for every hour of labor. Enhancing the social average standard, due to increases in labor productivity, provokes the innovative capitalist to obtain a value equivalent to *x* for twice as many commodities. In contrast, the less productive capitalist will receive less value for his *x* commodities, half of the *x* value.

This circumstance implies two situations. Firstly, that the capitalists using the new production technique will continue to obtain a value equivalent to *x* but will receive it by producing twice as many goods; this happens even when the number of goods produced per hour of labor has increased and the amount of labor time required per unit of goods lessens. That is, the total value produced in one hour of labor, after the technique became widespread, will remain the same. Secondly, those capitalists who continue producing with the less productive technique will only receive half the value; this happens because their production method becomes anachronistic to the new social abstract standard. As a result, they will receive less value for their work hours since each hour of their handwork is equivalent to only half of the abstract social hour (Postone 1996).

This example serves to identify two simultaneous processes due to accumulation. First, the need to increase labor productivity in the production process responds mainly to the abstract structure based in SNLT. This abstract structure exerts coercion over capitalists driving them to continually introduce more efficient methods because it is the only way to realize the value of the commodities they have produced. However, in doing so, capitalists trigger a contradiction, insofar as their efforts to be more productive lead to a continual updating of the abstract social standard; their efforts only reassert the abstraction that dominates them.[4]

On the other hand, the continual reduction in the amount of labor time necessary for production does not allow to overcome abstract labor as the value of commodities. Instead, it results in its continuous reaffirmation as value and its centrality as a social mediator.[5] Moreover, the reaffirmation of abstract labor involves a qualitative transformation of labor-time that is not reflected by the linear movement of hours and years. Namely, one hour of work before introducing a more productive method will be less dense than an hour of work after the introduction of a new production method. This qualitative transformation of time involves a more concentrated (or denser) time-based measure at capital's service due to accumulation. One hour in the past will be less dense than one hour in the future, even when every day still has 24 hours and people perceive they have only this number of daily hours available (Briales

2018). These two processes are interesting for the conceptualization of labor precariousness for the following purposes.

Firstly, accumulation and the Reserve Army of Labor represent a manifestation of technical and personal domination exerted by capitalists and the impersonal, abstract structure dominating capitalists' decisions to comply with social abstract standard currently in society. Furthermore, labor precariousness represents the product of a social mechanism that subordinates individual capitalists and workers.

Secondly, due to the constant reaffirmation of social labor time as the magnitude of value, the reduction of labor time resulting from accumulation does not imply a generalized saving in social labor time. Instead, it translates into an unequal distribution of working time and, therefore, a profound restructuring of the working class (Postone 2007) in which precariousness becomes a normal phenomenon.[6] Hence, the unequal distribution of labor means that employed workers will confront a severe intensification of their working hours, more demanding working days, alongside the increasing risk of becoming unemployed. Conversely, for the Reserve Army of Labor, this process will involve an increasing scarcity of employment, growing unstable working conditions, and salaries below the social minimum.

Uneven distribution of labor time among workers causes waged workers to spend more time at work and to reduce the time dedicated to everyday out-of-work activities. Overworking assures them to keep their not only job but also enough money to hire other people to do these activities. This evolves into a conflicting dynamic because if wage workers want to keep hiring other people to do their out-of-work activities, they will have to spend even more time at work. Therefore, accumulation involves the reproduction of a process where the fewer time waged workers have available for out-of-work-related activities, the more they will have to resort to other people to take them over. Simultaneously, unequal distribution of working time generates a new layer of workers desperate to take on any job: The Reserve Army of Labor. This situation leads them to take on the jobs that cover up for the overworked and those who do not have enough time to carry out their out-of-work activities and that are usually poorly remunerated.[7] This new layer usually refers to the floating overpopulation that finds itself between jobs or the latent and stagnant layers who have been exerted from accumulation over long periods. The jobs the surplus population take on are usually related to the existence of overworked and very busy people (Moruno 2018).[8] It is not surprising that most precarious jobs relate to the service reproduction sphere, and mostly carried out by women since they are the ones who bear most of out-of-work duties and who enjoy the least free time.

Thirdly, the continuous updating of the current social standard by which capitalists evaluate their productivity involves a continual readjustment of the working hour's material content as well as an acceleration of time. This process happens even when the total value produced and the unit of measure (i.e., the working hour) remain.[9] The former example showed that before introducing the new method, the social working hour was determined on *x* goods. However, after the new method became widespread, the working hour was adjusted to higher material content, *2x* goods. Consequently, accumulation results in the densification of working time. The working hour's densification is significant since it implies that abstract domination inserted into accumulation allows capitalism to establish a continually renewed time discipline over workers, which reflects not only at work but also out of work. This time discipline entails an impersonal, abstract form of domination.

In a capitalist economy, time is fundamental as it represents an abstract and social mechanism that exerts coercion to material production and determines the social life of all individuals by operating as self-discipline that regulates behavior and coordinates them with the social structure imposed by capital.[10] Accumulation, therefore, sets in place a time-based dynamic that reproduces in an omnipresent and inevitable way, even when every hour seems to be the same length to capitalists and workers (Briales 2018). Capital accumulation involves a continuous actualization of a rhythm, a temporal standard, by which individuals govern their work and out-of-work life. It represents a temporal standard set by capital and internalized[11] by all individuals. It is internalized since it involves a moral character by which individuals feel compelled to meet schedules and carry out activities more intensively and efficiently. The process of individuals internalizing this ever-changing time discipline is extraordinary because external, abstract coercion becomes a coercion exerted by itself (Safranski 2017).

Time compression influences all individuals in a capitalist society but impacts workers significantly. Those employed develop an inclination to dedicate most of their available time mainly to work[12] and to reduce their free time to a minimum, just for fear of not complying with time standards and therefore being dismissed from work. For precarious workers, it means losing control over their own time, at least for two reasons.

Firstly, because precarious workers live in constant uncertainty, whether they will be employed or not, so they lose control of what constitutes their working time and leisure time (Standing 2011).[13] The border between these two times becomes blurry since capitalists expect that the floating, latent, and stagnant overpopulation will be available when needed, no matter the day, hour, or the conditions of the employment they have to take on. Their time becomes subordinated to others' decisions, and therefore, their lives revolve around the principle of total availability.

Secondly, because time discipline dominates their lives even when expelled temporarily or permanently from accumulation.[14] The fact that abstract social structure continues to dominate the lives of precarious workers coerces them to desperately seek to occupy their "passive" time, without even matter what kind of activity they have to engage in or whether they have to take on multiple jobs (Moruno 2018). This situation happens not only because the time dedicated to work remains the mechanism for procuring an income to consume and live, but because staying productive and following discipline will enable them to remain competitive, employable, and suitable for accumulation, as well as socially accepted. Subjectively, this situation translates into the loss of autonomy over their own time. The boundaries between working time and leisure time dissolve, so precarious labor entails a situation of continued uncertainty regarding both present and future existence. The precarious workers' time subordinates to the time of others since their lives configure around the uncertainty of whether they will be able to cover up for others' demands.

Due to these characteristics, precarious labor represents a form of manifestation of the impersonal, abstract structure imposed by capital accumulation, associated with an uneven distribution of working time, a time discipline emanating from the centrality of SNLT, and a compression of time that constantly coerces the Reserve Army of Labor. Furthermore, precarious labor involves a subjective feeling of losing control over time and the difficulties involved in the subordination of all their available time as the constant uncertainty to make decisions for the present and the future.

CONCLUSION

Labor precariousness is embedded in capitalist societies. It emerges from technical changes that increase social labor productivity, from the personal domination exerted by capitalists over workers, and from the impersonal, abstract, and social mechanism that dominates over capitalists, workers, and the Reserve Army of Labor. This abstract mechanism, grounded on the centrality of SNLT, involves a contradiction since while accumulation reduces the amount of working time required for production simultaneously reaffirms labor as the social abstract structure that determines people's lifes, actions and worldviews.

This contradiction results in the uneven distribution of the working time among all workers, enabling a profound restructuring of the working class. Inside this structure, the Reserve Army of Labor represents a layer of workers that subordinate their time to cover up those who overwork and do not have enough time to do their out-of-work activities. Furthermore, accumulation establishes a time-discipline that constantly densifies time and that becomes internalized by all capitalist society members. This process leads the Reserve Army of Labor to lose control over their time, to revolve around a principle of total availability to capitalist demands, and to accept any job even when it implies the risk of precarious existence and the uncertainty of subordinating all their available time. Thus, labor precariousness represents a manifestation of abstract domination, primarily an impersonal domination of the Reserve Army of Labor by time.

NOTES

1. Marx ([1981] 1991) associated the latent population with the rural peasant population, stripped of its means of production due to the primitive accumulation process, which resulted in the migration from rural to urban spaces boosting the emerging capitalist relations. Today, it would correspond to the population that unceasingly becomes salaried workers due to expanding capital into new territories such as rural peasants, day laborers, and rural migrants.

2. This confrontation means that all the decisions taken by individual capitalists occur inside a social capitalist dynamic, so all individual decisions made by capitalists are subject to the whole.

3. As "the law of gravity asserts itself when a person's house collapses on top of him" (Marx [1867] 1976,168).

4.

> If the satisfaction of a given amount of material needs formerly required a certain expenditure of time and human effort which has later been reduced by half, then without any loss of material comfort the scope for spiritual activity and enjoyment has been simultaneously extended by as much. . . . But, again the way in which the booty, that we win from old Kronos himself in his most private domain, is shared out is still decided by the dice-throw of blind, unjust Chance. (Schulz cited by Marx [1844] 2018)

5. According to Postone (1996), the constant reconstitution of abstract time identity involves a dialectic of transformation and reconstitution. It consists of a process by which the centrality of work reasserts labor as value and SNLT as its magnitude, even when working time per unit of product reduces due to accumulation. This means that labor reasserts as the social mediator by excellence in capitalist societies. This role is since no one consumes what they produce. All the products of labor operate as the means necessary to access the product of others, that is, all people in capitalist society depend on the production of others to subsist.

6. An illustration of this situation arises when accumulation expands from local to global spaces. When the abstract structure bases on a global social-time measure, accumulation confronts capitalists with even higher labor productivity rates, and therefore, labor precariousness becomes severe. The outcome of this global accumulation process is that it becomes challenging for capitalism to create enough jobs. As capital reproduces, there is a shift toward creating more precarious jobs and even less stable labor conditions.

7. This new layer surges alongside a process in which leisure and reproduction activities become profitable for capitalization.

8. It is worth recalling Aristotle's definition of slaves, considered as animated objects whose function was to liberate free men from necessity and therefore as non-time (Moruno 2018). As a parallel, precarious workers liberate others from the necessity to do their out-of-work activities. These workers are vital to facilitate capital accumulation since their existence guarantee the continuity of an overworking society.

9. "The same amount of work, therefore, performed for the same amount of time, always produces the same amount of value, regardless of any change in productivity" (Marx cited by Postone 1996, 288).

10. In Grundrisse, Marx considered time to be one of the most fundamental elements in capitalism. To plan production and other economic activities, society needs to distribute time. Meanwhile, individuals must divide and calculate their time to, on the one hand, acquire the knowledge they need and in the appropriate amounts for that society and, on the other hand, to satisfy the varied demands of all their activities (Marx [1971] 2007, 101).

11. Thompson (1967) confirms that time discipline in capitalism is tied to a particular moral character that allows the internalization of external coercion. In capitalism, waste of time is unbearable and morally unacceptable. In *The Poor Man's Family Book*, Baxter advises: "Let the time of your sleep be so much only as health requireth; For precious time is not to be wasted in unnecessary sluggishness"; "quickly dress you"; "and follow your labours with constant diligence" (Baxter, cited by Thompson, 1967, 88). The triumph of capital accumulation, according to Kurz (2014), is to colonize free time and impose working time as a guide to individual and collective existence.

12.

> The working day contains the full 24 hours, with the deduction of the few hours of rest without which labor-power is absolutely incapable of renewing its services. Hence it is self-evident that the worker is nothing other than labor-power for the duration of his whole life, and that therefore all his disposable time is by nature and by right labor-time, to be devoted to the self-valorization of capital. Time for education, for intellectual development, for the fulfilment of social functions, for social intercourse, for the free play of the vital forces of his body and his mind, even the rest time of Sunday (and that in a country of Sabbatarians!)—what foolishness! . . . capital oversteps not only the moral but even the merely physical limits of the working day. It usurps the time for growth, development and healthy maintenance of the body. (Marx [1867] 1976, 375)

13. Standing (2011) argues that precarious workers, which he perceives as a class, suffer due to the compression and acceleration of working time, which emanates from the workforce's re-commodification and like Polanyi's workforce concept of fictitious commodities. The idea presented here differs from that since all employed workers are subject to an abstract structure that forces them to work in excess. In this sense, precarious workers' time becomes subordinated to everyone else's time.

14. Any individual under an abstract social norm of time will always experience time as social, even when it is separated from society. Marx ([1867] 1976) discusses a similar situation when referring to Robinson Crusoe, the castaway in Defoe's novel. Robinson comes ashore on a lonely island in the South Pacific and finds that he must allocate his time to realize different activities to meet his various needs. He believes that he must conscientiously allocate his time to survive and to keep his sanity. From the shipwreck, Mr. Crusoe has saved his watch, ledger, ink, and pen. Like a good Englishman, he begins to calculate his time and keeps count of the working time not just to meet his needs but also to maintain a link to his world. In Robinson's consciousness, necessity compels him to divide his time with precision, so an external coercion becomes a way of life, even outcasted. A similar situation happens with precarious workers because even when expelled from accumulation time, discipline still runs the various aspects of their lives.

BIBLIOGRAPHY

Briales, Álvaro. 2018. "La expropiación del tiempo: claves para una sociología histórica de la dominación capitalista." *Sociología Histórica* 9: 564–92.

Choonara, Joseph. 2020. "The Precarious Concept of Precarity." *Review of Radical Political Economy* 52(1): 427–46.

Choonara, Joseph. 2019. *Insecurity, Precarious Work and Labour Markets. Challenging the Orthodoxy.* Switzerland: Palgrave Macmillan. Springer Nature.

Engels, Friedrich. (1845) 1993. *The Condition of the Working Class in England.* Oxford: Oxford University Press.

Foster, John Bellamy, Robert W. McChesney and R. Jamil Jonna. 2011. "The Global Reserve Army of Labor and the New Imperialism." *Monthly Review* 63(6): 1–31.

Gorz, André. 1997. *Miserias del presente, riqueza de lo posible.* Argentina: Editorial Paidós.

Jonna, R. Jamil and John Bellamy Foster. 2015. "Marx's Theory of Working-Class Precariousness—Its Relevance Today." *Alternate Routes: A Journal of Critical Social Research* 67(11): 21–45.

Kurz, Robert. 2014. "Luces de progreso." In *El absurdo mercado de los hombres sin cualidades. Ensayos sobre el fetichismo de la mercancía* edited by Anselm Jappe, Robert Kurz and Claus Peter Ortlieb, 83–93. La Rioja: Pepitas de calabaza.

Mariña, Abelardo. 2019. "Tendencias a largo plazo de la acumulación de capital y crisis estructurales: una perspectiva marxista de las ondas largas." In *La naturaleza contradictoria del capitalismo contemporáneo. Ensayos de Economía Política* (forthcoming), edited by Sergio Cámara. México: Universidad Autónoma Metropolitana-Azcapotzalco.

Marx, Karl. (1844) 2018. *Manuscritos de economía y filosofía.* Madrid: Alianza Editorial, S.A.

Marx, Karl. (1971) 2007. *Fundamentos elementales para la crítica de la economía política. Borrador 1857–1858. Volumen 1.* México: Siglo XXI.

Marx, Karl. (1867) 1976. *Capital, Volume I.* London: Penguin.

Marx, Karl. (1981) 1991. *Capital, Volume 3.* London: Penguin.
Morris, William. (1887) 2013. *Cómo vivimos y cómo podríamos vivir.* La Rioja: Pepitas de Calabaza.
Moruno, Jorge. 2018. *No tengo tiempo. Geografías de la precariedad.* Spain: Ediciones Akal.
Postone, Moishe. 1996. *Time, Labor and Social Domination. A Reinterpretation of Marx's Critical Theory.* Cambridge: Cambridge University Press.
Postone, Moishe. 2007. *Marx reloaded. Repensar la teoría crítica del capitalismo.* Madrid: Traficantes de sueños.
Safranski, Rüdiger. 2017. *Tiempo. La dimensión temporal y el arte de vivir.* Barcelona: Tusquets Editores. Kindle.
Standing, Guy. 2011. *The Precariat. The New Dangerous Class.* London: Bloomsbury Academic.
Thompson, E. P. 1967. "Time, Work-Discipline and Industrial capitalism." *Past and Present* 38: 56–97.

Part II

UNDERDEVELOPMENT, IMPERIALISM, AND THE INDUSTRIAL RESERVE ARMY OF LABOUR IN LATIN AMERICA AND BEYOND

Chapter 6

Marx's General Law and the Development of Underdevelopment

Lorenzo Fusaro

INTRODUCTION: MARX'S ERROR?

Robert Brenner's seminal article "The Origins of Capitalist Development: a Critique of Neo-Smithian Marxism" published in 1977 in the *New Left Review* counts as one of the most established (and accepted) critiques of dependency theory, and its author, in the words of Howard and King (1992, 210), as being the "strongest critic of Baran, Frank and Wallerstein."[1] Brenner's article aims chiefly at criticizing dependency theory's and world systems theory's analysis of the transition to capitalism. Yet, in doing so, he also seems to dismantle dependency theory's central claim adopted by Frank and Wallerstein that capitalism produces both development and underdevelopment, and that the two are causally interrelated. Indeed, dependency theory, and in particular its radical strand, among which we count the works of Theotonio Dos Santos, Ruy Mauro Marini, and Gunder Frank, underlines the dual or contradictory nature of capitalist development and argues that capitalist modernity should be conceptualized as including both development and underdevelopment (Katz 2016; Kay 1991). In this sense, and as Dos Santos (1978, 304–5) has stressed, "underdevelopment" ceases to be seen as a phenomenon that stands "outside" or "before" capitalism. It is capitalism itself, as Gunder Frank's (1967, 9) famous expression goes, that results in "the development of underdevelopment."

In order to outline his critique, Robert Brenner actually starts from Marx and Engels' supposed error in the *Communist Manifesto* in envisaging world-wide capitalist expansion, accompanied by "a process of capital accumulation and economic development more or less following the pattern of the original homelands of capitalism" (Brenner 1977, 25). Brenner's critique suggests that, contra Marx, "capitalist expansion through trade and investment *failed* to break the old modes of production . . . or actually to strengthen the old modes" (1977, 26, author's emphasis). The continuing existence of precapitalist modes of production is crucial for Brenner's argument, as "underdevelopment" resulted, and still results, from a *lack* of capitalist relations of production. His well-known thesis suggests that development is a consequence of specific class structures, capitalist class structures, here understood as entailing the separation of producers from the means of production and the formation of the commodity "labour power." For it is only under capitalist relations of production, Brenner argues, that an economy has the incentive, even *the necessity*, to develop the forces of production (Brenner 1977, 32). Here the establishment of capitalist relations of production is understood as deriving from the "class struggle" whereby the latter can have contrasting outcomes. Thus, in England, according to Brenner, class conflict did indeed lead to the establishment of capitalist relations of production resulting in "development." By contrast, in other places such as Eastern Europe or Latin America, this was not the case (Brenner 1976; 1977, 78), leading to "underdevelopment" in these regions. It is therefore not capitalism but the absence of capitalist relations of production that results in underdevelopment.

Following Brenner's view, Marx—at least when writing the *Manifesto*—was hence wrong in maintaining that capitalist expansion would lead to the adoption of capitalist relations of production across the globe and that this would lead to development. But does this truly amount, as Brenner would have it, to Marx thinking that, on a global level, the establishment of capitalist relations of production would lead to "a process of capital accumulation and economic development"? And does the establishment of capitalist relations of production represent a *sufficient* condition for development? What if the establishment of capitalist relations of production does not guarantee economic development and can therefore also lead to "underdevelopment," as Latin American Marxists also thought?

Even a superficial reading of the *Communist Manifesto* suggests that Brenner's claims might be problematic and that Marx and Engels' analysis might be seen as anticipating the later elaboration provided by Latin American Marxists centered on the development of underdevelopment. Marx and Engels pointed to elements that, as we shall see further, would later be entailed within Marx's general law of capitalist accumulation, stating that the development of capital, while proportionally developing the proletariat, does not necessarily guarantee that the latter is fully absorbed into the production process, thus opening the possibility that a very large part of it might fall into poverty—a condition that is usually associated with "underdevelopment," as we shall see. As Marx and Engels put it:

> In proportion as the bourgeoisie, i.e., capital, is developed, in the same proportion is the proletariat, the modern working class, developed—a class of labourers, who live only so long as they find work, and *who find work only so long as their labour increases capital.* These labourers, who must sell themselves piecemeal, are a commodity, like every other article of commerce, and are consequently exposed to all the vicissitudes of competition, to all the fluctuations of the market. (*Marx-Engels-Werke*, Bd.4, 468, author's emphasis)[2]

As a result, Marx and Engels assert later in the same text that "the unceasing improvement of machinery" that characterizes capitalist development "makes their [the proletariat's] livelihood more and more precarious," eventually condemning them to pauperism, noting that "pauperism develops more rapidly than population and wealth" (*Marx-Engels-Werke*, Bd. 4, 473).

To be sure, Marx and Engels' assertions in the *Manifesto* are not as elaborate as those put forward by Marx in *Capital*, yet the observations within the former text seem to suggest that Brenner's claims are at least questionable, while pointing to the validity of some of the assertions made by dependency theory, that is, that capitalist development itself (and not the lack thereof) produces poverty and "underdevelopment." In the following section, I will critically engage with explanations of the occurrence of underdevelopment provided by dependency theory and political Marxism. In section "Marx's General Law, Underdevelopment, and Latin America," I shall return to Marx's general law of capitalist accumulation, arguing that Marx provided an analysis of the "development of underdevelopment" that might overcome the weaknesses of the aforementioned theories. Hence, I will maintain that following Marx's law, capital accumulation proportionally develops the proletariat, while also pointing out that a large part thereof (the so-called reserve army of labour) is ultimately not directly involved in the production process. Following Marx, this has the tendency to result in low levels of income, poverty, and income inequality—in short, "underdevelopment." By way of illustration, and considering Latin America's reserve army of labour, I will show that it still accounts for 60–70% of the (potentially) working population. Furthermore, in section "Further Research: Dependency, Forms of State, and Class Struggle," I will point to further research concerning the implications these insights might have when considering dependency, the specificities of Latin American states, and the class struggles that occur within the region.

THE LIMITATIONS OF DEPENDENCY THEORY AND POLITICAL MARXISM

While dependency theory presents several variants that restrain the possibility of generalizing its main theses, it is, I believe, probably fair to suggest that the systemic condition of underdevelopment is largely explained by the *transfer of surplus* from the periphery to the center (Salgado 2005), and the implications this had by heavily influencing the economic structure of subordinated economies. Initially, following the majority of the mentioned works, the transfer of surplus is related to the processes of "primitive accumulation," here (in my view, wrongly) understood as an accumulation of wealth to be used to kick off capitalist accumulation. According to this reading, economic development in 16th- and 17th-century Europe was largely based on the "pillaging" of colonial territories. In order to substantiate this argument, one might recall, for example, that relying on J. H. Elliot's account, Perry Anderson (1974, 90) contended that under Philip II's rein (1556 to 1598) colonial bullion represented 20–25% of Spain's revenues. Ernest Mandel, based on data provided by various authors, concluded that the overall transfer of resources from the colonies represented one billion pounds, which, according to his calculations, equaled "more than the total value of capital invested by the whole of European industry up to 1800" (Mandel 1971, author's translation). Relying on Enrique Semo, Augustín Cueva (1977, 13) speaks of "primitive *des-accumulation*" in Latin America, maintaining that the region was deprived of the means to enable primitive accumulation to take place in the continent itself. Yet, the transfer of surplus that resulted in the development of the center and the underdevelopment of the periphery is argued to be a persistent feature of the capitalist world economy. The central theoretical framework adopted to capture the transfer of surplus is that of *unequal exchange*, the explanation for which has varied over the years and has been further substantiated by Marxist economists. While Emmanuel's (1972) analysis focused on low wages and higher rates of exploitation in the periphery as enabling a transfer of surplus toward the center, the theory has since more largely focused on technological and productivity differences between center and periphery (Shaikh 1991; Carchedi 1991; Astarita 2009). As a result of higher technology and productivity within the center compared to the periphery, surplus is ultimately transferred toward the former. It should be noted that even Ruy Mauro Marini's *Dialectica de la dependencia* (1972) is ultimately also based on unequal exchange. For, here, capitalists in the "periphery" tend to make up for the losses derived from unequal exchange by "super-exploiting" the workers. Most recently, and partially following the above framework, John Smith (2016) has identified the transfer of surplus from the "Global South" toward the "Global North" as a distinctive feature of imperialism in the 21st century. Further, Adam Morton and Andreas Bieler concluded that "because capitalist expansion has historically taken place within an already existing international states-system, state spaces have become locked into relations of unequal exchange, in which surplus is transferred from peripheral spaces to advanced capitalist spaces due to different productivity rates" (2014, 42).

The critique of dependency theory came from the ranks of the *Dependentistas* themselves as José Serra and Fernando Cardoso (1978), in a polemic with Ruy Mauro Marini, eventually questioned the core of dependency theory—that development is bound up with underdevelopment (Hernández López 2005, 22). Moreover, within Western Marxism, it was Robert Brenner, whose crucial text was mentioned in the introduction, who claimed that through focusing on the sphere of exchange in conceptualizing capitalism, the theory strongly departed from Marx's analysis of the capitalist mode of production (see also Wood 1999). Relatedly, it has been argued that the theory's characterization of "capitalism" comes closer to the description of a mercantilism system characterized by a zero-sum game—the center accumulates at the expense of the periphery. Further, it has been argued that exploitation among *nations* and not classes became the central focus of analysis, and that at least part of the proletariat within the "center" (the so-called labor aristocracy) profited from the exploitation of its "fellow" proletarians in the periphery (Kay 1991; Larrain 1989; Howard and King 1992).

Brenner certainly deserves credit for criticizing the conceptualization of the capitalist mode of production put forward by some, albeit not all, dependency theorists. As mentioned before, processes of "primitive accumulation" are here understood as the accumulation of wealth able to start capitalist accumulation. However, Marx's discussion in chapter 24, "The Secret of Primitive Accumulation," clearly demonstrates how primitive accumulation refers primarily to the separation of human beings from their means of production, thus creating the specific social relations that characterize the capitalist mode of production. Yet, it is important to underline that this critique mainly applies to the conceptualization of capitalism put forward by Gunder Frank and later Immanuel Wallerstein, as Latin American Marxists such as Ruy Mauro Marini, Theotonio Dos Santos, and Augustín Cueva present an analysis of capitalism that is far more grounded in Marx's *Capital*. But what in my opinion remains a major issue of concern is dependency theory's insistence on "unequal exchange" in order to explain the "development of underdevelopment," and this makes the theory indeed vulnerable to the aforementioned critique. Following Marx in *Capital* (*Marx-Engels-Werke*, Bd. 23, 158, 583), I do not aim at denying the existence of such processes, yet I want to question how far these can be made responsible for the "development of underdevelopment." As is evident in any "model" that attempts to reconstruct processes of unequal exchange between the "center" and "periphery" (with peripheral countries producing goods at lower levels of technology or being characterized by lower wages compared to the "center"), the assumption is that the proletariat, generally and abstractly conceived, is actually *always integrated within direct capitalist production*—the periphery here always "produces," and part of the surplus is transferred to the "center." But what if part of the proletariat (and a very large part thereof), as I will show when discussing Marx's general law, while being *integrated* within capitalism, is actually *excluded* from participation in capitalist production, thereby falling into the realm of "poverty"?

By contrast, political Marxism's explanation for the occurrence of underdevelopment as a result of a *lack* of capitalist relations of production is highly problematic. Interestingly enough, this argument was very well known to dependency theorists. "Supposedly," Gunder Frank critically writes:

> Only one part of the economy has been importantly affected by intimate economic relations with the "outside" capitalist world, and that part, it is held, became modern, capitalist, and relatively developed precisely because of this contact. The other part is widely regarded as variously isolated, subsistence-based, feudal or pre-capitalist, and therefore more underdeveloped. (1969, 5).

The same point is made by Dos Santos: "up to very recently social science in our countries has understood Latin America as an underdeveloped region in which underdevelopment has been produced by the survival of a feudal economy and society" (1978, 289).

Bear in mind that the absence of capitalist relations of production during the colonial and early postcolonial periods might indicate that, at first sight, Brenner's argument *appears* to be valid—during this period, as the literature generally argues and as Keen and Haynes conclude "all colonial labor systems rested in varying degrees on servitude and coercion" (2009, 82). Even after the revolutions for independence, according to Bulmer Thomas, "the labour market changed only slightly":

> Slavery was abolished in those republics where it was of little consequence (e.g., Central America) but retained where it played a crucial role in production (e.g., Brazil, Cuba, and Peru). Tribute was abolished at first, but it was often restored when it became clear that the Indian labourer no longer had the same incentive to seek paid work. The *mita* was finally ended, but debt peonage and antivagrancy laws remained in place and were even adopted in those frontier areas, such as the Argentine pampas, where they had not previously been applied. For the Indian majorities in Mexico, Guatemala, Peru, and Bolivia, independence brought no perceptible change, and Black slaves in independent Brazil were in much the same position as their counterparts in the Spanish colonies of Cuba and Puerto Rico. (1995, 30)

But what about the subsequent fully "modern" period? Can we deny the eventual establishment of capitalist relations of production? If that is not the case, how to explain the *persistence* of "underdevelopment" *despite* the establishment of capitalist relations of production following Brenner's argument?

To be sure, and as mentioned previously, up to the mid- or late 19th century, the economic structure (not so the superstructures after independence characterized by the emergence of "modern" national states) remains largely typified by precapitalist relations of production. Yet, this incongruence between economic structure (precapitalist) and superstructures (capitalist) undoubtedly started to change from the late 19th century onward as Latin American states generally unleashed brutal processes of "primitive accumulation," here understood as the separation of human beings from their means of production. As if anticipating *in nuce* what Gramsci would later elaborate on, Marx outlines the role of the state in fostering the transition to capitalism: "they all employ the power of the state, the concentrated and organized force of society, to hasten, hot-house fashion, the process of transformation of the feudal mode of production into the capitalist mode, and to shorten the transition" (*Marx-Engels-Werke*, Bd. 23, 779). Augustín Cueva has thus well captured the violent intervention of the newborn, formally independent, oligarchic states "implanting the capitalist mode of production in a context that thus far was feudal or based on slavery." As Cueva recalls, the oligarchic states' policies and programs were about

> expropriating direct producers (the primary but not exclusive aspect of primitive accumulation), [they were] also simultaneously about transforming these producers "freed" of all propriety into labour power, making them available to the haciendas, plantations, mines, etc., the *sine qua non* for initiating capitalist production. The laws against "vagrancy" are responsible for shackling that pauper and vagrant labour power, which has nevertheless not yet internalized its conversion into a commodity. And the oligarchic state intervenes repressively not only to fill this "subjective lacunae," but also to convert, when necessary, a good part of still independent producers into a proletariat *sui generis*. (1977, 135)[3]

The long-term result is the unquestionable persistence and endurance of underdevelopment *despite* the eventual establishment of capitalist relations of production. As an approximate or proxy indicator for the latter, consider that already by the late 1970s, Latin America displayed levels of urbanization (63.9%) comparable to Europe (68.6%) or the United States (77.9%) (Fajnzylber 1983, 170). This leads us to strongly question Brenner's thesis. Moreover, we might address the same concerns to the author that Brenner originally raised against dependency theory by labeling it "neo-Smithian" or "liberal." For, similarly to liberal explanations for "underdevelopment," it seems that also for Brenner, it is a *lack of capitalism* that generated and generates underdevelopment. Further, and again following liberal accounts and methodological nationalism, developments within one country seem to be largely insulated from developments in other countries. As we will attempt to demonstrate in the next section, Marx's general law might be able to resolve the problems associated with the discussed theories, for on the one hand it captures (actually anticipates) the valuable contribution dependency theory (the understanding of capitalism as including development and underdevelopment) without falling into the problems associated with its conceptualizations of the capitalist mode of production. On the other hand, it retrieves (again, anticipates) interesting insights from Brenner's argument without proposing a "liberal" understanding of development and underdevelopment.[4]

MARX'S GENERAL LAW, UNDERDEVELOPMENT, AND LATIN AMERICA

In outlining Marx's general law, it is necessary to consider that the reading of *Capital* adopted here starts from the idea that Marx's method of exposition involves the "rising from the abstract to the concrete," or from the "simple to the complex." Therefore, starting from very general and abstract determinations, more concrete and complex determinations are introduced (Callinicos 2009; 2014). The latter will mediate the most abstract laws without invalidating them. Moreover, and relatedly, we understand part 7 of *Capital* as depicting capital accumulation at a very high level of abstraction, or we might say at the *global level* by considering capital as "total social capital" (*Marx-Engels-Werke*, Bd. 23, 653). We therefore wish to stress that Marx is not analyzing a single capitalist nation (Sunkel and Paz 1970; Marini 1972; Pradella 2014).

What, then, are Marx's general conclusions concerning capitalist accumulation on a world scale? We might summarize them, in Marx's words, as follows: "Accumulation of wealth at one pole is, therefore, at the same time accumulation of misery, agony of toil slavery, ignorance, brutality, mental degradation, at the opposite pole, *i.e.,* on the side of the class that produces its own product in the form of capital" (*Marx-Engels-Werke*, Bd. 23, 675).[5] Thus, the accumulation of capital on a word scale increases wealth on one pole, and, at the same time, misery on the other. Were we to put it along the terminology associated with dependency theory, we might say that, indeed, on a world scale, development is accompanied by underdevelopment. Yet, in order to grasp Marx's assertion, it is worth presenting the general law in full:

> The greater the social wealth, the functioning capital, the extent and energy of its growth, and, therefore, also the absolute mass of the proletariat and the productiveness of its labour, the greater is the industrial reserve army. The same causes which develop the expansive power of capital, develop also the labour-power at its disposal. The relative mass of the industrial reserve army increases therefore with the potential energy of wealth. But the greater this reserve army in proportion to the active labour-army, the greater is the mass of a consolidated surplus-population, whose misery is in inverse ratio to its torment of labour. The more extensive, finally, the lazarus-layers of the working-class, and the industrial reserve army, the greater is official pauperism. *This is the absolute general law of capitalist accumulation.* Like all other laws it is modified in its working by many circumstances, the analysis of which does not concern us here. (*Marx-Engels-Werke*, Bd. 23, 674)

In section 1, Marx unveils that the capitalist mode of production has its own demographic laws and that the accumulation of capital is accompanied by an increase of its variable part, hence that part of capital invested in labor-power. The "growth of capital," Marx writes, "involves growth of its variable constituent or of the part invested in labour-power," or, in other words, "accumulation of capital is, therefore, increase of the proletariat" (*Marx-Engels-Werke*, Bd. 23, 642). As Marx has shown, the creation of the proletariat, that is, the separation of human beings from their means of production, is an utterly violent process in which "conquest, enslavement, robbery, murder, in short, force, play the greatest part" (*Marx-Engels-Werke*, Bd. 23, 744). Further, as later Marxists demonstrated, processes of "primitive accumulation" are persistent features of the capitalist economy (Bonefeld 1988).

While in section 1 Marx argues that the proletariat increases as capital is accumulated, in section 2, he maintains that the proletariat included in capitalist production tends to decrease relatively as accumulation progresses. This, according to Marx, is due to the law for the organic composition of capital to rise, that is, "the law of the progressive growth of the constant part of capital in comparison with the variable part" (*Marx-Engels-Werke*, Bd. 23, 660). This law builds on Marx's concept of "relative surplus value production," and ultimately on the operation of the law of value as, following the law of value, every capital *must* expand and increase the productivity of labor in order to continue to exist on the market. With the progression of capitalist accumulation, accompanied by an increase of the productivity of labor, the variable part of capital decreases relative to the constant part. It is important to underline that this reduction of the variable part is *relative* as, in absolute terms, the employed workforce can increase. As Marx emphasizes throughout this chapter, the concentration and centralization of capital, also fueled by credit, further increase this tendency.

As a consequence, and as Marx goes on to argue in section 3, capitalist accumulation results in the creation of what he refers to as a "relative surplus labouring population" or the "industrial reserve army of labour." Importantly, not only is this "surplus labouring population" a *product*, but also it represents "a condition of existence of the capitalist mode of production." For it is only thanks to its existence that capital can find what it needs for its reproduction (*Marx-Engels-Werke*, Bd. 23, 661). Hence, Marx emphasizes that the existence of a surplus population grants capital the necessary flexibility that enables its expansion (*Marx-Engels-Werke*, Bd. 23, 661). A further central function it plays is related to the determination of *wages*, as their fluctuation is ultimately determined by the expansion and retrenchment of the industrial reserve army, and the relation it has with the "active" working population. The existence of a reserve army makes sure that, even in periods of accelerated accumulation, the demands for labor and possible wage rises are kept in check (*Marx-Engels-Werke*, Bd. 23, 669).

It is in section 4 that Marx finally distinguishes different "forms of existence" of this part of the proletariat labeled surplus-population, while noting that "every worker belongs to it during the time when he is only partially employed or wholly unemployed" (*Marx-Engels-Werke*, Bd. 23, 670). It is important to note here that being part of the proletariat—which, following Engels's definition, consists of being part of "the class of modern wage labourers who, having no means of production of their own, are reduced to selling their labour power in order to live" (*Marx-Engels-Werke*, Bd. 4, 462)—by no means guarantees that wage workers are continuously absorbed within the capitalist production process. They are "internal" to, and part of, capital but can completely or partially remain "external" or excluded from the direct capitalist process of production. Hence, Marx distinguishes between "the floating, the latent, and the stagnant" surplus-population, while also describing that workers might *flow* from one category to another (notice Marx's recurrent analogies to liquids throughout this section). The first category comprises workers who are "sometimes repelled, sometimes attracted again in greater masses, so that the number of those employed increases on the whole, although in a constantly decreasing proportion to the scale of production" (*Marx-Engels-Werke*, Bd. 23, 670). The "latent" surplus population refers to that section of the proletariat, which, following innovations within one sector of the economy, is made redundant while without being absorbed by the rest of the economy. The third category, Marx writes, "forms a part of the active labour army, but with extremely irregular employment," into which workers from the first and second categories might fall. Finally, Marx focuses on "the lowest sediment of the relative surplus-population" that "dwells in the sphere of pauperism," and that might count as a fourth category in which all categories of unemployed or semi-employed workers previously discussed *might* drop into. Aside from the *Lumpenproletariat*, that is, "vagabonds, criminals, prostitutes" (*Marx-Engels-Werke*, Bd. 23, 673), it consists of the following three sub-categories: first, those able to work; second, orphans and pauper children; and third, "the demoralized, the ragged, and those unable to work, chiefly people who succumb to their incapacity for adaptation, an incapacity which results from the division of labour; people who have lived beyond the worker's average life-span; and the victims of industry" (*Marx-Engels-Werke*, Bd. 23, 673).

By way of illustration, we might refer to calculations made by John Bellamy Foster, Robert W. McChesney, and R. Jamil Jonna (2011, 21) who attempt to quantify the global reserve army of labour using data and categories ("vulnerably employed," "unemployed," and "economic inactive population") provided by the International Labour Organization (ILO). They show that between 1997 and 2011, the *global* reserve army of labour stood at roughly 65% of the global workforce, noticing a slight decline between the years 2000 and 2009 followed by a slight increase thereafter. Using the authors' methodology reveals that Latin America's reserve army of labour stood at a staggering 70% of the total workforce at the beginning of the new millennium, and declined to approximately 60% in 2014 in order to increase again (see figure 6.1). For the sake of comparison, it is worth bearing in mind that in the United States, the industrial reserve army of labour (calculated using the same methodology) stood at 28%, displaying a noticeable increase to close to 35% starting with the 2008–2009 economic crisis.

To be sure, and as the authors admit, there might be objections in considering all "vulnerable employment" (the ILO understands this as the sum of "own-account workers" and "contributing family workers," all of which are largely informal, insecure, and badly paid jobs) as the reserve army of labour. Yet, vulnerable employment in its different facets is part of Marx's category of "stagnant" surplus-population, whereby it should be noted that even Marx's text includes *Hausarbeit* [homework] in the latter category (*Marx-Engels-Werke*, Bd. 23, 673). Consider that even more conservative estimates would not alter the fact that we are dealing with an enormous proportion of the proletariat that is not or only partially included in the capitalist production process. This is also manifest in other historical calculations that merely consider "underemployment" for Latin America as a whole, and that show that this phenomenon concerned 46% of the total working population in 1950 (for Mexico, it was 56.9%; Brazil, 48%; and Bolivia, 68%, while in Argentina, underemployment stood at "only" 22%). While the period 1950–1980 was characterized by a slight amelioration with total underemployment standing at 38% in 1980, the 1990s (the last set of data provided) was characterized by further deterioration (Bértola and Ocampo 2012, 192).

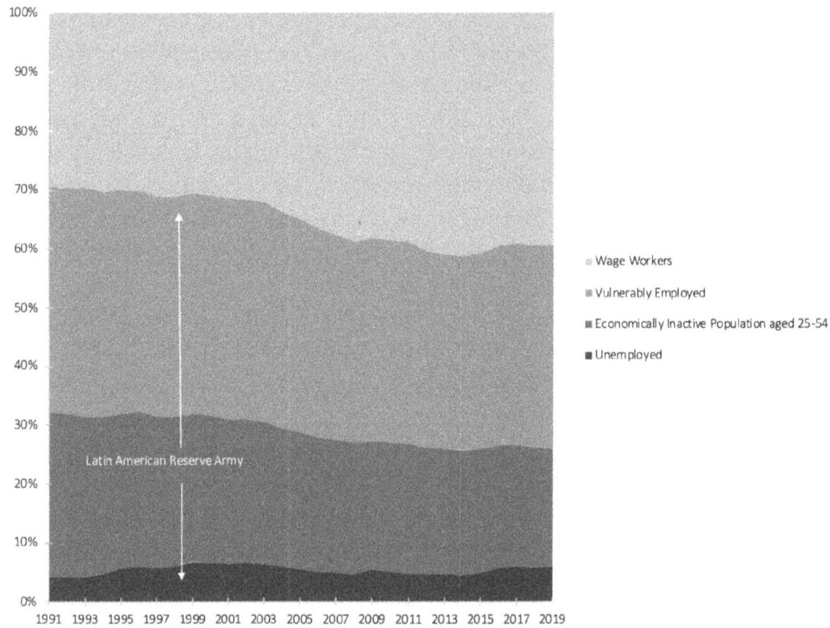

Figure 6.1 The Latin American Workforce and Reserve Army (1991–2019). *Source*: ILO (2020) using the methodology adopted by Foster, McChesney, and Jonna (2011).

As recent studies further demonstrate, and as Marx anticipated, the existence of such a large reserve army of labour or surplus population is associated with very high levels of poverty. Thus, according to the 2016 UNPD report on the region, in 2002, 42% (i.e., 214 million) of Latin America's population was living in income poverty (UNPD 2016, 24). While the report indicates that the number decreased substantially, reaching 142 million in 2013, it also notes that most people escaping absolute poverty are still subjected to economic vulnerability, meaning that falling back into extreme poverty is likely (UNPD 2016, 18), unless governments prevent it by, among other things, "expanding social protection systems to guarantee universal coverage and combat the variety of risks that arise during the life cycle" (UNPD 2016, 37). In addition, and again as anticipated by Marx's law, the region presents very high levels of income inequality with the Gini coefficient standing at 0.5 (UNPD 2016, 6). Moreover, following Marx's law, one might also expect that in regions where the surplus population is particularly large, constant capital (capital invested in machinery etc.) is particularly low relative to the available workforce. Even if not using Marxist categories, data provided by Reyes and Sawyer (2016, 60) show that in 2013, the capital stock to labor (which here only includes wage workers, making the estimate far higher than it would be if they considered the reserve army in full) stood at 2,864, whereas in high-income countries, it stood at 13,614.

Adopting Osvaldo Sunkel's (1970) definition of underdevelopment associated with low levels of income, poverty and low levels of capital relative to the available workforce might retain that Marx's general law provides an explanation for its occurrence. But more than this, I believe that Marx's general law of capitalist accumulation seems to offer a possible solution that enables very valid elements from the discussed theories to be retained without falling into the problems we have identified in both the dependency theory and political Marxism: first, it offers, as dependency theory does (and contra Brenner), an analysis that comprehends capitalist modernity as including the interrelated moments of development and underdevelopment. Here, underdevelopment is not due to a lack of capitalist relations of production—on the contrary, it is the very presence of capitalist relations of production that creates development and underdevelopment, while the latter is a "condition of existence" for capital accumulation. Moreover, the theory is fundamentally grounded in Marx's analysis of the capitalist mode of production and its "inner laws of motion." Thus, capitalism is not understood as a mercantilist system characterized by a zero-sum game, nor does it remain static. Importantly, exploitation among classes and not nations remains the central focus of analysis. Marx's analysis further suggests that the idea of a "worker aristocracy" that would profit from exploitation is seemingly groundless, as the general law of capitalist accumulation presents what we might refer to as a lose-lose situation. The negative effects on that part of the population that is excluded from the direct production process do not need any further clarification. But what about the "active" or directly involved population? As Marx puts it, to be a "productive worker" or, by way of extension, part of the "active population" is "not a piece of luck, but a misfortune" (*Marx-Engels-Werke*, Bd. 23, 532). Indeed, as a result of the increase in relative surplus value production, the level of exploitation of employed workers increases, that is, an even greater amount of the value produced is appropriated by capital. In addition, the condition of the active proletariat deteriorates independently from changes in wages or income (*Marx-Engels-Werke*, Bd. 23, 675). Apart from higher levels of exploitation, in chapter 23, Marx also summarizes the effects of capitalist accumulation on the "active population" discussed in earlier chapters of *Capital*:

> All means for the development of production undergo a dialectical inversion so that they become means of domination and exploitation of the producers; they distort the worker into a fragment of a man, they degrade him to the level of an appendage of a machine, they destroy the actual content of his labour by turning it into a torment; they alienate from him the intellectual potentialities of the

> labour process in the same proportion as science is incorporated in it as an independent power; they deform the conditions under which he works, subject him during the labour process to a despotism the more hateful for its meanness; they transform his life-time into working-time, and drag his wife and child beneath the wheels of the juggernaut of capital. (*Marx-Engels-Werke*, Bd. 23, 674)

Finally, and albeit this might occur at a concrete level of analysis, underdevelopment does not exclusively rest on the transfer of surplus or "unequal exchange"—it is included within capitalism but excluded from the direct process of capitalist production that constitutes the realm of poverty and "underdevelopment" as previously described.

FURTHER RESEARCH: DEPENDENCY, FORMS OF STATE, AND CLASS STRUGGLE

Following Marx's general law, I attempted to show that Marx provided an analysis of the development of underdevelopment. The insights thus gained call for further research in different areas, among which, relying especially on the work of Antonio Gramsci, I shall refer to three. First, the analysis presented invites a rethinking of the concept of dependency in a way that avoids focusing too strongly on the transfer of surplus. Second, I believe that the specific way in which capitalism developed in Latin America also resulted in specific forms of states typified by the exercise of power in the form of domination and *exclusion*. This, in opposition to hegemony characterized by subordination by *inclusion*, we encounter in "Western" or "central" liberal states. Finally, I wish to raise thoughts on the implications for class struggle. In particular, I wish to point to the contradiction revolution-restauration that might characterize the politics of the reserve army of labour and further inform the analysis of present-day experiences.

Underdevelopment and Dependency

So far, following Marx's general law, I have only maintained that capitalism, operating on a world scale, produces development and underdevelopment, and that the latter is a necessary condition for the former. At a descriptive level of analysis, I have shown that Latin America is a site where poverty and underdevelopment are located. At the same time, we do not yet know the reasons that can account for the uneven geographical distribution of poverty, and hence underdevelopment. The challenge, therefore, following Marx's method, is to introduce the necessary mediations that can enable us to discern how "underdevelopment" has to be understood and explained at a more concrete level of analysis. "Descending" to the level of the word market and international relations, we encounter, of course, the concept of "dependency" that might be understood as a mediating moment of the law of value at the global level.

Dos Santos comprehends dependency in "the first place . . . as a conditioning situation," and hence one in which "a certain group of countries have their economy conditioned by the development and expansion of another economy" (1978, 304, author's translation). But, consistent with dependency theory's understanding of "underdevelopment," the author focuses almost exclusively on exploitation and surplus extraction. In his words, "... the dominant countries have a technological, commercial, capitalist and sociopolitical predominance over dependent countries (with predominance of some of these aspects in the various historical moments) that allows them to impose *conditions of exploitation and to extract some of the surplus* produced internally" (Dos Santos 1978, emphasis added).

But as I have attempted to show earlier, while surplus extraction might play an important role, this remains too restrictive to an explanation. It is therefore probably worth introducing Gramsci's analysis of international relations that interestingly anticipates the themes encountered in Dos Santos, without, however, limiting dependency to the extraction and transfer of surplus. As I have shown elsewhere, Gramsci presents a "dialectical" understanding of international relations that is also concerned with the idea that national states are mutually conditioned while also differentiating between a hierarchy among them (Fusaro 2017; 2019). Hence, Gramsci introduces the concept of *hegemonic states and subordinated or dependent states*, with the former typified by what we might refer to as *relative geopolitical autonomy* (achieved, ultimately, militarily), and the latter, such as Italy or Latin American states, by a lack thereof. What characterizes a hegemonic state, then, is "its ability to impress upon state activity an autonomous direction, of which other states need to support the influence and repercussion," maintaining that "the line of a hegemonic state (hence of a great power) does not oscillate because it does determine the will of others and it is not determined by them" (Gramsci 2001, Q.13, §32, 1629).

Thus understood, dependency starts from politico-military subordination. It also enables a discernment of ways in which core states (or hegemonic states) might mediate the law of value—which produces development and underdevelopment—by diverting its negative effects to subordinated or dependent states. Indeed, as Gramsci also warned, it is the inability of capitalist development in a given country to deliver the goods (e.g. development and jobs) that might create the basis for "organic crises" and crises of the state as a whole (Gramsci 2001, Q.1 §127, 116; Q. 13 §23, 1603). The existence of an excessive reserve army of labour and poverty (something that Gramsci discusses explicitly) can hence turn into a sociopolitical problem that might threaten the legitimacy of the ruling classes and the established order in core countries. As Giovanni Arrighi argued, core states are hence interested in maintaining poverty and related protest movements outside their jurisdiction, outlining that "as long as . . . movements of protest take place outside the jurisdiction of the core states, the legitimacy of these states is not threatened and may even be strengthened by them" (Arrighi and Piselli 1987, 734).

This initial discussion of the concept of dependency therefore suggests rethinking the concept by analyzing the *different contradictions* presented in *Capital*. Subaltern or dependent states might therefore not only be differently integrated into the core or hegemonic nation's circuit of capital (and hence as providers of raw materials, labor-power, production sites, market for realization, etc.), necessary for the containment of rival states for geopolitical reasons. In addition, and very importantly, dependent nations should also be understood as *loci* to where the contradictions of capital accumulation can be "outsourced."

Forms of State

The persistent condition of underdevelopment is characterized by a very large fraction of the population being integrated within capitalism, but excluded from direct production, and this also invites reflection on the specificities of Latin American states. Following Gramsci again and his analysis of the "normal" exercise of hegemony in "Western" liberal states as being characterized by the (economic, political, and cultural) *inclusion* of subaltern groups by means of coercion and consensus (Frosini 2016) calls for further reflection when considering Latin American states. If, at the structural level, capitalist modernity (and not the absence thereof) in Latin America is characterized by *exclusion* of large masses from the direct production typified by conditions of poverty and underdevelopment, then we might expect different forms of states and differences in the exercise of power compared to those we find within "developed" countries.

Indeed, as both Gramsci and Poulantzas invite us to reflect on, the articulation of the superstructures cannot be analyzed in isolation from the economic structure that might take different forms in time and space. Hence, Poulantzas's theorization of the state is, in the words of the author, "bound up with the periodization of capitalism into distinct stages and phases." "Authoritarian statism," for example, following Poulantzas again, "seems to correspond to the current phase [1970s] of imperialism and monopoly capitalism in the dominant countries, in the way that the liberal state referred to the competitive stage of capitalism and the various forms of interventionist state to the previous phases of monopoly capitalism" (2014, 204). The identification of different "forms" or "typologies" of capitalist states has not only a temporal dimension, for it is also bound to the spatial dimension that corresponds to the different mode of insertion within the capitalist world economy. Hence, *in passim*, the author notes that "in the zone of dominated countries, for example in Latin America, we are witnessing the emergence of a new form of dependent state, which itself manifested in diverse regimes, involves significant points of dissimilarity with the new form of state in the dominant countries" (2014, 204).

I wish to argue that Latin America's historically subordinated position within the capitalist world economy called for, and indeed found, a corresponding "political model" based on the exercise of power in the form of domination and exclusion, that, in turn, has been used to reinforce the continent's countries' subordinate economic position. Notably, Gramsci suggested distinguishing between "East" and the "West" (2001, Q.7, §16, 866). Here, I am suggesting a distinction between "North" (developed) and "South" (underdeveloped), where the different positions within the capitalist world economy have resulted in different "political models" or different sorts of "capitalist modernity" (see also Marcos 2018).

Class Struggle

But in light of the earlier reading of the general law, I wish to also point to further research that might help to draw light on the nature of contemporary struggles in "underdeveloped" or "dependent" countries, for example, those that were responsible for the so-called pink tide in Latin America. In particular, I wish to draw attention to our statement that the proletariat increases proportionally with the accumulation of capital, while a great part of it remains excluded from direct capitalist production. Following this conceptualization of the "border" as designating the inclusion within capitalism but exclusion from direct participation, I wish to reflect on the possibility that some struggles of the proletariat that dwells outside direct participation might be interpreted as attempts to "enter" capitalist production, broadly understood, rather than overcome capitalism.

Interestingly, both Marx and Gramsci drew attention to the fact that social struggles might actually reinforce capitalism rather than overcome it. Hence, in the *Manifesto*, Marx and Engels express the idea that it is only at a certain stage of development that the proletariat is going to struggle *against* capital or the bourgeoisie, while in earlier stages, its struggles and victories are "victories for the bourgeoisie" (*Marx-Engels-Werke*, Bd. 4, 470). While reaching, eventually, far more pessimistic conclusions compared to those Marx and Engels would reach in the *Manifesto*, Gramsci's discussion of the *subalterns* in the *Notebooks* also highlights different stages that subaltern groups should go through before they become self-conscious, autonomous, and "leading." In doing so, Gramsci reflects upon the limitations and the contradictory nature as well as the difficulties of struggles pursued by subaltern groups, also arguing that they might actually reinforce the hitherto prevailing forms of domination (Gramsci 2001, notebook 25, in particular).

In Latin America, the problematic surrounding the political consciousness of the enormous masses that fall into the reserve army of labour has been taken up especially by *marginalistas*. Hence, Cristóbal Kay (1989), following Quijano (1977) and Nun (1972), maintains that the mobilization of marginal groups might have contrasting outcomes—on the one hand, it is argued that marginalized groups represent a revolutionary potential as they witness the limitations of the capitalist mode of production and its impossibility for providing them with stable jobs and adequate levels of income. Yet, on the other hand, it is argued that the vulnerable position of marginal groups as well as their lack of organization can lead to reactionary politics. As Kay reports, they can easily fall victim "to the paternalism and clientelism of state sponsored organisations" or the "manipulation of populist politicians," leading to "desperate violent actions which are self-defeating." More generally, Kay continues, they might represent "a disposable mass for political manipulation by charismatic leaders from the right and left as they are vulnerable to short-term promises" (Kay 1989, 105–6). An analysis of the mass mobilizations that lead to the establishment of left-leaning governments as well as their social basis from the aforementioned perspective, that is, one that dwells on the reserve army of labour and its contradictory consciousness, might be helpful in shedding further light when analyzing the contradictions of contemporary processes. Importantly, it might further inform that significant strand within the literature that does indeed refer to the binomial "revolution-restauration" and the related Gramscian concept of "passive revolution" in order to describe both the achievements and limits of left-leaning governments in Latin America (Modonesi 2012; Webber 2017).

CONCLUSION

This chapter aimed at recovering one crucial chapter of Marx's *Capital*, the general law of capitalist accumulation, arguing that it represents an insightful analytical tool for understanding the occurrence of "underdevelopment" within the capitalist international political economy. Unlike Brenner, who argued that "underdevelopment" is due to a lack of capitalist relations of production, it has been put forward that—as Latin American Marxists argued—it is the very presence of capitalist relations of production that produces "underdevelopment." Our textual interpretation of Marx's general law suggests that capital has the tendency to increase the proletariat proportionally to its own expansion. However, and as Marx's discussion highlighted, not all the proletariat thus produced (the surplus-population or reserve army of labor) is actually participating in the actual capitalist process of production. This, following Marx, implies that, on a world scale, large sections of the population present low levels of income, poverty, and a lack of access to capital that can be largely seen as depicting "underdevelopment." When it comes to Latin America, I have shown that within the region, the reserve army of labour accounts for 60–70% of the potential working population, and that the region, as Marx anticipated, presents very high levels of poverty, income inequality, and low levels of capital relative to the available workforce.

Hence, and differently from Latin American Marxists associated with dependency theory, I have argued that it is not unequal exchange and surplus extraction, despite their concrete existence, that explain the persistence of "underdevelopment," but that for dependency theory and for Marx, "underdevelopment" is both a consequence and condition of the existence of capitalist development—the existence of a surplus population offers flexibility to the operation of capitalism and is a crucial factor for the determination of the fluctuation in wages. Also, I have argued that capitalist accumulation should be comprehended as resulting in a lose-lose situation for the proletariat as a whole, independently from their location in the "center" or the "periphery."

Following the insights thus gained, I pointed to three areas where further research might be needed. First, I suggested that the analysis presented invites us to rethink the concept of dependency that avoids a strong focus on the extraction of surplus and that considers the different and multiple contradictions that characterize the capitalist process of accumulation. Second, I also suggested considering that the specific way in which capitalism developed in Latin America also resulted in specific forms of states typified by the exercise of power in the form of domination and exclusion. Finally, I have raised thoughts on the implications that the existence of a very large reserve army of labor and its contradictory consciousness might have on the class struggle. In particular, I pointed to the contradiction "revolution-restauration" that might characterize the politics of the reserve army of labor and further inform the analysis of present-day experiences.

NOTES

1. This chapter is a slightly modified and updated version of the chapter "The Development of Underdevelopment Before and Beyond Dependency Theory and Political Marxism: Rereading Marx's General Law of Capitalist Accumulation" (Fusaro 2019a) published in *Latin American Marxisms in Context: Past and Present.* Published with the permission of Cambridge Scholars Publishing. I wish to thank Alejandro González for his help in the collection of the data concerning the industrial reserve army of labour in Latin America.

2. When referring to Marx's *Capital* and other works by Marx and Engels, I follow the German original within the *Marx-Engels Werke*, providing the English translation. Unlike the English editions of *Capital*, within the *Marx-Engels Werke*, "The General Law of Capitalist Accumulation" is chapter 23 (and not 25, as in the English editions).

3.

> no se trata sólo de llevar adelante la tarea de expropiación de los productores directos (aspecto primero pero no único de la acumulación originaria), sino también y simultáneamente la de transformación de esos productores 'liberados' de toda propiedad en fuerza de trabajo a disposición de las haciendas, plantaciones, minas, etc., *requisito sine qua non* para el arranque de la producción capitalista. Las leyes contra la 'vagancia' son las encargadas de aherrojar esa mano de obra ya paupérrima y vagabunda, pero que sin embargo no ha interiorizado todavía su proceso de conversión en mercancía.

4. Both Nun (1970) and Quijano (1978) returned to Marx's general law of capitalist accumulation stimulating a very important debate among Latin American Marxists. While Marx's insights are here applied to characterize specific features of underdeveloped countries, the authors, in my view (and contrary to the task undertaken in this chapter), do not interpret Marx's general law as a general *explanation* for underdevelopment.

5. Notice the similarity with Hegel's assertions in the *Lectures on the Philosophy of Right*, according to whom the emergence of poverty is a symptom of the workings of civil society: "The emergence of poverty is actually a consequence of civil society, and *it grows necessarily out of it*. Riches without measure and limits are accumulated on the one side, poverty and misery on the other side. The increase of wealth and poverty keeps the same pace" (Hegel 1974, VPR, 193, author's translation and emphasis).

BIBLIOGRAPHY

Anderson, Perry. 1974. *Passages From Antiquity to Feudalism*. London: New Left Books.

Arrighi, Giovanni, and Fortunata Piselli. 1987. "Capitalist Development in Hostile Environments: Feuds, Class Struggles, and Migrations in a Peripheral Region of Southern Italy." *Review Fernand Braudel Center* 10, no. 4: 649–751.

Astarita, Rolando. 2009. *Monopolio, Imperialismo y Intercambio Desigual*. Madrid: Maia.

Bértola, Luis, and Ocampo, José Antonio. 2012. *The Economic Development of Latin America since Independence*. Oxford: Oxford University Press.

Bieler, Andreas Morton, and Adam David Morton. 2014. "Uneven and Combined Development and Unequal Exchange: The Second Wind of Neoliberal 'Free Trade'?" *Globalizations* 11, no. 1: 35–45.

Bonefeld, Werner. 1988. "Class Struggle and the Permanence of Primitive Accumulation." *Common Sense* 6: 54–65.

Brenner, Robert. 1976. "Agrarian Class Structure and Economic Development in Pre-Industrial Europe." *Past and Present* 70, no. 1: 30–75.
———. 1977. "The Origins of Capitalist Development: a Critique of Neo-smithian Marxism." *New Left Review* 104: 25–92.
Bulmer, Thomas. 1995. *The Economic History of Latin America since Independence.* New York: Cambridge University Press.
Callinicos, Alex. 2009. *Imperialism and Global Political Economy.* Cambridge: Polity.
———. 2014. *Deciphering Capital.* London: Bookmarks.
Carchedi, Guglielmo. 1991. *Frontiers of Political Economy.* London; New York: Verso.
Cardoso, Fernando, and Enzo Faletto. 1969. *Dependencia y Desarrollo en América Latina: Ensayo de lnterpretación Sociológica.* México D.F.: Siglo XXI editores.
Cueva, Agustín. 1977. *El Desarrollo del Capitalismo en América Latina.* México: Siglo XXI Editores.
Dos Santos, Theotonio. 1978. *Imperialismo y Dependencia.* México: Era.
Emmanuel, Arghiri. 1972. *Unequal Exchange: A Study of the Imperialism of Trade.* New York; London: Monthly Review Press.
Fajnzyblber, Fernando. 1983. *La industrialisación trunca de América Latina.* México D.F.: Editorial Nueva Imagen.
Foster, John Bellamy, Robert McChesney, and Ramil Jonna. 2011. "The Global Reserve Army of Labour and the New Imperialism." *Monthly Review* 63, no. 06: 1–31.
Frank, Gunder. 1969. *Underdevelopment or Revolution.* New York: Monthly Review Press.
———. 1967. *Capitalism and Under-development in Latin America: Historical Studies of Chile and Brazil.* New York: Monthly Review Press.
Frosini, Fabio. 2016. "L'egemonia e i "subalterni": utopia, religione, democracia." *International Gramsci Journal* 2, no. 1: 126–66.
Fusaro, Lorenzo. 2019. *Crises and Hegemonic Transitions: From Gramsci's* Quaderni *to the Contemporary World Economy.* Boston and Leiden: Brill.
———. 2019a. "The Development of Underdevelopment Before and Beyond Dependency Theory and Political Marxism: Rereading Marx's General Law of Capitalist Accumulation." In *Latin American Marxisms in Context: Past and Present*, edited by Peter Baker, Irina Feldman, Mike Geddes, Felipe Lagos and Roberto Pareja. Newcastle: Cambridge Scholars.
———. 2017. "Why China is Different: Hegemony, Revolutions and the Rise of Contender States." *Research in Political Economy* 32: 181–219.
Gramsci, Antonio. 2001. *Quaderni del Carcere* (edizione critica dell'Istituto Gramsci a cura di Valentino Gerratana). Torino: Einaudi.
Harvey, David. 2010. *A Companion to Marx's Capital.* London: Verso.
Hegel, Friedrich. 1974. *Vorlesungen über Rechtsphilosophie.* Stuttgart: Frommann Verlag.
Hernández López, Roberto Carlos. 2005. "La Dependencia a Debate." *Revista de Estudios Latinoamericanos* 40: 11–54.

Howard, Michael Charles, and John Edward King. 1992. *A History of Marxian Economics, Volume II, 1929–1990*. Princeton, NJ: Princeton University Press.
International Labour Organisaiton. 2020. *World Employment and Social Outlook: Trends 2020*. Geneva: ILO.
Katz, Claudio. 2016. "El surgimiento de las Teorías de Dependencia." http://www.rebelion.org/noticia.php?id=214869.
Kay, Cristóbal. 1991. "Reflections on the Latin American Contribution to Development Theory." *Development and Change* 22, no. 1: 31–68.
———. 1989. *Latin American Theories of Development and Underdevelopment*. London and New York: Routledge.
Keen, Benjamin, and Keith Haynes. 2009. *A History of Latin America*. Boston, MA; New York: Houghton Mifflin Harcourt.
Larrain, Jorge. 1989. *Theories of Development: Capitalism, Colonialism and Dependency*. Cambridge: Polity Press.
Mandel, Ernest. 1971. "La acumulación originaria y la industrialización del tercer Mundo." http://www.rebelion.org/noticia.php?id=51090.
Marcos, Beatriu. 2018. "*Pensamiento político converso* en la Castilla del siglo XV y su impronta en la Modernidad hispánica: Teología política y pensamiento republicano en el *Defensorium unitatis christianae* de Alonso de Cartagena." PhD diss., UAM México.
Marini, Ruy Mauro. 1972. "Dialéctica de la Dependencia." *Sociedad y Desarrollo* 1: 35–51.
———. 1978. "Las razones del neodesarrollismo." *Revista Mexicana de Sociología* 40, no. extraordinario: 57–106.
Marx, Karl, and Friedrich Engels. 1956–1990. *Marx-Engels-Werke* (forty-three volumes). Berlin: Dietz Verlag.
Modonesi, Massimo. 2012. "Revoluciones pasivas en América Latina. Una aproximación gramsciana a la caracterización de los gobiernos progresistas de inicio de siglo." In *El Estado en América Latina: continuidades y rupturas*, 139–66, edited by Mabel Thwaites Rey. CLACSO-ARCIS: Santiago de Chile.
Nun, José. 1969. "Superpopolación relativa, ejercito industrial y masa marginal." *Revista Latinoamericana de Sociologia* 5, no. 2: 178–236.
Poulantzas, Nicos. 2014. *State, Power, Socialism*. London: Verso.
Pradella, Lucia. 2014. *Globalisation and the Critique of Political Economy*. London: Routledge.
Quijano, Anibal. 1983. "Imperialism and Marginality in Latin America." *Latin American Perspectives* 10, no. 3: 76–85.
———. 1977. *Imperialismo y "marginalidad" en América Latina*. Lima: Mosca Azul Editores.
Reyes, Javier, and Charles Sawyer 2016. *Latin American Economic Development*. London; New York: Routledge.
Salgado Garilla, José Guadalupe. 2005. *América Latina en la conformación de la economía-mundo capitalista: Las transferencias de excedente en el tiempo largo de la historia y en la época actual*. México: UNAM.

Serra, José, and Fernando Cardoso. 1978. "Las desventuras de la dialéctica de la dependencia." *Revista Mexicana de Sociología* 40, no. extraordinario: 9–55.

Shaikh, Amwar. 1991. "Competition and Exchange Rates: Theory and Empirical Evidence." http://www.anwarshaikhecon.org/sortable/images/docs/publications/international_trade/1991/Competition%20and%20Exchange%20Rates.pdf.

Smith, John. 2016. *Imperialism in the Twenty-First Century. Globalization, Super-Exploitation, and Capitalism's Final Crisis*. New York: Monthly Review Press.

Sunkel, Osvaldo, and Pedro Paz. 1970. *El subdesarrollo latinoamericano y la teoría del subdesarrollo*. México D.F.: Siglo XXI editores.

United Nations Development Programme. 2016. *Regional Human Development Report for Latin America and the Caribbean. Multidimensional progress: well-being beyond income*. New York: UNDP.

Webber, Jeffery R. 2017. *The Last Day of Oppression, and the First Day of the Same: the Politics and Economics of the New Latin American Left*. London: Pluto.

Wood, Ellen. 1999. *The Origins of Capitalism: A Longer View*. London; New York: Verso.

Chapter 7

Bordering the Surplus Population across the Mediterranean

Imperialism and Unfree Labor

Lucia Pradella and Rossana Cillo

INTRODUCTION

In August 2018, hundreds of workers took on the street of southern Italy against the killing of 16 African workers in two accidents in overcrowded vans on the way home from the fields (Bellizzi and Di Zanni 2018).[1,2] In Libya, Eritrean immigrants and refugees escaped detention camps and marched to Tripoli to oppose being sold like "slaves" (France24 2018). These two protests are closely linked to each other: many of the immigrants marching in Italy came through the desert, Libya and the Mediterranean; both protests, we argue in this chapter, were directed against conditions resulting from a unitary process of accumulation in which the neocolonial extraction of Libyan resources and the militarization of the European Union's (EU) borders facilitated a movement of vulnerable workers to Italy.

Too often, however, these two sides of a common story are not treated together. Since the late 1980s, the mobilizations of immigrant agricultural workers in Italy have made their conditions visible, highlighting their role as a reserve army of labour, a pool of underemployed and unemployed workers that allows farmers to meet the low production costs and just-in-time (JIT) demands of retail and agribusiness corporations (Avallone 2016; Borretti 2010; Colloca and Corrado 2013; Pugliese 2012). The 2018 Placido Rizzotto Observatory's survey revealed about 80 areas of "caporalato" (gangmaster system) and 55 areas of severe labor exploitation concentrated in Italy's South but spreading throughout the country. Between 400,000 and 430,000 agricultural workers are employed irregularly; 100,000 of whom risk being employed through a gangmaster or in conditions of severe exploitation (cf. Iovino 2018, 11–12).[3]

This points to a widespread condition of unfree labor, that is, labor extracted through the various forms of coercion and compulsion, including economic coercion, that deprive workers of "the type of 'free' choice they are believed to exercise in 'normal' labour markets." (Skrivankova 2010, 9).[4] A broad body of literature highlights the importance of the state in creating conditions for unfree labor through policies limiting labor mobility, deregulating the labor market, and empowering employers (LeBaron and Phillips 2019; Strauss and McGrath 2017; Yea 2017). As Nicholas De Genova (2013) argued, the spectacle of militarized border enforcement is geared toward immigrants' subordinated inclusion. By tying together residence permit and employment contract, Italian migration policies and the structures of the asylum system make immigrants more vulnerable to super-exploitation and unfree labor, enhancing the deregulation of the labor market (Basso 2010; Dines and Rigo 2015; Ferrero 2010; Oliveri 2015).

As we discuss in the next section, however, with a few notable exceptions (Avallone 2017; Domșodi 2019), the literature on labor exploitation in Italian agriculture conceptualizes the reserve army and the role of the state in national terms. This is the case despite recent important attempts at developing a Mediterranean outlook on Italian agriculture (Corrado et al. 2016). State-centric approaches are problematic in analyzing a sector that is dominated by national and multinational retail and agribusiness corporations, whose global operations—supported by the EU, World Bank, and International Monetary Fund—fuel the dispossession and emigration of workers then employed in forced labor enclaves in Europe (Araghi 2009; Boeckler and Berndt 2014; Fritz 2011; McMichael 2012).

In section "The Global Reserve Army of Labour, Imperialism, and Unfree Labor," we argue that Marx conceptualized the reserve army in global terms and anticipated contemporary studies of the role of imperialism in swelling its ranks (Foster et al. 2011; Patnaik and Patnaik 2016): a process that, for Tom Brass (2011), is key to the growth of unfree labor also in metropolitan countries. This perspective challenges the viewpoint that people on the move are really "undesirable" (Agier 2011), a "surplus humanity" of limited significance to capital (Li 2010). It sheds light on what Harsha Walia (2014) calls "border imperialism": the process by which contemporary imperialism securitizes the border against the immigrants it displaces with the goal of increasing their exploitation. Importantly, Marx conceptualized the role of the imperial state against the backdrop of the possibilities for international solidarity generated by this process.

In this light, this chapter aims to investigate the development of labor exploitation and unfree labor in Italian agriculture against the backdrop of

Italian and Western imperialism in Libya during the 2007–2008 global economic crisis and the 2011 uprisings of the Middle East and North Africa, up until 2018. Libya's ex-colonial power (1911–1947), Italy is both the main country of arrival for immigrants crossing the Mediterranean from Libya and the main recipient of Libyan energy (Greco and Oddo 2018). Italy is also leading EU cooperation with Libya on migration controls. This cooperation, according to several studies, strengthened Libya's security apparatus, undermined asylum-seekers' rights, and "illegalized" established migratory movements in the Sahel (Andrijasevic 2006, 2010; Brachet 2016; Bialasiewicz 2012; Paoletti 2010). As is well-known, renewed cooperation after 2011 fueled a brutal system of detention, extortion, and forced labor in Libya (CNN 2017; Phillips and Missbach 2017).

This system, we argue, needs to be situated within processes of neocolonial extraction of Libyan resources, and the resulting expansion of the reserve army of labour of Italian and EU capital in Libya (section "Border Imperialism in the Mediterranean"). This analysis highlights the interlinkages between immigrant workers' experiences of exploitation and unfree labor in Libya (section "Reserve Workers in Libya") and in Italian agriculture (section "Reserve Workers in Italy's Fields"), and sheds light on the role of the Italian and Libyan state and non-state actors in facilitating and enforcing this process, regulating and containing the conflicts it entails. If immigrants' experiences in Libya can play a disciplining role when they arrive in Italy, in fact, these experiences can also encourage them to reclaim their rights and freedom (section "The Resistance of Immigrant Workers").

This chapter presents the results of a study of unfree labor in Italian agriculture that started in 2012–2014 with a research funded by the European Commission. This included 21 interviews and two focus groups with trade-unionists, labor inspectors, and members of NGOs, employers' associations and agribusiness companies. Since then, we conducted more interviews with immigrants, trade-unionists, investigative journalists, antiracist activists, and labor inspectors (five in 2015 and 25 in 2019). In 2019, we widened our gaze to the experiences of immigrants on both sides of the Mediterranean, and conducted ten in-depth semistructured interviews with the immigrants who had arrived in Italy from Libya; three interviews with journalists, filmmakers, and bloggers with an expertise on Libya; six interviews with antiracist activists; three interviews with trade-unionists belonging to Flai-CGIL (Federation of Agro-Industrial Workers within the Italian General Confederation of Labour); and three interviews with Italian labor experts. This qualitative research helped us assess the secondary literature and a plethora of official reports, investigative articles, and online resources on Libya, including immigrants' own messages available online. Thousands of immigrants in Libya, in fact, use social media and WhatsApp to communicate with their families and the world. Their testimonies are available on several online platforms, including the radio program Exodus (Severgnini and Messina 2018) that broadcasts the oral and written messages that immigrants sent to its curators (Severgnini 2018).[5]

UNFREE LABOR IN ITALIAN AGRICULTURE

Since the late 1980s, several studies have shown that Italian agriculture went through a process of neoliberal restructuring and "super-marketization." The Italian government and the EU promoted the deregulation of the agricultural sector and the spread of entrepreneurial farming. As in other countries, trade liberalization, mergers, acquisitions, and global sourcing strategies reinforced Italian and foreign retailers, particularly supermarket chains, and large European processors (Corrado et al. 2016; McMichael and Friedmann 2007). These actors have now the power to influence where, how, by whom and at what price food is produced. Capital concentration increased the differentiation among farmers and the competitive pressures on small and medium farms (Corrado 2015). If processes of concentration are key, for Gaetano Martino (2018), their impact on labor can only be understood by looking at the production and distribution of value between labor, capital, and ground rent.

The sharp increase in labor productivity in the past two decades reduced the number of workers employed in agriculture, as well as the demand for skilled workers (Esposti and Merlino 2016; Mori 2018). While increased land productivity gave a competitive advantage to some producers, it also limited the possibility for farmers to contain fixed costs. In this context, one of the strategies pursued by farmers has been to lower wages and conditions (Magdoff et al. 2000; FCE 2002). As Martin (2011) pointed out, in mechanized agriculture, labor-power is considered the most "controllable" expense. The increased competitive pressure on small and medium farmers, concentrated in the South, has been presented as one of the main factors behind the diffusion of unfree labor. Some years ago, for example, the farmer organization Coldiretti denounced that in the labor-intensive Rosarno, citrus plantations multinational corporations like The Coca-Cola Company imposed production costs of €0.07 per kilo of oranges, way below cost price, leaving farmers no other choice (Garrappa 2016; Wasley 2012).

This strategy must be contextualized within the capitalist offensive against the workers' movement that took place in Italy since the end of the 1970s, and intensified in the 1990s, when Italy became a country of mass immigration.[6] As Brass (2011: 272) argued, the possibility for capital to draw upon a global reserve army through immigration and outsourcing is crucial to shifting the class balance of forces in its own favor, pushing down wages and conditions up to the point of depriving workers of the control over their own labor-power (see also Avallone 2017; Domşodi 2019).

According to CREA (Consiglio per la ricerca in agricoltura; Council for Research in Agriculture) sources, which also estimated irregular labor, between 1991 and 2015, immigrant workers grew from being 0.3% to 48% of the total agricultural workforce. As in other countries (Strauss and McGrath 2017), restrictive immigration policies (e.g., 1996 Turco-Napolitano Law and 2002 Bossi-Fini Law) did not stop immigration but made it more dangerous and expensive, and immigrants more vulnerable, multiplying stratifications along legal, ethnic, and gender lines (Basso 2010; Martin 2006). The "supermarketization" of Italian agriculture thus coincided with a process of internationalization, segmentation and precarization of the agricultural workforce, with conditions of unfree labor particularly affecting undocumented workers in irregular employment; EU immigrants, especially women (Palumbo 2016; Arci member, Caserta and Aiab representative, Rome 2013); and, more recently, refugees with humanitarian permits (Dines and Rigo 2015).

The growth of unfree labor is also linked to the expansion of formal and informal labor intermediation.[7] After declining in the 1970s and 1980s as a result of farm laborers' struggles and public placement policies, the gangmaster system has returned to being the main system of workforce recruitment and management in agriculture (Limoccia et al. 1997; Pugliese 2012) both in the South and, increasingly, in the North of Italy (Osservatorio Placido Rizzotto 2018; INPS and INAIL labor inspectors 2013). The *caporali* select the workers on behalf of agricultural employers in *mercati delle braccia* (laborer markets) in town squares, bars, roundabouts, and reception centers and on WhatsApp, and mobilize workers according to the demands of production cycles in different agricultural zones. Often immigrants themselves, gangmasters perform a variety of socially necessary tasks, like arranging transport and accommodation that are not provided by public policies (Corrado and Perrotta 2012; Filhol 2017; Perrotta 2014). The system varies according to the territorial context and has different hierarchical structures, with a minority of gangmasters colluding with criminal organizations. In some cases, control over workers is achieved with violent means, such physical segregation, seizure of documents, wage theft, sexual abuse, and murder (Osservatorio Placido Rizzotto 2018; Pugliese 2012). Despite its variations, the main aim of the system is disciplining and coercing workers into highly exploitative labor relations (Brass 2011; Domşodi 2019). Employment conditions depend on the specificities of local production systems. While in areas of mechanized greenhouse cultivation, employment and working times are more stable, the harvest of certain vegetables and fruits is concentrated in a few weeks or days: the working day is then generally very long (8–12 hours), while in other periods, laborers work short hours and intermittently

(MSF 2005; Pugliese 2012; Scotto 2016). Severely exploited laborers do not enjoy contractual and social rights and are paid much below the levels established by national collective agreements. Common forms of payment, albeit illegal, are a fixed "day wage," which allows employers to increase working hours, and "piecework"; workers, for example, receive €3–4 for picking a 375-kilo crate, which pushes them to speed up pace and work longer hours (Osservatorio Placido Rizzotto 2018). While *caporali* deduct a part of workers' pay, and gangmasters and employers deduct transport and housing costs, the latter sometimes become untraceable at the end of harvest (Caruso 2016; Garrappa 2016; Oliveri 2012).

A 2005 Doctors without Borders' survey into immigrant workers' health conditions—the most extensive study till date for geographical scope and sample size, confirmed by later studies (MSF 2008; Amnesty 2012; OIM-Italy 2010)—reported that only 5.6% of the immigrants who went to MSF mobile clinics were in a good state of health. The rest suffered from environmental factors, poor health and hygiene conditions, injuries, poisoning by pesticides, and working and housing conditions.[8] Women are often subjected to sexual violence by employers and gangmasters (Palumbo and Sciurba 2015). MEDU (2019) reported that of the 180 patients they visited in the summer 2019 in the Capitanata plain (Apulia), 5% and 8.5% manifested, respectively, signs of psychological distress and alcohol abuse, as well as psychosomatic symptoms due to the violence and tortures during their journey (especially in Libya), exploitation, and social uncertainty.

These conditions are not signs of Italian backwardness but characterize a sector that is largely industrialized and integrated into the world market. They can thrive also thanks to the high levels of undeclared work, which are tolerated if not encouraged by the Italian state through frequent tax amnesties and labor-inspection cuts (Cillo and Toffanin 2014). The lack of regulation leaves space to the illegal activities of criminal organizations. Since the late 1990s, these have started to operate throughout the entire agro-food chains and invest in highly profitable activities like logistics and commercialization, raising intermediate and final costs (Eurispes 2019a; Perone 2018).

While the process of agricultural restructuring over the past 30 years did not produce major conflicts among Italian farmers and workers, from the late 1980s, immigrants' levels of self-organization and unionization increased, prompting the birth of Italy's antiracist movement after the killing of the South African asylum-seeker Jerry Masslo in 1989 (Di Luzio 2006; Sciortino 2003). Intensified after the mid-2000s, immigrant struggles brought to light the responsibilities of retail and multinational corporations, and the role of state policies, organized crime, and the gangmasters. As discussed in section "The Resistance of Immigrant Workers," these movements played an important role in the introduction of legislation against the gangmaster system and severe exploitation (laws 138/2011 and 199/2016).[9] Several studies highlight that immigrant workers' mobilizations drew inspiration from the 2011 uprisings in North Africa and the Middle East (Corrado et al. 2016; Perrotta and Sacchetto 2012). So far, however, there is still little research on the impact of the NATO war against Libya and the militarization of EU borders on the sector. This lacuna, we contend, depends on an under-theorization of the relationship between the reserve army of labour, imperialism, and workers' agency, which is central to Marx's analysis.

THE GLOBAL RESERVE ARMY OF LABOUR, IMPERIALISM, AND UNFREE LABOR

In famous passages, Marx describes the foundational role of "the extirpation, enslavement and entombment of the indigenous population of [America] . . . and the conversion of Africa into a preserve for the commercial hunting of blackskins" (Marx 1976, 915). Marx did not see these processes, as David Harvey (2004) suggests, as abominations of the capitalist mode of production, belonging to a past history of "primitive accumulation." Along with the violent expansion of the world market, unfree labor is also a *result* of capitalist development (Marx 1981, 343). For Marx, in fact, it is capital accumulation as such with its tendency toward technological progress, and the concentration and centralization of capital—that generates a surplus population of displaced workers and direct producers. Far from being superfluous, this represents a *relative* surplus population: superfluous in relation to the current demand for labor-power in production but necessary to the accumulation process as such. This is therefore better defined as a reserve army of labour that puts pressure on employed workers, limiting their claims and resistance, allowing capital to increase exploitation and sustain profitability.

If the expansion of the reserve army is a systemic tendency, for Marx, colonialism and imperialism also play a crucial role in it. As accumulation proceeds, in fact, the appropriation of cheap raw materials and primary commodities becomes more important in order to reduce fixed costs and support profitability (Marx 1981, 203–204). This means that what has been defined as "extractivism"—activities that overexploit natural resources mainly destined to export, shaped in the period of formal colonialism (Hamouchene 2019; Rodney 1972)—is for Marx a permanent feature of accumulation. Colonial extraction, for Marx, also leads to the expansion of the reserve army of metropolitan capital, and this is another crucial factor that stems the tendency of the rate of profit to fall, as are the reduction of wages to below the value of the labor-power and the increase in the absolute exploitation of workers (cf. Patnaik and Patnaik 2016). In the colonies, for Marx (1981, 342, 344, 763), the latter was facilitated by the diffusion of slavery, bonded labor, and the oppression of small peasants. This was particularly evident in colonial India (Marx 1986, 235) and in Ireland, which was reduced to "an agricultural district of England," providing it with "corn, wool, cattle, industrial and military recruits" (Marx 1976, 860). Since these processes are only possible by crushing the resistance of the colonized and by shifting the class balance of forces (Brass 2011; Das 2012), capital has permanent recourse to colonial violence in order to ensure its reproduction (Cross 2013, 17; Pradella 2010).

Marx, therefore, did not assume, as Tania Murray Li (2010) maintains, that the reserve army would be fully incorporated into the active army: the former, in fact, takes on different forms in capital's uneven development in metropolitan and colonial countries. In *Capital*, he argues that while the floating surplus population comes and goes according to the business cycles, the latent one comprises the self-sustaining segments of the rural population both in England and its colonies. Interestingly, Marx describes agricultural laborers in England as "slaves of the landed proprietors and the farmers" (1976: 849). If land concentration and productivity advancements continuously converted them into a surplus population facing abysmal wages and living conditions, the gangmaster system allowed farmers to get a cheap "extra hand ready for extra work" during production peaks (Marx 1976, 853). Small peasants suffered the competition of capitalist farms and were always at risk of becoming surplus laborers. If, in England, surplus rural laborers were transformed into factory workers, in Ireland, the dispossessed rural population migrated to the towns but was *not* incorporated into the active workforce and was constantly sent back to the countryside (Marx 1976, 866). It was the lack of sufficient employment opportunities in Ireland that made them a reserve army for English capital, exploitable in Ireland or abroad, including in England. In order to contain the unrest of this surplus population, before the development of the welfare state, the British Empire combined a "terrorist legislation" against vagabonds and unemployed in England with the brutal militarization of Irish society (cf. Jones 2016). Anticipating Aimé Césaire's (1950) reflections on the "boomerang effect" of colonialism, Marx believed that socioeconomic and political conditions in Ireland rebounded on England as well. Not only was Ireland a laboratory for political repression in England (Marx 2010, 120), but also the British ruling classes used Irish immigration to create stratifications and divisions among workers, fomenting feelings of fear, hostility, and racism against the Irish, which helped justify British domination of Ireland and the super-exploitation of Irish workers in England, generating a downward competition among workers (Marx 1988, 474–475). But, for Marx, also the Irish struggle for emancipation rebounded on British politics. In the wake of a growing anti-colonial movement, Irish immigrants brought their aspirations into the labor movement in England, inspiring support for their liberation struggle. It is in the light of these possibilities for working class and anticolonial solidarities—this fusion of horizons and struggles transcending the state—that the role of the imperial state can be fully theorized. Neocolonial processes of resource extraction reduce employment opportunities in the countries affected, expanding the reserve army of metropolitan capital. This surplus population is contained through the multiplication of external and internal frontiers, which, as Fanon argued (1991, 39), enable the brutal submission and exploitation of the population. In a context of international migration, these conditions rebound on the reserve army in metropolitan countries. They facilitate the super-exploitation of immigrant workers and the diffusion of forms of unfree labor in Europe as well, enhancing the exploitation of the entire working class (cf. Cross 2013, 28; Nikolanikos 1975, 15–16). From this perspective, contemporary borders represent a mechanism of differential containment and exploitation of the surplus population mobilized by the global, uneven dynamic of capital accumulation. The violence of the borders, however, gives the impression that people on the move are really superfluous and undesirable, shifting the blame away from capitalist social relations onto innate characteristics of entire peoples: a naturalization of social inequalities that underpins processes of racialization (cf. Walia 2014, 61–63). The resulting view of the state as a self-enclosed entity reacting to global transformations—rather than enabling or enforcing them—legitimizes restrictive immigration policies and the criminalization of immigrants, who are cast as an external threat to both the state and the "national" working classes through deeply entrenched colonial and racist narratives (Bhattacharyya 2018, 129; Davies and Isakjee 2018). The bordering of the reserve army thus reinforces the international system of division of labor, obstructing the coming together of workers made possible by growing interdependence and labor cooperation, and by the new sources of structural power this generates (Silver 2003). If, for Marx (1988, 473), racism is the "secret" of the power of the ruling class, international solidarity is the key to workers' power.

BORDER IMPERIALISM IN THE MEDITERRANEAN

The 2007–2008 global economic crisis and the 2011 uprisings generated new possibilities for workers' solidarity across the Mediterranean and led to renewed efforts by imperialist powers to increase their appropriation of global resources. As in Egypt and Tunisia, the Libyan uprising was an expression of widespread social and political discontent (Kamat and Shokr 2013). But its violent repression by Gaddafi offered a NATO coalition including Italy the pretext to intervene militarily, preventing the radicalization and extension of the uprising. Started under the "Responsibility to Protect" framework, the war soon turned into a mission for regime change unveiling its crude neo-colonial motives (O'Sullivan 2017). Despite Libya's opening up since the 1990s, in fact, for Western leaders, Gaddafi's economic nationalism was an obstacle to the desired neoliberal reforms, while his foreign policy ambitions in Africa and economic relations with China were a source of political tension.[10]

Thanks to its diplomatic role in Libya's opening up and in the lifting of EU sanctions (2004), Italy had secured particularly profitable conditions to its main oil and gas corporation, ENI (Ente Nazionale Idrocarburi), which established joint-ventures with the Libyan National Oil Company (NOC) (Cardinale 2019, 350). Italy also initiated cooperation with Libya on migration controls. Through pressures and funding, in the 2000s, Italy and the EU pushed Libya to restrict its open-door policy toward its African neighbors, passing laws criminalizing immigrants and refugees indiscriminately, and building centers for their indefinite detention (Paoletti 2010, 127; Global Detention Project 2018). The multiplication of borders in the Sahel and Libya "illegalized" established intra-African migratory movements, strengthening smuggling networks, and reinforced racialized divisions between a "black" and a "white" Africa (Brachet 2016).

In order to foster this collaboration, Libyan authorities demanded reparations for the crimes of Italian colonialism, which they achieved in 2008 with the "Treaty of Friendship, Partnership and Co-operation." With its $5 billion reparations package (to be paid over 25 years, mainly by ENI), the Treaty favored Italian infrastructural investment in Libya and increased cooperation on migration controls, leading to joint patrolling operations in Libyan waters and pushbacks. In 2009, in fact, the third Berlusconi government significantly reduced work immigration quotas and passed a law criminalizing undocumented immigrants (Law No 94/2009).[11] While this pushed many immigrants to apply for asylum and obtain a humanitarian permit while waiting for the outcome, the Italian government also started illegally to drive both immigrants and asylum-seekers in international waters back to Libya (Andrijasevic 2010; Cuttitta 2014). In spite of this cooperation, however, Gaddafi still opposed Frontex and the Mediterranean Union as neocolonial projects (Paoletti 2010, 190). Despite rising unemployment from 2008, moreover, he still encouraged immigration from the rest of Africa: in March 2011, in Libya, out of a population of about 6.5 million, 2.5 million were immigrants. Black Africans performed the worst-paid jobs, and had come under increasing attack with the growth of institutional and popular racism (deHaas 2008; Kamat and Shokr 2013; Malakooti 2013; Pliez 2003).

In the words of the *New York Times*, the NATO war unleashed a "scramble for access to Libya's oil wealth," and intensified attempts by rival Western companies and states to control Libyan natural, financial, and human resources (Campbell 2013; Forte 2012). The neoliberal reforms implemented by the National Transition Council (NTC), and the immunity it granted to militias, exacerbated social divides and human-right abuses, generating a spiral of retribution that soon got out of western control. The killing of the U.S. ambassador in Benghazi in September 2012 signaled militias' refusal to be coopted by the West, as they began to compete for the control of Libyan resources, borders, and key installations, and became integrated into state institutions. This led to a breakdown of centralized state authorities amid ongoing civil war since 2014: a political fragmentation reinforced by competing imperialist and regional powers lending support to different militias in order to secure the extraction of Libyan resources (Capasso et al. 2019, 24). The Italian energy corporation ENI's presence too became more predatory. In the summer of 2014, the company interrupted the payment of colonial reparations (Greco and Oddo 2018, 201). To protect its fields and infrastructures, moreover, ENI struck deals with the Al-Ammu and Brigade 48 militias (Eaton 2018). Despite falling oil production, this guaranteed ENI an almost uninterrupted gas supply to Italy, increasing the income and profit margins of the Greenstream pipeline (Cardinale 2019, 351). As many other institutions and militias, moreover, those acting as ENI's security companies are engaged in the smuggling of petroleum, weapons, and human beings from Libya with the complicity of government officials in both sides of the country.[12] But the network of complicity goes beyond Libya. As the Procura di Catania's investigation "Dirty Oil" brought to light, the Al-Nasr Brigade leaders, in charge of Zawiya's "Oussama prison," collaborated with the Italian mafia and Maltese brokers to smuggle Libyan diesel into Italy (Sarzanini and Naddeo 2017).[13] This network was linked to Abdel-Rahman al-Milad, "Bija," Zawiya's coastguard commander and "undisputed leader of the human traffic trade," who used to receive funding and training from Italy and the EU (Porsia 2015). According to the Italian Petrol Union, illegal fuel trade accounts for 5–10% of total sales in Italy.[14] The Libyan Audit Bureau estimated that the smuggling of refined petroleum products (imported and distributed in Libya at subsidized price) cost the Libyan state around $20 billion between 2014 and 2017 (Noria Research 2019).

This neocolonial drain of Libyan resources has caused widespread impoverishment and insecurity, expanding the reserve army of labour of Italian and European capital. The 2011 war initiated a prolonged and unprecedented displacement crisis of Libyan citizens, who initially sought refuge within Libya and in neighboring countries.[15] Between 1.3 and 1.8 million immigrants, moreover, moved to home and neighboring countries, and, in small percentage, to Europe (Fargues 2017; UNHCR 2019, 16). The reopening of the Central-Mediterranean route after Gaddafi's defeat allowed larger numbers of African and then Syrian immigrants and refugees to embark to Europe.[16]

But Libya has not become a "transit country": since 2012, immigration has resumed. While East-African immigrants and refugees mostly intend to transit to Europe, a majority of West and Central Africans still arrive in Libya to work, building on a long tradition of circular migration (UNHCR 2019, 27, 4). This is the case despite widespread impoverishment (around a third of the Libyan population now lives on or below the poverty line), growing insecurity, an 80% decline in purchasing power due to rising inflation since 2014, the absence of basic public services, and environmental degradation (Capasso et al. 2019). As discussed in the next section, this situation disproportionately impacts on Sub-Saharan African immigrants and refugees, who embarked to Italy in larger numbers between 2014 and mid-2017 (UNHCR 2019, 28). In recent years, for the first time, a significant number of Libyan nationals have attempted to cross the Mediterranean for Europe.[17]

If in 2011 Italy stopped pushbacks and conceded humanitarian permits to those fleeing North Africa, it simultaneously led EU attempts to renew collaboration with the NTC on migration controls as part of broader talks to recover Italian investment in the country. Immediately after the killing of Gaddafi in October, the Friendship Treaty was reactivated, including the closure of all Libyan borders and pushbacks, this time under the responsibility of militias absorbed into, or affiliated with, the Libyan Ministries of Interior and Defense (Global Detention Project 2018, 21–23). Unsurprisingly, this collaboration empowered smuggling militias, making the migratory journey through and from Libya even more dangerous.[18] Subsequent Italian and EU missions in the Mediterranean only targeted low-level human smugglers (House of Lords EU Committee 2016), turning a blind eye to energy and weapon smuggling.

Mare Nostrum (MN), launched by Italy after two deadly shipwrecks in October 2013, did combine anti-smuggling operations and pushbacks with search and rescue (SAR) activities. But this strengthened a low-cost smuggling business model, with seaworthy vessels being replaced with dinghies only fit to reach its SAR zone (Tinti and Reitano 2017, 114–120). This caused increased mortality at sea, despite a record number of people rescued by MN. Things got even worse when the EU replaced MN with *Triton* and *Operation Sophia*, which delegated SAR activities first to inefficient commercial ships and then to NGOs (Heller and Pezzani 2016). *Mare Sicuro*, the main Italian naval operation since 2015, primarily aims at defending ENI's energy platforms and pipeline (Greco and Oddo 2018, 200).

After the April 2015 shipwreck, emigrants and refugees redirected their routes toward the Balkans and then collectively mobilized in Europe against this border regime (De Genova 2017, 3–5). After the EU-Turkey deal in March 2016, however, arrivals through the Central-Mediterranean route peaked again, and so did deaths.[19] Italy and the EU started to fund, train, and equip Libyan forces to patrol the sea and conduct "rescue" missions, and restricted the work of NGO vessels. In February 2017, EU leaders endorsed the memorandum of understanding between the Prime Ministers Gentiloni and al-Serraj, allowing the Libyan Coast Guard (LCG) to intercept and return immigrants bound for Italy. They also gave millions of Euros to the Government of National Accord (GNA) as part of the EU Fund for Africa, nominally to improve conditions in detention and boost the LCG's capacity. Despite all this, in May and June 2017, arrivals increased (23,000 each month). Then, in July and August, they plummeted (11,000 and 4,000 respectively). This drop was the result of deals that Italy's Interior Minister Marco Minniti and Secret Services struck with tribes and militias in West and South Libya, who decided to block almost all departures from the coast between Zawiya and Sabratha (Micaleff and Reitano 2017). In August, moreover, part of operation, Mare Sicuro was deployed to support Libyan forces and extended *into* Libyan waters.

The Italian government, therefore, started to collaborate directly with armed groups, superseding formal state authorities, and to exercise control over the LCG (Forensic Oceanography 2018). The al-Ammu militia spokesman defined this situation a "truce," dependent on continued support for the militias (Michael 2017). These deals, however, fueled internal rivalries, reinforcing a culture of predation. Despite being part of a broader attempt to curb the expansion of General Haftar's Libyan National Army, they ended up favoring it. As discussed in the next section, while continuing their other highly profitable smuggling activities, militias shifted their focus from human smuggling to a burgeoning business of detention and forced labor (Micaleff et al. 2019). The Italian Five Star-Lega government (June 2018–September 2019) fully supported these arrangements: it nominally handed over the coordination of rescue operations to the LCG, quadrupled assistance funding for it, and sought to prevent private vessels from docking immigrants in Italian ports. If the previous government had reinforced deportations and eliminated second-grade asylum appeals (Minniti-Orlando Decre 2017), the Salvini Decree (Law No 132/2018) abolished humanitarian protection, depriving most immigrants arrived in Italy after 2009 of their legal status, and boosted asylum rejections.

RESERVE WORKERS IN LIBYA

These economic and political developments have turned Sub-Saharan African immigrants into "a commodity to be captured, sold, traded and leveraged" (Tinti 2017). From mid-2017, the number of people caged in overcrowded prisons, intercepted, and returned to Libya increased, and periods of detention became longer. Members of the same militias conduct "rescue" operations in their coastguard capacity, run detention centers, and arrange boats to Europe. Immigrants claim that after "rescuing" them, militias beat, imprison, and subject them, especially women, to sexual violence. According to a Nigerian immigrant, the same people who run the prisons also ask for money to embark them on better boats for Europe: "They promise you that since they are organizing everything, nobody will catch you" (Zuwara, Libya 2018, Exodus 0, 15:49 min). An Ivorian immigrant and antiracist activist we interviewed reported from his own experience:

> Violence has two forms. They make you pay to get free and this induces the idea you have to leave. They put you in a cage and the same people offer you the possibility of going away. When you leave the coastguard knows it. This is the Libyan economy. (Caserta 2019)

Detention is a growing source of income. In addition to receiving hundreds of millions of Euros from the EU, militias force detainees to pay bribes were to be released (Micaleff et al. 2019; Tinti 2017). Detained indefinitely without legal support, immigrants face physical and psychological violence, torture, rape, and other ill-treatment, including malnutrition, sexual abuse, insufficient sanitation, racial and religious discrimination, and murder. This violence enhances militias' ability to extort money from detainees and their families. This situation, denounced by a plethora of international organizations (e.g., Amnesty International 2016; Global Detention Project 2018), was confirmed by all immigrants and experts we interviewed.

Detention centers also perform the function of labor reserves. Militias buy and sell their detainees or rent them out, to the highest bidder, forcing them to work without pay in order to secure their release. Employers themselves often go to detention centers looking for workers (Phillips and Missbach 2017; Gambian immigrant, Treviso 2019). According to Vincent Cochetel, UNHCR Special Envoy for the Central-Mediterranean, after 2017 militias started to sell more detainees for forced labor and sexual exploitation (Micaleff 2017, 35; Nielsen 2018). These conditions fueled repeated protests in detention centers and immigrants refusing to disembark.

Forced labor, however, is not confined to detention centers; it affects the majority of immigrants in the country, especially Sub-Saharan Africans, independently of their legal status. All the immigrants we interviewed denounced the lack of security in Libya, including the risk of being kidnapped, detained, abused, and killed.

> Libya is not a safe country. Many people have died. Slavery is visible. They shoot on the people on the street. (Ivorian immigrant, Caserta 2019)

The interpenetration of militias and state institutions allows employers not to pay workers with total impunity. According to the IOM (2017 2018), this now affects most sectors, including construction, agricultural and farm work, cleaning, car washing, gardening, housekeeping, and prostitution. For an investigative filmmaker we interviewed (2019), it also affects the energy sector. Immigrant's report of recruiters going to the laborer's market with their guns "chasing us as if we were slaves" (West-African immigrant, Tripoli 2018, Exodus 0, min. 4:34). Workers are frequently robbed on their way home by local gangs or arrested by police and militias. Our fieldwork highlighted several cases of immigrants who worked for a private employer, receiving shelter and food, without being paid or being robbed and kidnapped by armed gangs called by the employer. A Gambian immigrant we interviewed reported having worked for one year and seven months for a farmer: when he claimed his money, he was sold to the Asma Boys, a network of violent armed groups protected by militias and police. A Malian immigrant, who was 12 years old when first detained in Libya, told us the Asma Boys killed his brother and sold him to another group. "They sell you to these people. It's business" (Caserta 2019). According to a Libyan immigrant and an investigative filmmaker, we interviewed (2019), Libyans also suffer from attacks by Black African gangs.

Although not all immigrants wanted to go to Europe in the first place, they cannot find secure work in Libya or safe transit to Europe or their countries of origin. If they try to return home by land, they will almost certainly be kidnapped and sold as "slaves." The "voluntary return programmes" organized by the IOM, which is implementing EU border policies in the region (Brachet 2016), are one of the few ways for those in indefinite detention to get out of prison. But the number of flights is severely inadequate and, for Amnesty International (2017), the number of resettlement slots offered to those who cannot return to their home countries is "dismal." A Nigerian immigrant described the humiliation of returning home without reaching Europe and without financial support to start something in the country of origin (Zuwara 2018, Exodus 0, min. 18). In a collective video message circulated on WhatsApp, detainees in the Oussama prison (7 July 2018) denounced:

> They refuse to deport us. We told them that we want to go back to Africa but they refuse to deport us. They don't want us to go to Europe and also they don't want us to go back to our countries. . . . They are keeping us here for business. (Exodus 0, min 40)

Our fieldwork confirmed that even those immigrants who had not originally planned on going to Europe are trapped in a system that pushes them toward Europe (cf. Phillips and Missbach 2017). Half of the 7,048 immigrants interviewed by the IOM on the Central-Mediterranean route in 2016 and 2017, West Africans in particular, reported having worked during their journey without receiving the expected remuneration. This mostly happened in Libya, where they reported payments indefinitely delayed by employers or brokers, threats by armed individuals at the workplace, or having worked without remuneration as a way of being freed from detention (IOM 2016 [2017]). From the second half of 2017, the price of the journey sharply increased and the main nationalities of respondents changed. For Micaleff et al. (2019, 23) smugglers started leaning more heavily on ransoming and extortion. But still 42% of respondents, women in particular, reported having worked without agreed remuneration.

RESERVE WORKERS IN ITALY'S FIELDS

Most of the immigrants we interviewed told us that when they arrived in Italy, they felt safe, human again. Despite the severe exploitation and uncertainties, "You can start to have another dream, . . . the dream of being free."[20]

I was happy when I arrived in Italy. I think my future will change. No one can kidnap me.

> No one can come and catch me and put me into prison. There is law and regulations and everything, you know . . . [laughing]. (Malian immigrant, Caserta 2019)

Very often, immigrants join the ranks of the agricultural surplus population. Before the global economic crisis, Italian agriculture was a *transit sector* for many immigrants who often managed to move to the industrial or service sectors in Northern Italy or other North European countries (Pugliese 2012). Especially in the first years of the crisis, however, those immigrants who lost their jobs (and residence permits) in the North returned to agriculture, in a process of "re-ruralization" of migration (Puglies 2015). This, along with increasing arrivals from the Mediterranean after 2011, swelled the ranks of the agricultural reserve army. Given the sharp reduction in work quotas, many immigrants sought to get a regular status through asylum, as reflected in the sharp increase in the number of African agricultural workers with a humanitarian permit (Rigo 2018, 48).[21]

Employers used this situation to substitute workers and attack wages and conditions, counteracting the achievements of previous struggles. According to a trade-unionist from Salerno (2019), asylum-seekers have become "a very valuable commodity": "since they are provided with lodging and meals, employers lower their wages and put them in competition with other immigrants." In the Piana del Sele—"Italy's California" with highly mechanized greenhouse cultivation—for example, asylum-seekers are employed in a fairly continuous manner and with a regular contract[22] along with a core workforce of Italians and long-term immigrants from North Africa and Romania. Nevertheless, they receive lower-than-average wages of around €25–30 for a 10/11 hours working per day. This generated conflicts between Sub-Saharan African and Moroccan workers, who had improved their wages and conditions through strike action in 2006 (trade-unionist, Salerno 2019). In areas of seasonal harvest, like Latina, asylum-seekers from Nigeria, Mali, and Senegal only come for the harvest, and work for up to 12 hours a day, 7 days a week, for €2.5–3 an hour. They are replacing Punjabi immigrants, who had improved their wages (€5 an hour) through their mobilizations in 2016 (trade-unionist, Latina 2019).

One of our interviewees highlighted similar conflicts taking place in Rosarno among African workers with a work permit and the "huge reserve army" of asylum-seekers (anti-racist activist and labor expert, Rosarno 2019). An activist from the Castel Volturno area (2019) reported that average wages seem to have declined from about €35–30 for 8/12 hours working per day before 2008 to about €15–20. Very often, moreover, employers feel they can avoid paying workers at all, either physically assaulting or denouncing for extortion of those workers who claim their wages. Several interviewees in the Treviso province (in Italy's North East) reported asylum-seekers working irregularly in poultry farms under Moroccan gangmasters or being hired through temporary work agencies in grape-picking with contractual irregularities and underpayments. This points to a general employers' practice of underreporting days worked in order to pay lower taxes and contributions, depriving workers of access to welfare benefits (trade-unionist, Foggia 2019; anti-racist activist, Treviso 2019). Francesco Carchedi (2018: 280, 223) reports cases of asylum-seekers and Roma seasonal immigrants working for abysmal salaries, including of €1 an hour or less.

If, in some cases, the quality of the reception system and solidarity networks can limit or prevent extreme forms of exploitation, the Salvini Decree (2018) increased the vulnerability of asylum-seekers by excluding them from the decentralized state reception system (SPRAR) and cramming them into emergency reception centers (CAS) very often located in isolated rural areas (Corrado 2018; two labor experts 2019). For a trade-unionist (Salerno 2019), the Decree will produce "a reserve labour army of irregular immigrants in agricultural areas." Many asylum-seekers who lost their humanitarian permit are trying to obtain a work permit by working for free in exchange for fake contracts that cost up to €500–600 (trade-unionist, Foggia 2019).

The majority of our interviewees in 2019 pointed to the "disciplining role" played by immigrants' experiences in Libya. These represent a collective trauma, both physical and psychological, immigrants rarely talk about if not asked the right questions and surrounded by a network of solidarity (anti-racist activist Catania 2019). According to a trade-unionist, conditions in Italy are still seen as an improvement compared to what they suffered before:

> Living in a reception centre, even if decent living conditions are not provided, is considered a good accommodation if compared with the situation in Libya; working for few Euros a day, even if exploited, and sending remittances to the family in the country of origin, is considered an improvement compared to the enslavement in Libya. (Latina 2019)

In the light of his own experience and engagement with thousands of immigrants in the Castel Volturno area, an Ivorian activist told us this is a natural attitude after a traumatic situation, but also a sign of lack of integration (Caserta 2019). After reporting situations of underpayment and lack of payment, for example, a Malian asylum-seeker told us:

> The wage is good, but I don't need it. If they don't pay me that's not a problem. Because I am in Italy. I am not beaten. Before I was in prison all the time, in Nigeria, in Libya. But here I am not in prison, I eat, I sleep well. God willing. (Treviso 2019)

Most of the immigrants we interviewed, however, stressed the importance of their newly acquired formal freedoms for improving their situation individually and, in some cases, collectively.

THE RESISTANCE OF IMMIGRANT WORKERS

This feeling has animated some of the most important immigrant workers' struggles in Italy over the past decade. In September 2008, after the killing of six African workers by a Camorra commando in Castel Volturno, hundreds of African immigrants took onto the streets in protest against exploitation, organized crime, and institutional racism, demanding the killers be brought to justice. The protesters received sustained support by local antiracist associations active in the area, like the ex-Canapificio social center (anti-racist activist, Caserta 2019; Filhol 2016). The same December, another uprising erupted in Rosarno after two Ivorian workers were wounded by gunfire on the way "home" from the citrus groves. One year later, in January 2010, after some Italians open fired on three African workers, a second uprising erupted in Rosarno (Corrad 2011). If both uprisings took place in the period of "low-intensity expulsion" at the end of the orange harvest (Borretti 2010), the second one involved workers from Northern Italy used for employment in unionized contexts as well as Africans coming from the unionization of the Piana del Sele and the politicization in Castel Volturno (Terranova 2010).

"We will be remembered," they wrote in Rosarno before the police deported about 2,500 of them to other cities to "protect" them from the pogroms that followed their second uprising. As Antonello Mangano highlighted (2010), these uprisings were crucial political events. African workers saw them as part of a secular struggle for emancipation. "Rosarno gave us courage, the conscience that conditions had to change" (Ivorian activist, Caserta, December 2019). The Rosarno uprisings led to the first independent organization of immigrant agricultural workers in Italy: the "African Workers' Assembly of Rosarno." In March 2010, they organized a national strike of immigrants evoking the French and U.S. "days without immigrants," which mobilized about 300,000 immigrants all over the country (Caruso 2015). In October, immigrant workers in the Castel Volturno area, with the support of the Ex-Canapificio social-center, organized a strike against undeclared work and illegal hiring, which involved about 35 roundabouts and 1,000 workers demanding minimum wages and regularizations (*Kalifoo Ground* Strike; anti-racist activist, Caserta 2019).

In July 2011, at the height of the "North Africa Emergency," about 400 immigrants from the Maghreb and Sub-Saharan Africa, housed at the Masseria Boncuri center in Nardò (Apulia), started a 13-day strike against low wages and the gangmaster system. More than half the immigrants housed there had some form of humanitarian protection: many were fleeing conflicts in the Sudan, Ivory Coast, and Libya, while a significant part of Tunisians had just arrived in Italy after the fall of Ben Ali (Perrotta and Sacchetto 2012, 20–21). The concentration of workers in the Masseria Boncuri, run by a supportive association (Nigro 2012), and the unionization experiences of the immigrants coming from Northern Italy played an important role in the strike, as did the inspiration of the North African uprisings. For Tarek, a Tunisian worker who spoke at a workers' assembly, workers' self-organization and unity was key. "In Tunisia we autonomously drove away any dictatorship [laughing] . . . and in a similar way . . . we can do similar things here; it is our right" (in Perrotta and Sacchetto 2012, 36). "This is no longer the age of slavery" (ivi, p. 34): those coming from Libya wanted to reclaim their formal rights to bargain directly with the employers and be treated like all other workers.

Taking place at the height of the watermelon harvest, the strike manifested the agency of asylum-seekers, who used their structural power to affect the suppliers of big German retailers. As in other sectors, the reorganization of the agricultural production cycle along with JIT principles and the concentration of the harvest enhance the disruptive power of workers, whose strikes and blockades can affect the entire supply chain (Silver 2003). Thanks to support from the union Flai-CGIL and antiracist associations (Brigate di Solidarietà Attiva 2012), the strike had a major impact. But Flai-CGIL pushed for an institutional solution to the gangmaster system rather than generalizing the strike. As Di Bartolo (2013, 25) argued, this is in line with the legalistic approach of Flai-CGIL's intervention among immigrant agricultural workers. By focusing on the gangmaster as a matter of criminal concern, the law against illegal hiring that passed in September 2011 and the law against severe exploitation in 2016 (199/2016) failed to tackle the socio-economic roots of the system of labor exploitation in Italian agriculture, and to empower immigrant workers against it (Rigo 2015).

After 2011, grassroots organization and trade-unions became more prominent (Andretta 2017), also in the Italian countryside. In August 2011, the African Workers' Assembly of Rosarno and workers and militants from Nardò gave birth to the collective Campagne in Lotta (ND) to coordinate and support the self-organization of immigrant workers in the Italian agro-food sector. This led to numerous pickets and local demonstrations, especially in the Capitanata and Gioia Tauro (Rosarno) plains, for better working conditions, decent housing, and regularizations. Between 2015 and 2017, thanks to the collaboration between Campagne in Lotta and the independent union Si-Cobas (Sindacato Intercategoriale Cobas), these struggles started to converge with the logistics movement, the most sustained workers' movement in Italy since 2008, mainly led by immigrant workers organized with grassroots unions (Cillo and Pradella 2018). In August 2016, for example, several hundred workers, mainly from North Africa, picketed the gates of the local Anglo-Japanese multinational corporation Princes (Mitsubishi), a manufacturer of canned tomatoes exported to the United Kingdom, blocking tomato processing in Foggia for six hours (Annibale 2016). Struggles of this kind shifted attention from the gangmaster system to multinational corporations, and flowed into two national demonstrations linking demands for better salaries and regularizations to a critique of the role of borders in the exploitation of workers across the Mediterranean (Campagne in Lotta 2016). Grassroots unions and organizations, however, are very fragmented and divided (antiracist activist and labor expert, Rosarno 2019). The murder of the Unione Sindacale di Base (USB) trade-unionist Soumayla Sacko and the killing of 16 agricultural workers in 2018 have only sparked localized strikes but not a unitary national response.

CONCLUSION

The 2011 uprisings in the Middle East and North Africa resonated in the struggles of immigrant workers in the fields of southern Italy, pointing to the global scope of their experience of exploitation and struggle for emancipation. Marx's conceptualization of the *global* reserve army of labour highlights the connection between exploitation, accumulation, and unfree labor, and contextualizes the role of the imperial state against the backdrop of the conflicts and possibilities for workers' solidarity generated by the uneven development of capitalism. This helps explain why, in the wake of the global economic crisis and the 2011 uprisings, we witnessed an intensification of inter-imperialist conflicts for the appropriation of global resources.

After the 2011 NATO intervention, the system of neocolonial resource extraction that imposed itself in Libya caused widespread impoverishment and social insecurity, empowering militias involved in fuel, weapon, and human smuggling. Similarly to Marx's example of Ireland, Libya has come to play a role of labor reserve for Italy, even if the majority of those trying to cross the Mediterranean do not originate in Libya itself. The decline in arrivals since July 2017 depends on the direct collaboration between the Italian state and armed groups, and on the Italian navy extending its operations into Libyan waters in a clearly neocolonial fashion. This boosted a brutal system of detention and forced labor that, while trapping immigrants in Libya, pushes them toward Europe. As three African immigrants just landed in Sicily protested:

> In Libya slavery has been reinstated. Europe caused it. It allowed it to happen and benefits from it. In case of necessity, Europe has got reserve slaves just overseas. (in Severgnini 2018)

In assessing the role of the Italian state in creating the conditions for unfree labor, therefore, we need to consider the full scope of its activities, including those carried out in Libyan territory or devolved to Libyan state and non-state actors. The same is true with regard to the impact of migration, labor-market, and business-empowering policies on unfree labor in Italy. Agribusiness and retail corporations operating in Italy benefited from the continuing importation of gas and workers from Libya, whose vulnerability was enhanced by the violence experienced in Libya and by Italy's increasingly restrictive immigration and asylum policies. The expansion of the agricultural reserve army after 2007–2008 and 2011 enabled employers to substitute part of the workforce with immigrants with a status of asylum-seekers, undermining the achievements of previous labor struggles. In this context, formal and informal labor intermediation is expanding.

If unfree labor must be understood in a continuum of exploitation (Lerche 2007), our analysis highlights the inter-linkages between immigrants' experiences of unfree labor in Libya and Italy. The former can play a disciplining role, as they make labor conditions in Italy seem an improvement. But the comparison between the two can also lead immigrants to try and assert their formal rights and realize their "dream to be free." As the example of Nardò shows, the reorganization of agricultural production along JIT principles increases workers' power at the point of production. Solidarity between active and reserve workers can disrupt entire value chains. But so far unions with great associational power like CGIL have focused on legal campaigns, without leveraging on workers' structural power, while a series of radical and relatively successful struggles have not managed to overcome local boundaries.

The Five Star-Lega government was quite aware of the potential of workers' struggles. In the wake of a loudly proclaimed "migration crisis," the then Interior Minister Salvini not only denied the existence of torture in Libya, "closed" Italian ports, and abolished the humanitarian permit but also included in his Security Decrees provisions targeting road blockades. The Italian government thus tried to disempower those immigrants from Africa and the Middle East—important nodes of the global class struggle today—who have animated the most radical labor struggles of the past 10 years in agriculture and logistics. While these workers appealed to Italian workers for solidarity, the narrative of a "migration crisis" reinforced racist and divisive arguments, shifting attention away from global power relations and the role of imperialism in the general worsening of labor and living conditions in Italy. If this helps explain the present divisions and weaknesses of the labor movement in the country, it also indicates the political questions that need addressing in order to realize its potential strength.

NOTES

1. Part of this work was supported by ISEC (Prevention of and Fight against Crime Programme, funded by the Directorate-General Home Affairs, European Commission, European Union) HOME/2011/ISEC/ AG/THB/4000001962. We would like to thank the editors of this special issue, Nick Bernards and Susanne Soederberg, and the three anonymous *Geoforum* referees for their helpful comments. We are grateful to all those who supported or contributed to our research: the comrades of the ex-Canapificio (Caserta) and Rete Cittadinanza Solidale (Vittorio Veneto), Majed Akhter, Andrea Bartoli, Pietro Basso, Roberta Benato, Alex Callinicos, Imma D'Amico, Ruggero Da Ros, Dariush Doust, Vincenzo Fiano, Elisa Greco, Giulio Iocco, Mamadou Kovassi Idris, Paolo Novak, Michelangelo Severgnini, Timothy Wai, Angela Wigger, and Lea Ypi. A heartfelt thank to all the immigrants who were so kind to share their stories with us. We dedicate this work to realization of their, and our, dream to be free.

2. This chapter was originally published as "Bordering the Surplus Population across the Mediterranean: Imperialism and Unfree Labour in Libya and the Italian

Countryside" (Pradella and Cillo 2020) in *Geoforum*. Reprinted with permission from Elsevier.

3. Estimates of irregular employment are obtained by processing ISTAT (Italian National Institute of Statistics) data on the irregularity rate of annual work units and employment contracts. Estimates of undeclared work, at risk of serious labor exploitation, are obtained by crossing this first dataset with (Italian National Social Security Institute's (INPS) data about workers who are officially employed less than 50 days a year and therefore do not meet the minimum requirements to access unemployment benefits (cf. Iovino 2018, 11–12).

4. The concept of "unfree labor" is broader than that of "forced labor" prevailing in policy circles, which fails to recognize exploitation as constitutive in capitalist labor relations as well as the continuum of different forms of exploitation ranging "from decent work through minor and major labour law violations, to extreme exploitation in the form of forced labour" (Skrivankova 2010, 9; see also: LeBaron 2015; Lerche 2007; Strauss and McGrath 2017).

5. Michelangelo Severgnini got in touch with hundreds of immigrants on social media and WhatsApp, checking from their geolocalization that they are in Libya. We also consulted testimonies through the Guardian journalist Sally Hayden's and Sarita Fratini's blog (Fratini, ND).

6. Understanding how this shift took place is an area of further research that also requires a deeper examination of the dynamics of profitability and ground rent in Italian agriculture.

7. Formal labor intermediation includes national and international temporary work agencies, cooperatives, posting of workers, and seasonal work programs (Avallone, 2016; Brass, 2011; Corrado 2017; Oliveri, 2015; Osservatorio Placido Rizzotto, 2018; Potot, 2010). In Italy, it is mainly used by large companies in Northern regions (Interviews: HR manager, Ferrara province 2013; Quality manager, Verona province 2013).

8. Immigrants often live in makeshift shelters or stables in the fields, abandoned houses, huge informal ghettos, or reception centers often located in areas with a large concentration of agricultural activities (Nigro 2012; Sanò and Piro 2017).

9. They also pushed the actors involved in the export of Italian products to try and clean up the "Made in Italy" label through private certifications and ethical codes (Caruso and Pagano 2018)

10. Campbell (2013); Martinez (2017: 131); Nkrumah (2000); Pliez (2002); Pradella and Rad (2017: 2416); st John (2008).

11. This law was subsequently revoked by the Renzi government in 2016.

12. Eaton (2018: 15); Mannocchi (2017); Micaleff (2017); Michael (2017); Liga (2018); Noria Research (2019); Zaptia (2018). In June 2017, the UN Council passed Resolution 2362, which made those who illicitly export petroleum from Libya subject to international sanctions.

13. The Santa Paola-Ercolano family, involved in this traffic, used to control the logistics of agro-food chain in Sicily (Eurispes 2019b)

14. Giliberto (2019); Serrao (2019). See also: Mottola (2018).

15. In 2011, about 550,000 Libyans were uprooted within the country and 660,000 moved abroad. At the end of 2016, between 500,000 and 1.5 million Libyans were exiled (Bradley et al., 2016: Loc. 54, 907, 974 and 1205).

16. Arrivals in Italy through the Central-Mediterranean route increased from an average of below 40,000 in the 2000s (4,300 in 2010, also because of the deal with Gaddafi) to 62,692 in 2011 and 170,100 in 2014 (Baldwin-Edwards and Lutterbeck 2018).

17. UNOCHA (2019: 12–3). According to the UNHCR database, between 2015 and 2018, arrivals of Libyan immigrants in Italy increased from 0.36% to 1.80% of total arrivals. But many arrivals are not reported (Furlanetto 2019).

18. Micaleff (2017: 42–3); Micaleff and Reitano (2017: 11); Monzini et al. (2015); Porsia (2015); UNSMIL (2018).

19. In 2016, arrivals from Libya climbed to 181,000. Year 2016 was also the deadliest year on record, with more than 5,000 people killed while crossing (UNHCR).

20.

> Who leaves Libya and arrives in Italy, even if they don't have anything here, they find a freedom . . . the freedom to walk with your head up, to say what you think. The person feels human again. Here we experience the fact of racism. Sure, maybe you will be insulted but in Libya you can be kidnapped, killed, wounded. The person who arrives in Italy is safe: this is the first thing that matters. You can start to have another dream. This is what people don't understand. The dream of being free, of having a calm mind. Because in Libya you cannot sleep at night, you are scared of sleeping, going out, going shopping on your own. They beat you, you cannot react: this is Libya. Many people prefer to die at sea than stay in Libya. (Ivorian immigrant and anti-racist activist, Caserta 2019)

21. Between 2007 and 2017, asylum applications increased from 13,310 to 130,119, and then declined to 53,596 in 2018 (Ministero dell'Interno 2019).

22. Most asylum-seekers are hired with a regular contract, as employers fear criminal convictions according to the legislation against extreme exploitation and the gangmaster system.

BIBLIOGRAPHY

Agier, M. 2011. *Managing the Undesirables: Refugee Camps and Humanitarian Government.* Wiley, London.

Amnesty International. 2012. *'We Wanted Workers but We Got Humans Instead': Labour Exploitation of Agricultural Migrant Workers in Italy.* Amnesty International, London.

Amnesty International. 2016. *EU Risks Fuelling Horrific Abuse of Refugees and Migrants in Libya.* Amnesty International, London. https://www.amnesty.org/en/press-releases/2016/06/eu-risks-fuelling-horrific-abuse-of-refugees-and-migrants-in-libya/.

Amnesty International. 2017. *Libya's Dark Web of Collusion: Abuses Against Europe-Bound Refugees and Migrants.* 11 December. Amnesty International, London.

Andretta, M. 2017. Neoliberalism and Its Discontents in Italy: Protests Without Movement? In: Della Porta, D., Andretta, M., Fernandes, T., Romanos, E., O'Connor, F., Vogiatzoglou, M. (Eds.), *Late Neoliberalism and its Discontents in the Economic Crisis*. Palgrave, London, pp. 201–242.

Andrijasevic, R. 2006. *How to Balance Rights and Responsibilities on Asylum at the EU's*. Southern Border of Italy and Libya. COMPAS Working Paper No. 27. University of Oxford. Oxford.

Andrijasevic, R. 2010. From Exception to Excess: Detention and Deportations across the Mediterranean Space. In: De Genova, N., Peutz, N. (Eds.), *The Deportation Regime: Sovereignty, Space and the Freedom of Movement*. Duke University Press, Durham, NC, pp. 147–165.

Annibale, F. 2016. Foggia, lo sciopero generale e la lotta dei braccianti. Articolo 21.

Araghi, F. 2009. The invisible hand and the visible foot: Peasants, dispossession and globalization. In: Akram-Lodhi, A. H., Kay, C. (Eds.), *Peasants and Globalization: Political Economy, Rural Transformation and the Agrarian Question*. Routledge, New York, pp. 111–147.

Avallone, G. 2016. The land of informal intermediation: the social regulation of migrant agricultural labour in the Piana del Sele, Italy. In: Corrado, A., de Castro, C., Perrotta, D. (Eds.), *Migration and Agriculture. Mobility and Change in the Mediterranean Area*. Routledge, London, pp. 241–254.

Avallone, G. 2017. *Sfruttamento e resistenze. Migrazioni e agricoltura in Europa, Italia, Piana del Sele*. OmbreCorte, Verona.

Baldwin-Edwards, M., and Lutterbeck, D. 2018. Coping with the Libyan migration crisis. *Journal of Ethnic and Migration Studies*, https://doi.org/10.1080/1369183X .2018. 1468391.

Basso, P. (Ed.). 2010. *Razzismo di stato. Stati Uniti, Europa, Italia*. FrancoAngeli, Milan.

Bhattacharyya, G. 2018. *Rethinking Racial Capitalism: Questions of Reproduction and Survival*. Rowman & Littlefield, Lanham.

Bellizzi, T., and Di Zanni, C. 2018. *Foggia, scontro frontale tra un furgone e un tir: morti dodici migranti*. In arrivo il premier. La Repubblica, 2018, 6th August edition https:// bari.repubblica.it/cronaca/2018/08/06/news/foggia_scontro_frontal e_tra_furgoni_cinque_migranti_morti-203524785/.

Bialasiewicz, L. 2012. Off-Shoring and Out-Sourcing the Borders of Europe: Libya and EU Border Work in the Mediterranean. *Geopolitics* 17 (4), 843–866.

Boeckler, M. and Berndt, C. 2014. B/ordering the Mediterranean: Free Trade, Fresh Fruits and Fluid Fixity. In: Gertel, J., Sippel S.R. (Eds.), *Seasonal Workers in Mediterranean Agriculture. The Social Costs of Eating Fresh*. Routledge, London, pp. 23–33.

Borretti, B. 2010. Da Castel Volturno a Rosarno. Il lavoro vivo degli immigrati tra stragi, pogrom, rivolte e razzismo di stato. In: Basso, P. (Ed.), *Razzismo di stato. Stati Uniti, Europa, Italia*. FrancoAngeli, Milan, pp. 493–522.

Brachet, J. 2016. Policing the desert: The IOM in Libya beyond war and peace. *Antipode* 48 (2), 272–292.

Bradley, M., Fraihat, I., and Mzioudet, H. 2016. *Libya's Displacement Crisis: Uprooted by Revolution and Civil War*. Georgetown University Press, Washington DC.

Brass, T. 2011. *Labour Regime Change in the Twenty-First Century: Unfreedom, Capitalism and Primitive Accumulation.* Brill, Leiden.

Brigate di solidarietà attiva, Nigro, G., Perrotta, M., Sacchetto, D., Sagnet, Y. 2012. Sulla pelle viva. Nardò: la lotta autorganizzata dei braccianti agricoli. DeriveApprodi, Rome. Campagne in Lotta, ND. Chi siamo. http://campagneinlotta.org/chi-siamo/.

Campagne in Lotta. 2016. Roma 12 novembre: manifestazione nazionale contro il regime di controllo della mobilità e contro lo sfruttamento. http://campagneinlotta.org/ roma-12novembre-manifestazione-nazionale-contro-il-regime-di-controllo-della-mobilita-e-contro-lo-sfruttamento/.

Campbell, H.G. 2013. *Global NATO and the Catastrophic Failure in Libya.* Monthly Review Press, New York.

Capasso, M., Czerep, J., Dessì, A., Sanchez, G. 2019. Libya Country Report. Report, Project EU-LISTCO.

Carchedi, F. 2018. Il lavoro indecente nel settore agricolo. Casi di studio territoriali. In: Osservatorio Placido Rizzotto (Ed.), *Agromafie e caporalato. IV Rapporto.* Bibliotheka Edizioni, Rome, pp. 141–305.

Caruso, F.S. 2015. *La politica dei subalterni. Organizzazione e lotte del bracciantato migrante nel Sud Europa*, DeriveApprodi, Rome.

Caruso, F.S. 2016. Dal caporalato alle agenzie di lavoro temporaneo: i braccianti rumeni nell'agricoltura mediterranea. *Mondi Migranti* 3, 51–64.

Caruso, F.S., and Pagano, U. 2018. Salute e alimentazione nel Corporate Food Regime. *Salute e società* XVII 3, 57–71.

Cardinale, R. 2019. The profitability of transnational energy infrastructure: A comparative analysis of the Greenstream and Galsi gas pipelines. *Energy Policy* 131, 347–357.

Césaire, A. 2000 [1950]. *Discourse on Colonialism.* Monthly Review Press, New York.

Cillo, R., and Pradella, L. 2018. New immigrant struggles in Italy's logistics industry. *Comparative European Politics* 16 (1), 67–84.

Cillo, R., Toffanin, T. 2014. *Corporate Social Responsibility to Prevent Human Trafficking Immigrant Workers in Italian Agriculture—A Mapping.* Ca' Foscari University, Venice. https://www.unive.it/pag/fileadmin/user_upload/dipartimenti/filosofia/doc/laboratori/laris/library/cillo-toffanin.pdf.

Colloca, C., and Corrado, A. 2013. Trasformazioni meridionali: migranti e aree rurali. In: Colloca, C., Corrado, A. (Eds.), *La globalizzazione delle campagne. Migranti e società rurale del sud Italia*, FrancoAngeli Editore, Milan, pp. 13–29.

Corrado, A. 2011. Clandestini in the Orange Towns: Migrations and Racisms in Calabria's Agriculture. *Race/Ethnicity: Multidisciplinary Global Contexts* 4 (2), 191–201.

Corrado, A. 2015. Lavoro straniero e riorganizzazione dell'agricoltura familiare in Italia. *Agriregionieuropa*, 11 (43) https://agriregionieuropa.univpm.it/it/content/article/31/43/lavoro-straniero-e-riorganizzazione-dellagricoltura-familiare-italia#footnoteref13_7a6j632.

Corrado, A. 2017. Migrant crop pickers in Italy and Spain. Heinrich Böll Foundation, Berlin. https://www.boell.de/sites/default/files/e-paper_migrant-crop-pickers-in-italy-and-spain_1.pdf.

Corrado, A. 2018. Is Italian Agriculture a "Pull Factor" for Irregular Migration—and, If So, Why? Open Society Foundations. https://www.opensocietyfoundations.org/sites/default/files/is-italian-agriculture-a-pull-factor-for-irregular-migration-20181205.pdf.

Corrado, A., de Castro, C., and Perrotta, D. (Eds.). 2016. *Migration and Agriculture. Mobility and Change in the Mediterranean Area*. Routledge, London.

Corrado, A., and Perrotta, D. 2012. Migranti che contano. Percorsi di mobilità e confinamenti nell'agricoltura del Sud Italia. *Mondi Migranti* 3, 103–128.

CREA. 1991–2016. *Annuario dell'agricoltura italiana. Consiglio per la Ricerca in agri-coltura e l'analisi dell'Economia Agraria (ex INEA)*, Rome.

Cross, H. 2013. *Migrants, Borders and Global Capitalism: West African Labour Mobility and EU Borders*. Routledge, Abingdon.

Cuttitta, P. 2014. From the Cap Anamur to Mare Nostrum: Humanitarianism and Migration Controls at the EU's Maritime Borders. In: Matera, C., Taylor, A. (Eds.), *The Common European Asylum System and Human Rights: Enhancing Protection in Times of Emergencies*. CLEER, The Hague, pp. 21–38.

Das, R. J. 2012. Reconceptualizing Capitalism: Forms. *Review of Radical Political Economics* 442), 178–200.

Davies, T., and Isakjee, A. 2018. Ruins of Empire: Refugees, Race and the Postcolonial Geo-graphies of European Migrant caMps. *Geoforum* 102, 214–217.

De Genova, N. 2013. Spectacles of Migrant 'Illegality': The Scene of Exclusion, the Obscene of Inclusion. *Ethnic Racial Studies* 36 (7), 1180–1198.

De Genova, N. (Ed.). 2017. *The Borders of Europe. Autonomy of Migration, Tactics of Bordering*. Duke University Press, Durham, NC.

De Haas, H. 2008. The Myth of Invasion: The Inconvenient Realities of African Migration to Europe. *Third World Quarterly* 29 (7), 1305–1322.

Di Bartolo, F. 2013. Dalle lotte sociali alla globalizzazione delle rivolte Il movimento bracciantile nelle zone capitalistiche del Mezzogiorno. Meridiana 77, 175–201.

Di Luzio, G. 2006. *A un passo dal sogno. Gli avvenimenti che hanno cambiato la storia dell'immigrazione in Italia*. Besa, Nardò.

Dines, N.,and Rigo, E. 2015. Postcolonial citizenships and the 'refugeeization' of the work-force: migrant agricultural labour in the Italian Mezzogiorno. In: Ponzanesi, S., Colpani, G. (Eds.), *Postcolonial Transitions in Europe: Contexts, Practices and Politics*. Rowman & Littlefield, Lanham, pp. 151–172.

Domşodi, D. 2019. Labour Relations and Labour Structures in MEDITERRANEAN capitalism. Caporalato and Romanian migration in the Southern Italian agriculture. *Studia UBB Sociologia* 64 (1), 127–142.

Eaton, T. 2018. *Libya's War Economy: Predation, Profiteering and State Weakness*. Middle East and North Africa Programme Research Paper. Chatham House, London.

Esposti, R.,and Merlino, C. (Eds.). 2016. *Lavoro e impresa nell'agricoltura italiana*. CIA, Ancona.

Eurispes. 2019a. Agromafie. 6° Rapporto sui crimini agroalimentari. Eurispes, Rome https://eurispes.eu/wp-content/uploads/2019/02/eurispes_coldiretti_osservatorio_-sintesi_6_agromafie.pdf.

Eurispes. 2019b. Mafia nei mercati ortofrutticoli. Eurispes, Rome https://www.leurispes. it/mafia-nei-mercati-ortofrutticoli-sud-pontino-epicentro-della-filiera-criminale/.

Fanon, F.1991. *The Wretched of the Earth*. Grove Weidenfeld, New York.

Fargues, P. 2017. Mass Migration and Uprisings in Arab Countries: An Analytical Frame-Work. In: Luciani, G. (Ed.), *Combining Economic and Political Development: The Experience of MENA*. Brill-Nijhoff, Boston, pp. 170–183.

FCE (Forum Civique Européen). 2002. *Le Goût amer de nos fruits et légumes—L'exploitation des migrants dans l'agriculture intensive en Europe*. Information et Commentaires, Limans.

Ferrero, M. 2010. Il "Pacchetto sicurezza": dall'integrazione subalterna degli immigrati, alla loro criminalizzazione. In: Basso, P. (Ed.), *Razzismo di stato. Stati Uniti, Europa, Italia*. FrancoAngeli, Milan, pp. 423–438.

Filhol, R.. 2016. When migrants meet squatters: The case of the movement of migrants and refugees in Caserta. In: Mudu, P., Chattopadhyay, S. (Eds.), *Migration, Squatting and Radical Autonomy*. Routledge, London, pp. 232–247.

Filhol, R.. 2017. Du « caporale » au « caponero ». L'intermédiation de main-d'œuvre agricole migrante en Italie du Sud. *Mélanges de l'École française de Rome—Italie et Méditerranée modernes et contemporaines*. 129 (1) https://journals.openedition.org/ mefrim/3333#tocto1n4.

Forensic Oceanography. 2018. Mare Clausum. Italy and the EU's Undeclared Operation to Stem Migration Across the Mediterranean. Report. University of London. https:// www.osservatoriodiritti.it/wp-content/uploads/2018/05/italia-libia-report.pdf.

Forte, M. 2012. *Slouching Towards Sirte: NATO's War on Libya and Africa*. Baraka Books, Montreal.

Foster, J. B., McChesney, R. W., and Jonna, R. J. 2011. The Global Reserve Army of Labor and the New Imperialism. *Monthly Review* 63 (6). https://monthlyreview.org/2011/11/01/ the-global-reserve-army-of-labor-and-the-new-imperialism/.

France24. 2018. "Help us get out of this hell"! Migrants Hold Rare Protest in Libya. The Observers. https://observers.france24.com/en/20180822-libya-migrants-rare-protest-eritrea-ethiopia.

Fratini, S., ND. Sarita Libre. Blog. https://saritalibre.it/chi-sono/.

Fritz, T. 2011. Globalising Hunger: Food Security and the EU's Common Agricultural Policy (CAP). FDCL-Verlag, Berlin https://www.tni.org/files/cappaperfinal-web.pdf.

Furlanetto, V. 2019. Sbarchi fantasma, così arriva in Italia l'80% dei migranti con barchini e contatti Facebook. Il Sole 24 Ore, 29th September edition. https://www.ilsole24ore.com/art/sbarchi-fantasma-cosi-arriva-italia-l-80percento-migranti-barchini-e-contatti-facebook-AC8UyRn.

Garrappa, A. M. 2016. The citrus fruit crisis: value chains and 'just in time' migrants in Rosarno (Italy) and Valencia (Spain). In: Corrado, A., de Castro, C., Perrotta,

D. (Eds.), *Migration and Agriculture. Mobility and Change in the Mediterranean Area*. Routledge, London, pp. 111–127.

Giliberto, J. 2019. Il buco del mercato nero del petrolio. Il sole 24 ore, 2nd October edition. https://www.ilsole24ore.com/art/il-buco-mercato-nero-petrolio-ACXo1do.

Global Detention Project. 2018. Immigration Detention in Libya: "A Human Rights Crisis." Global Detention Project.

Greco, A., and Oddo, G. 2018. *Lo stato parallelo. La prima inchiesta sull'ENI tra politica, servizi segreti, scandali finanziari e nuove guerre*. Chiarelettere, Milan.

Harvey, D. 2004. The 'New' Imperialism and Accumulation by Dispossession. *Socialist Register* 2004, pp. 63–87 https://socialistregister.com › index.php › srv › article › download.

Hamouchene, H. 2019. *Extractivism and Resistance in North Africa*. Transnational Institute, Amsterdam.

Heller, C., and Pezzani, L. 2016. Ebbing and Flowing: The EU's Shifting Practices of (Non-)Assistance and Bordering in a Time of Crisis. Near Futures Online. Accessed online, 28 April 2019 at: http://nearfuturesonline.org/ebbing-and-flowing-the-eus-shifting-practices-of-non-assistance-and-bordering-in-a-time-of-crisis/.

House of Lords EU Committee. 2016. EU Operation Sophia Failing to Disrupt People Smuggling, Says Committee. https://www.parliament.uk/business/committees/committees-a-z/lords-select/eu-external-affairs-subcommittee/news-parliament-2015/operation-sophia-report-publication/.

IOM. 2016. Analysis: Flow Monitoring Surveys—The Human Trafficking and other Exploitative Practices Prevalence Indication Survey (May–September 2016).

September 2016. https://migration.iom.int/docs/Analysis_-_Flow_Monitoring_and_Human_Trafficking_Surveys_in_the_Mediterranean_and_Beyond_-_6%20_October_ 2016.pdf.

IOM. 2017. Analysis: Flow Monitoring Surveys—The Human Trafficking and other EXploitative Practices Prevalence Indication Survey (February–May 2017). June 2017. https://migration.iom.int/docs/Analysis_Flow_Monitoring_and_Human_Trafficking_Surveys_in_the_Mediterranean_and_Beyond_14_June_2017.pdf.

IOM. 2018. Analysis: Flow Monitoring Surveys—The Human Trafficking and other Exploitative Practices Prevalence Indication Survey (2017). January 2018. https://migration.iom.int/docs/FMS_CT_Analysis_male%20female_Central_Eastern_2017.pdf.

Iovino, R. 2018. L'infiltrazione delle mafie e della criminalità nella Filiera agroalimentare. In: Osservatorio Placido Rizzotto (Ed.), *Agromafie e caporalato. IV Rapporto*. Bibliotheka Edizioni, Rome, pp. 10–18.

Jones, R. 2016. *Violent Borders: Refugees and the Right to Move*. Verso, London.

Kamat, A., and Shokr, A. 2013. Libya: A Revolution Contested. In: Prashad, V., Amar, P. (Eds.), *Dispatches from the Arab Spring: Understanding the New Middle East*. University of Minnesota Press, Minneapolis.

LeBaron, G. 2015. Unfree Labour Beyond Binaries: Insecurity, Social Hierarchy and Labour Market Restructuring. International Feminist Journal of Politics 17 (1), 1–19.

LeBaron, G., and Phillips, N. 2019. States and the Political Economy of Unfree Labour. *New Political Economics* 24 (1), 1–21.
Lerche, J. 2007. A global alliance against forced labour? Unfree labour, neo-liberal globalization and the international labour organization. *Journal of Agrarian Change* 7 (4), 425–452.
Li, T.M. 2010. To make live or let die? Rural dispossession and the protection of surplus populations. *Antipode* 41 (1), 66–93.
Liga, A. 2018. *'Playing with Molecules': The Italian Approach to Libya*. Ifri, Paris.
Limoccia, L., Leo, A., and Piacente, N. 1997. *Vite bruciate di terra. Storie, testimonianze, proposte contro il caporalato e l'illegalità*. Gruppo Abele, Turin.
Magdoff, F., Buttel, F.H., and Bellamy Foster, J. (Eds.). 2000. *Hungry for Profit. The Agribusiness Threat to Farmers, Food, and the Environment*. Monthly Review Press, New York.
Malakooti, A. 2013. *Mixed Migration: Libya at the Crossroads*. UNHCR, Tripoli.
Mangano, A. 2010. *Gli africani salveranno l'Italia*. Rizzoli, Milan.
Mannocchi, F. 2017. How Libya's Oil Smugglers Are Bleeding Country of Cash. Middle East Eye, 2017, 13th February edition https://www.middleeasteye.net/news/how-libyas-oil-smugglers-are-bleeding-country-cash.
Martin, P. 2006. Immigration Reform: Implications for Agriculture. *Western Economics Forum*. https://core.ac.uk/download/pdf/6407443.pdf.
Martin, P. 2011. *California Hired Farm Labor 1960–2010: Change and Continuity*. Report. University of California https://migrationfiles.ucdavis.edu/uploads/cf/files/2011-may/martin-california-hired-farm-labor.pdf.
Martinez, L. 2017. *The Libyan Paradox*. Columbia University Press, New York.
Martino, G. 2018. Una riflessione sulle filiere di valore e sul lavoro gravemente sfruttato in agricoltura. In: Osservatorio Placido Rizzotto (Ed.), *Agromafie e caporalato. IV Rapporto*. Bibliotheka Edizioni, Rome, pp. 119–140.
Marx, K. 1976. *Capital: A Critique of Political Economy, Volume 1*. Penguin, London.
Marx, K. 1981. *Capital: Volume 3*. Penguin, London.
Marx, K. 1986. English Atrocities in China (10 April 1857). In: Marx, K., Engels, F., (Eds.), *Collected Works, Volume 15*. Lawrence & Wishart, London, pp. 232–235.
Marx, K. 1988. Marx to Sigfrid Meyer and August Vogt. In Marx, K., Engels, F., (Eds.), *Collected Works, Volume 43—Marx and Engels: 1868–1870*. Lawrence and Wishart, London, pp. 471–476.
Marx, K. 2010. Confidential Communication. In Marx, K., Engels, F., (Eds.), *Collected Works, Volume 21—Marx and Engels: 1867–1870*. Lawrence and Wishart, London, pp. 112–124.
McGrath, S. 2017. Unfree labour. In: Richardson, D., Castree, N., Goodchild, M.F., Kobayashi, A., Liu, W., Marston, R. A. (Eds.), *The International Encyclopedia of Geography*. Wiley, London, pp. 1–8.
McMichael, P. 2012. *Development and Social Change: A Global Perspective*. Pine Forge Press, Thousand Oaks, CA.

McMichael, P., and Friedmann, H. 2007. Situating the Retailing Revolution. In: Burch, D., Lawrence, G. (Eds.), *Supermarkets and Agri-food Supply Chains. Transformations in the Production and Consumption of Foods*. Edward Elgar, Cheltenham, pp. 291–319.

Medici Senza Frontiere. 2005. *I frutti dell'ipocrisia. Storie di chi l'agricoltura la fa.* Di nascosto, Sinnos, Rome.

Medici Senza Frontiere. 2008. Una stagione all'inferno. Rapporto sulle condizioni degli immigrati impiegati in agricoltura nelle regioni del Sud Italia. Report. MSF, Rome http://archivio.medicisenzafrontiere.it/allegati/pubblicazioni/rapporti/una_stagione_all_inferno.pdf.

MEDU. 2019. *La cattiva stagione. Rapporto sulle condizioni di vita e di lavoro dei braccianti nella Capitanata*. MEDU, Rome.

Micaleff, M. 2017. *The Human Conveyor Belt: Trends in Human Trafficking and Smuggling in Post-revolution Libya*. Global Initiative Against Transnational Organized Crime, Geneva.

Micaleff, M., and Reitano, T. 2017. *The Anti-Human Smuggling Business and Libya's Political End Game*. Global Initiative Against Transnational Organized Crime, Geneva.

Micaleff, M., Horsley, R., and Bish, A. 2019. *The Human Conveyor Belt Broken—assessing the collapse of the human-smuggling industry in Libya and the central Sahel*. Global Initiative Against Transnational Organized Crime, Geneva.

Michael, M. 2017. Backed by Italy, Libya Enlists Militias to Stop Migrants. APNews, 2019, 29th August edition https://www.apnews.com/ 9e808574a4d04eb38fa8c688d110a23d.

Ministero dell'Interno. 2019. I numeri dell'asilo. Quaderno statistico dal 1990 al 2018. Ministero dell'Interno. Rome http://www.libertaciviliimmigrazione.dlci.interno.gov.it/sites/default/files/allegati/quaderno_statistico_per_gli_anni_1990-2018.pdf.

Monzini, P., Aziz, N.A., and Pastore, F. 2015. *The Changing Dynamics of Cross-border Human Smuggling and Trafficking in the Mediterranean*. Istituto Affari Internazionali, Rome.

Mori, S. 2018. The *Agricultural Migrant Labourer Caught Between Exploitation and Irregularity: Stories from Southern Europe*. Centro Internazionale Crocevia. Report. Nielsen, N., 2018. Libyan militia cash in on EU's anti-smuggling strategy. EUobserver. https://euobserver.com/migration/143003.

Nigro, G. 2012. Lavori in corso. Pratiche e idee per la liberazione del lavoro migrante. In: Brigate di solidarietà attiva, Nigro, G., Perrotta, M., Sacchetto, D., Sagnet, Y., Sulla pelle viva (Eds.), *Nardò: la lotta autorganizzata dei braccianti agricoli*. DeriveApprodi, Rome, pp. 76–100.

Nikolanikos, M. 1975. Notes Towards a General theory of Migration in Late Capitalism. *Race and Class* XVII 1, 5–17.

Nkrumah, G. 2000. Tapping the Global Economy. Al-Ahram Weekly On-line, 14–20 December, No. 512, http://weekly.ahram.org.eg/2000/512/ec3.htm.

Noria Research. 2019. Predatory economies in eastern Libya. The Dominant Role of the Libyan National Army. Global Initiative Against Transnational Organized

Crime, Geneva. https://globalinitiative.net/wp-content/uploads/2019/06/GITOC-Predatory-Economies-Eastern-Libya-WEB.pdf.

OIM-Italy. 2010. *Praesidium V. Rapporto sulla situazione dei migranti presenti nella provincia di Caserta e nell'area di Castelvolturno.* OIM, Rome.

Oliveri, F. 2012. Enacting Rights from Below: Migrant Farmworkers' Struggles in Nardò, Southern Italy. In: Walthrust Jones, N. (Ed.), *Diversity and Turbulence in Contemporary Global Migration.* Brill, Leiden, pp. 37–43.

Oliveri, F. 2015. Giuridificare ed esternalizzare lo sfruttamento. Il caso dei lavoratori immigrati nella vitivinicoltura senese. In: Rigo, E. (Ed.), *Leggi, migranti e caporali. Prospettive critiche e di ricerca sullo sfruttamento del lavoro in agricoltura.* Pacini Giuridica, Pisa, pp. 47–67.

Osservatorio Placido Rizzotto (Ed.). 2018. *Agromafie e caporalato. IV Rapporto.* Bibliotheka Edizioni, Rome.

O'Sullivan, S. 2017. *Military Intervention in the Middle East and North Africa. The Case of NATO in Libya.* Routledge, London.

Palumbo, L. 2016. *Trafficking and Labour exploitation in Domestic Work and the Agricultural Sector in Italy.* EUI, San Domenico di Fiesole.

Palumbo, L., and Sciurba, A. 2015. Vulnerability to Forced Labour and Trafficking: The Case of Romanian Women in the Agricultural Sector in Sicily. *Anti-Trafficking Review* 5, 89–108.

Paoletti, E. 2010. *The Migration of Power and North-South Inequalities. The Case of Italy and Libya.* Palgrave MacMillan, London.

Patnaik, U., and Patnaik, P. 2016. *A Theory of Imperialism.* Columbia University Press, New York.

Perone, G. 2018. I costi della criminalità organizzata nel settore agroalimentare italiano. *Moneta e Credito* 71 (281), 35–64.

Perrotta, D. 2014. Vecchi e nuovi mediatori. Storia, geografia ed etnografia del caporalato in agricoltura. *Meridiana* 79, 193–220.

Perrotta, D., and Sacchetto, D. 2012. 'Un piccolo sentimento di vittoria'. Note sullo sciopero di Nardò. In: Brigate di solidarietà attiva, Nigro, G., Perrotta, M., Sacchetto, D., Sagnet, Y., Sulla pelle viva (Eds.), *Nardò: la lotta autorganizzata dei braccianti agricoli.* DeriveApprodi, Rome, pp. 9–55.

Phillips, M., and Missbach, A. 2017. Economies of transit: exploiting migrants and refugees in Indonesia and Libya. *International Journal of Migration and Border Studies* 3 (2/3), 139–157.

Pliez, O. 2002. Vieux réseaux et nouvelles circulations entre les deux rives du Sahara. *Revue Méditerranée* 99, 31–40.

Pliez, O. 2003. La Libye sommée de définir une politique migratoire. *Annuaire de l'Afrique du Nord* 41, 195–202.

Porsia, N. 2015. The Exploitation of Migration Routes to Europe: Human Trafficking Through Areas of Libya Affected by Fundamentalism. In: European Foundation for Democracy (Ed.), *Libya's fight for survival. Defeating Jihadist networks.* European Foundation for Democracy, Brussels, pp. 73–87.

Potot, S. 2010. La précarité sous toutes ses formes: concurrence entre travailleurs étrangers dans l'agriculture française. In: Morice, A., Potot, S. (Eds.), *De l'ouvrier immigré au travailleur sans papiers: les étrangers dans la modernisation du salariat.* Karthala, Paris, pp. 201–223.

Pradella, L. 2010. *L'attualità del Capitale: Accumulazione e impoverimento nel capitalismo globale.* Il Poligrafo, Padua.

Pradella, L., and Rad, T.S. 2017. Libya and Europe: imperialism, crisis and migration. *Third World Quarterly* 38 (11), 2411–2427. https://doi.org/10.1080/01436597.2017.1350819.

Pugliese E. (Ed.). 2012. *Diritti violati. Indagine sulle condizioni di vita dei lavoratori in aree rurali del Sud Italia e sulle violazioni dei loro diritti umani e sociali.* Dedalus, Napoli.

Pugliese, E. 2015. Introduzione: Quaranta anni di cambiamenti del lavoro in Italia. *Sociologia del Lavoro* 138, 9–34.

Rigo, E. 2015. Lo sfruttamento come modo di produzione. In: Rigo, E. (Ed.), *Leggi, mi-granti e caporali. Prospettive critiche e di ricerca sullo sfruttamento del lavoro in agricoltura.* Pacini Giuridica, Pisa.

Rigo, E. 2018. Migration, knowledge production and the humanitarian agenda in times of crisis. *Journal of Modern Italian Studies* 23 (4), 507–521.

Rodney, W. 1972. *How Europe Underdeveloped Africa.* Pambazuka Press, OXford.

Sanò, G., Piro, V. 2017. Abitare (ne)i luoghi di lavoro: il caso dei braccianti rumeni nelle serre della provincia di Ragusa. *Sociologia del Lavoro* 146 (2), 40–55.

Sarzanini, F., and Naddeo, F. 2017. Gasolio rubato in Libia da miliziani dell'Isis e rivenduto in Italia ed Europa: 6 arresti. Corriere della Sera, 2017, 18th October edition. https:// corrieredelmezzogiorno.corriere.it/catania/cronaca/17_ottobre_18/gasolio-rubato-libia-venduto-italia-ed-europa-nove-arresti-73d0b250-b3cb-11e7-a16e-c85a3b50cb84.shtml.

Scotto, A. 2016. Tra sfruttamento e protesta: i migranti e il caporalato agricolo in Italia meridionale. *REMHU* 24 (48), 79–92.

Sciortino, R. 2003. L'organizzazione del proletariato immigrato in Italia. In: Basso, P., Perocco, F. (Eds.), *Gli immigrati in Europa.* FrancoAngeli, Milan, pp. 376–406.

Serrao, G. 2019. Quanto vale il mercato illegale dei carburanti. AGI, 23 May 2019. https://www.agi.it/blog-italia/energia-e-sostenibilta/mercato_illegale_carburanti-5527404/post/2019-05-23/.

Silver, B. 2003. *Forces of Labour: Workers' Movements and Globalization Since 1870.* Cambridge University Press, Cambridge.

Skrivankova, K. 2010. *Between Decent Work and Forced Labour: EXamining the Continuum of EXploitation.* Joseph Rowntree Foundation, York.

St John, R.B. 2008. The Changing Libyan Economy: Causes and Consequences. *Middle East Journal* 62 (1), 75–91.

Strauss, K. McGrath, S. 2017. Temporary Migration, Precarious Employment and Unfree Labour Relations: Exploring the 'Continuum of Exploitation' in Canada's Temporary Foreign Worker Program. *Geoforum* 78, 199–208.

Terranova, G. 2010. Rivolta di Rosarno, riflessione a Sociologia. http://www.fattialcubo. it/rivolta-di-rosarno-riflessione-a-sociologia/.

Tinti, P. 2017. Nearly There, But Never Further Away. Foreign Policy, 2017, 5th October edition http://europeslamsitsgates.foreignpolicy.com/part-3-nearly-there-but-never-further-away-libya-africa-europe-EU-militias-migration.
Tinti, P., and Reitano, T. 2017. *Migrant, Refugee, Smuggler, Saviour*. OXford University Press, New York.
UNHCR, Operational Portal: Refugee Situations. https://data2.unhcr.org/en/situations/ mediterranean.
UNHCR. 2019. Mixed Migration Routes and Dynamics in Libya in 2018. UNHCR, Geneva. https://reliefweb.int/sites/reliefweb.int/files/resources/impact_lby_report_miXed_ migration_routes_and_dynamics_in_2018_june_2019.pdf.
United Nations Office for Coordination of Humanitarian Affairs, 2019. Humanitarian Needs Overview. Libya. UNOCHA, Geneva. https://reliefweb.int/sites/reliefweb.int/ files/resources/2019_lby_hno_draftv1.1.pdf.
UNSMIL, OHCHR. 2018. Desperate and Dangerous: Report on the human rights situation of migrants and refugees in Libya. United Nations Support Mission in Libya and Office of the High Commissioner for Human Rights. https://www.ohchr.org/Documents/ Countries/LY/LibyaMigrationReport.pdf.
Walia, H. 2014. *Undoing Border Imperialism*. AK Press, Oakland.
Wasley, A. 2012. Coca Cola Challenged Over Orange Harvest Linked to 'Exploitation and Squalor'. *The Ecologist*, 2012, 24th February edition https://theecologist.org/2012/ feb/24/coca-cola-challenged-over-orange-harvest-linked-exploitation-and-squalor.
Yea, S. 2017. The Art of Not Being Caught: Temporal Strategies for Disciplining Unfree Labour in Singapore's Contract Migration. *Geoforum* 78, 179–188.
Zaptia, S. 2018. $ 750 m worth of fuel is stolen: Sanalla. Libya Herald, 2018, 19th April edition https://www.libyaherald.com/2018/04/20/750-m-worth-of-libyan-fuel-is-stolen-sanalla/.

AUDIO AND VIDEO MATERIALS

CNN. 2017. People for sale. Where Lives Are Auctioned for $400. https://edition.cnn.com/ 2017/11/14/africa/libya-migrant-auctions/index.html.
Mottola, G. 2018. Nero come il petrolio. Video documentary, Report Rai, 19 November 2018. https://www.rai.it/programmi/report/inchieste/Petrolio-nero-94706fc8-0526-4d7b-aa5c-a40329de851a.html.
Severgnini, M. 2018. Schiavi di riserva. https://www.youtube.com/watch?v=V64286Qq-9M.
Severgnini, M., and Messina, P. 2018. EXODUS—Fuga dalla Libia. https://vimeo.com/ exoduslibya/videos.

Chapter 8

Marini within Its Limits

A Critique of Super-exploitation as a Structural Mechanism of Accumulation in the Periphery

Matari Pierre Manigat

INTRODUCTION

For Ruy Mauro Marini, the super-exploitation of labor constitutes a "structural mechanism" of accumulation in the Latin American formations of dependent capitalism. This means that the labor force is permanently paid below its value. This chapter demonstrates the inconsistency of this hypothesis with the generalization of wage labor. Super-exploitation in Marini's sense necessarily implies the existence of social forms of production not yet subject to the law of value, and of noncapitalist forms that contribute to the maintenance of workers. We present the argument in four sections.

After briefly contextualizing the formulation of Marxist dependency theory (1), we set out the genealogy of the concept of super-exploitation in Marx (2) to show how Marini's definition as a "structural mechanism" of accumulation contradicts the conditions of generalized wage labor (3). As a conclusion, we delimit the scope of Marini's concept to the colonial and capitalist formation periods in the economic history of Latin America (4).

THE CONTEXT OF THE FORMULATION OF MARXIST DEPENDENCY THEORY

The contradictions of Import Substitution Industrialization (ISI) opened a series of criticisms of the "economic programming" of the Economic Commission for Latin America (ECLAC) and the theories of modernization.

The problem of "dependency" brought together these critics that can be divided—for analytical clarity—into two main currents: the structuralist dependency theory and the Marxist dependency theory. The structuralist dependency theorists broke with ECLAC at an essential point: they no longer considered the classes and social strata that emerged from ISI as agents of structural reforms (Kay 1989). On the other hand, for Marxist authors, the dependent character of the Latin American bourgeoisies implied that only a socialist revolution could take on and complete the tasks of development.

Both structuralist and Marxist dependency theorists noted that the periods of greatest economic growth in Latin America coincided with moments of rupture or crisis in the world market (e.g., the two world wars and the Great Depression). This was the manifestation of a certain way of articulation between development and underdevelopment, whereby both phenomena are mutually determined. In this sense, the merit of Paul Baran's seminal book consisted in analyzing the "morphology of underdevelopment" as a consequence of colonialism and imperialism (Baran 1957). His considerations were appropriated by Marxist dependency theorists to define the concept of dependency as a "complement" to the theory of imperialism (Osorio 1994, 167). Among those scholars, Marini defined dependency as "a relationship of subordination among formally independent nations, in which the relations of production of subordinated nations are modified or recreated to ensure the expanded reproduction of dependency" (Marini 1973, 5). More profoundly, however, the critique of the assumptions of the theory of modernization and of ECLAC's developmentalism concealed a debate on the historical formation of capitalism in Latin America. This discussion faced two great perspectives.

The first emphasized the conditions of production and the forms of existence of labor that characterize economic systems (i.e., modes of production). It highlighted the conflicts that occurred within the colonial economic regimes as factors that determined the formation of capitalism. In Marxist orthodoxy, the "fundamental law of development of feudalism" formulated in the Union of Soviet Socialist Republics (USSR) in the 1950s largely sustained this approach to economic and social history in the "backward" countries. These theses—analogous in their fundamental perspective, although different in their results—stumbled when they turned to the specificities of the world market. However, the peculiarity of the economic history of Latin America lay, precisely, in its subordinate insertion into the world market since the European Conquest in the 16th century.

This difficulty contributed to the success of a second perspective developed by the dependency school. Its merit lay in making it impossible to study any problem in the economic history of the region independently of the influences of the world market. However, dependency scholars did not provide a definitive answer to the problem of the historical formation of capitalism in the region. The subsequent split into two strands—Structuralist dependency theory and Marxist dependency theory—largely reflected that dispute. Structuralist and Marxist dependency theorists also diverged when discussing the nature of the social forces destined to or capable of leading a social transformation. While the structuralist dependency theorists represented the radical voices of developmentalist projects, the Marxists rejected any possibility for self-centered development within the limits of capitalism. The former emphasized a problem of a socio-political nature: they did not consider the "national bourgeoisies" and the social strata that emerged from industrialization to be agents of developmental structural reforms. However, this did not prevent the continuation of an "associated dependent development" based on a "dependent industrial development" as argued by Fernando Henrique Cardoso, its main representative (Cardoso 1972, Cardoso and Magnani 1974, 3–32). For Marxists, the political dilemma facing the Third World countries was the following: Capitalist underdevelopment or socialist revolution? as summarized by André Gunder Frank (1968).[1]

This position turned the so-called Marxist dependency into a common theoretical platform for all Marxist currents that did not share the fundamental economic theses and the class alliances proposed by the communist parties affiliated with the *Kominform*: Castro-Guevaristas (*foquismo*), Trotskyists, Maoists, etc. Probably, that the most radical theoretical position—in the sense of pointing out the absolute impossibility of exiting underdevelopment within the framework of capitalism—was the Maoist thesis that opposed the "bourgeois nations" to the "proletarian nations" (Lichtheim 1971, 161–179).

As a matter of fact, the earlier polemic was a sort of Latin American "remake" of the controversy over the problems of "transition to capitalism"; a debate that intensified with the publication of *Studies in the Development of Capitalism* by Maurice Dobb in 1946. From a methodological point of view, the problem consisted of determining the status of the social relations of production and of the relations of exchange, respectively, in the definition of a mode of production. While the relations between the direct producer and the owner of the means of production constitute the cornerstone of the problem for Dobb, Paul Sweezy, his principal critic, dissociated the social relations of production from the definition of the mode of production (Sweezy 1950, 44). This is the thesis that most influenced and shaped Marxist thought in postwar America. In the United States, for example, Harry Magdoff (historian and co-editor of the Monthly Review with Sweezy) explained that "the existence of slavery [in the South of the Union] does not make it a slave society, not even in the southern region of the country. Slavery in the United States was, indeed, a special feature of U.S. capitalism" (1965: 134–135). In Latin America, the Sweezy-Magdoff perspective, which defines capitalism as a system of production for the market, allowed some theorists to establish the incorporation into the world market as the central criterion for defining the character of colonial economies. Dobb himself acknowledged the echoes of his debate with Sweezy in the controversy over the character of modes of production in Latin America:

> On the one hand, there is the tendency to give greater weight to market influences; that is, to the relationships within the sphere of exchange between producers and final consumers of the product and the forms of this exchange. It was argued that this would have provided the dynamic impetus to change feudal society; and these relationships were the main criteria to characterize a given society as "feudal" or "capitalist" in any period. We cannot avoid seeing analogous trends today in Gunder Frank's writings on the economy of colonial or semi-colonial dependent countries. (Dobb 1972, 8)

For Sweezy's critics, it is a methodological error to try to define a mode of production without starting from the form of social existence of labor (Takahashi 1976). As a result, it was logical that the same complaint was raised (Puiggrós 1965, Laclau 1968, Brewer 1980, Howard and King 1992) to dependency theorists who projected that perspective in Latin America (Frank 1967). The formulation of most of these criticisms of dependency "circulationism" called for studies of the "articulation of modes of production" in a given social formation, in Louis Althusser's sense. But Marxist dependency theory did not limit itself to saying that producing for the world market turned Latin America into a capitalist space. Sergio Bagú (1949) was, maybe, the first to support the hypothesis of a Latin American colonial capitalism. The specificity of Marxist dependency theory was—following Baran this time—to connect the discussion with the considerations about the reciprocal determination between development and underdevelopment. This latter concern presided over a series of works that contributed to the emergence of a dependency problem: Emmanuel (1959), Furtado (1969), Amin (1970), Cardoso and Faletto (1969), Frank (1967) and Marini (2012: 58–60). If Marini's thesis stood out, it was, among other reasons, because his central concept—the super-exploitation of labor—rooted this concern transversally to all dependency-related thought in the particularities of the conditions of labor.[2] Therefore, it was necessary to deduce all the implications "of the link to the world market [for] the internal organization of labour" (Marini 1973, 48).

SUPER-EXPLOITATION IN MARX'S THEORY

The theory of exploitation and the study of the forms of production of surplus value derive from the distinction between the value of labor and the value of labor-power. While absolute surplus value is produced by the prolongation or intensification of the working day (based on an invariable technical mode of production), relative surplus value is produced by reducing the necessary labor time thanks to advances in labor productivity (as long as they affect the production of consumer goods for the working class). Whatever the case, wage—a specific form of income for a specific producer—conceals capitalist exploitation because it formally stipulates that the totality of the labor carried out (Piece Wages) or of the workday carried out (Time Wages) is being remunerated. But the theoretical confusion of the value of labor-power and the value of labor entails much more than a concealment of the process of exploitation. According to Marx, it supports "all the mystifications of the capitalistic mode of production" and "all the apologetic shifts of the vulgar economists" (Marx 1967, 540). Instead, it is because the wage is not the price of labor, but the price of labor-power that makes the capitalist dream of being able to get labor without buying it. The problem is:

> If the labourers could live on air they could not be bought at any price. The zero of their cost is therefore a limit in a mathematical sense, always beyond reach, although we can always approximate more and more nearly to it. The constant tendency of capital is to force the cost of labour back towards this zero. (Marx 1967, 596)

Marx locates this "constant tendency of capital" in the wage form itself. Hence, the importance of a systematic study of this specific form of income—a task whose broad guidelines were only outlined by Marx.[3] For example, some forms of time-wage—the differences between normal hours and overtime rates—compel workers to extend the working day beyond what is normally established. Similarly, certain conditions of the labor market—high unemployment, relative disorganization of workers, and so on—make it possible to improve the profitability of capital, increasing the rate of exploitation by remunerating the labor force below its value. Finally, differences in the standard of living between countries also serve as tools to force (depending on the situation) a reduction in high standards and therefore in wages. Those kinds of blackmails are possible since the quantity and quality of the use values that enter the consumption of the workers of the different countries have a relative dimension—a "historical and moral" dimension. In short, capital has a wide range of tools to increase the degree of exploitation of labor-power beyond what the absolute and relative surplus value methods allow. In studying the production of surplus value:

> It was constantly presupposed that wages are at least equal to the value of labour power. Forcible reduction of wages below this value plays, however, in

> practice too important a part. . . . It, in fact, transforms, within certain limits, the labourer's necessary consumption fund into a fund for the accumulation of capital. (Marx 1967, 595)

Yet supposing that wages represent an average of the values of labor-power is not an ideal type arbitrarily forged by the researcher, nor is it the fortuitous result of a correlation of strength between social classes. It is a relationship that is objectively imposed on capital by the need to ensure the reproduction of the wage-earning class. The issue is that the historical formation of wage labor conditions implies the continuing disappearance of domestic forms of production. The extraction of surplus labor, whatever its modality, cannot permanently violate the law of exchange of equivalents that governs the sale and purchase of labor-power. If wages must replenish the wear and tear of the workforce, it is a consequence of the transformation of labor-power into a commodity, regardless of the place that each country occupies in the international division of labor. Marx even goes so far as to illustrate his considerations on the transformation of labor-power into commodity with the struggle for the abolition of various forms of serfdom in Hungary before the revolution of Cuza, or in the Mexico of Maximilian of Habsburg (Marx 1867, 178).

Finally, Marx specifies as follows the implications of differences in the level of productivity and wages for national differences in exploitation rates. For the author of *Theories of Surplus Value*, countries where labor productivity is higher record better nominal and real wages. Reciprocally, countries with lower labor productivity, in order to compete, are forced to extend the working day. This extension of the working day

> is the case in countries (such as Austria, etc.) where the capitalist mode of production is already in existence but which have to compete with far more developed countries. Wages can be low here partly because the requirements of the worker are less developed, partly because agricultural products are cheaper or—this amounts to the same thing as far as the capitalist is concerned—because they have less value in terms of money. Hence the quantity of the product of, say, 10 hours' labour, which must go to the worker as necessary wages, is small. If, however, he works 17 hours instead of 12 then this can be made good. In any case because in a given country the relative value of labour falls in proportion to its productivity, it must not be imagined that wages in different countries are inversely proportional to the productivity of labour. In fact exactly the opposite is the case. The more productive one country is relative to another in the world market, the higher will be its wages as compared with the other. In England, not only nominal wages but real wages are higher than on the Continent. The worker eats more meat; he satisfies more needs. This, however, only applies to

> the industrial worker and not the agricultural labourer. But in proportion to the productivity of the English workers their wages are not higher. (Marx 1863, 252)

SUPER-EXPLOITATION AND REPRODUCTION OF WORKFORCE IN MARINI

In his *Dialectics of Dependency*, Marini subordinates his considerations on the capitalist exploitation of workers in Latin America to the problem of unequal exchange between imperialist and dependent nations. His concept of super-exploitation—that is, the permanent remuneration of the labor force below its value—roots both phenomena in the conditions of production.

> The problem posed by unequal exchange is not that of counteracting the transfer of value that it implies, but rather that of compensating for a loss of surplus value, and that, unable to prevent it at the level of market relations, the reaction of the dependent economy is to compensate it at the level of internal production. (Marini 1973, 38)

The reception of Marini's thesis gave rise to a whole series of criticisms, beginning with his identification of the production of absolute surplus value with super-exploitation in Marx's sense (transformation of a part of the worker's consumption fund into an accumulation fund). For the author of the *Dialectics of Dependency*, intensification of labor, prolongation of the working day, and expropriation of part of necessary labor are all mechanisms that "lead to labour power being paid below its value and therefore correspond to a super-exploitation of workers" (Marini 1973, 42). But most critics attacked Marini's method. For example, Cardoso and Serra (1978) objected that Marini had superimposed an international division of the forms of production of surplus value on the international division of labor; as a result, Marini removed any possibility of producing relative surplus value in the dependent economies. A correlate to this criticism is that Marini subordinated the very possibility of relative surplus value in the North to super-exploitation in the South (Singer 1980). For his part, Cueva (1974) criticized the substitution of class contradictions for contradictions between nation-states. Finally, Valenzuela (1997) points out the inconsistency of establishing a positive correlation between technological progress and an increase in the degree of super-exploitation. Most of these criticisms have been answered by Marini himself (1978), by his disciples (Sotelo Valencia 2012, Días Carcanholo y Correa 2021, 531–532) or by other Marxist dependency scholars (Bambirra 1978, Dos Santos 2002). More recently, Katz (2017) argues that "dependency theory does not require a concept of super-exploitation."[4] Almost all these criticisms and responses were limited to complaints about the "correct" definitions of the different forms of production of surplus value, as well as their different modalities of articulation, depending on whether it is considered at a general and abstract (theoretical) level of analysis or at a concrete level (the global economy as a structured and hierarchical totality).

But an essential problem remains. It is necessary to explain the very possibility of permanently overexploiting labor under capitalist conditions of production, even when these are dependent. Some critics of Marini, such as Paul Singer and Carton de Grammont (1985), have pointed out this insufficiency in Marini's thesis. They did not develop it further because they subordinated it to other problems: the underconsumption of workers for Singer, and the question of the transfer of value between the peasant economy and the industrial sector for Carton de Grammont. The latter correctly deduces that "the total value of labour power is equal to the wage paid by the capitalist plus the value extracted from the peasant production unit" (Carton 1985, 90–91).

However, explaining the very possibility of permanently overexploiting labor implies reconsidering the definitions of the forms of social existence of labor proposed by Marini. For Marini, wage labor differs from servitude and slavery because in the latter case, the owner appropriates the "total time of the worker's existence," while in the former, it is "the time of his existence usable for production, leaving the worker to take care of his non-productive time" (Marini 1973, 44). The problem is that the difference between forms of social existence of labor also implies a differentiation of the particular modes of reproduction of labor. In addition, Marini's whole book ignores the particular modes of reproduction of labor-power associated with each mode of social production. A social mode of production is differentiated not only by the mode of exploitation but also by the way in which the worker ensures his conditions of existence.

The hypothesis of super-exploitation requires that a part of the necessary labor be carried out outside the wage relationship. As a result, the presence of domestic forms of production—individually or collectively owned—is a sine qua non for considering super-exploitation to be a structural mechanism of capital accumulation in dependent formations, as defined by Marini. By contrast, from the moment in which the worker is a proletarian who has nothing but his or her labor-power, the permanence of super-exploitation would represent exhaustion and, in the long run, a progressive extinction of the wage-earning class. Super-exploitation in Marini's sense is inconceivable under fully developed capitalist conditions. Hence, rather than a structural mechanism of accumulation in dependent capitalism, it is more of a structural mechanism of accumulation in the various colonial regimes.

THE HISTORICAL SCOPE OF THE MARINI MODEL

Super-exploitation shaped the horizon of the economic and social history of the colonial regimes in the Americas. The submission of the colonial economies to the world market acted as a spur to the exploitation of labor. In that sense, as the dependency theorists noted, the world market played a crucial role in determining the goals and methods of production. However, the possibility of super-exploitation in Marini's sense was established by the conditions of reproduction of the labor force. It was precisely in the Ibero-American colonial empires that the domestic forms of production—individual and collective—marked a spatial and temporal distinction between labor that produces the subsistence goods needed by the workers and labor that produces the surplus, that is, between the *necessary labor* and the *surplus labor*. This distinction, particularly clear in plantation economies based on slavery, was less discontinuous in economies structured around tribute payable by serf-Indians, as in much of the Spanish empire.

The reproduction of the colonial system as a whole depended on the conservation of these forms and spaces of production, as well as the possibility that the direct producer dedicates a certain amount of time to labor there. Therefore, the existence of these lands owned either individually or collectively by the workers directly or indirectly determined how workers' remuneration was fixed. Directly, because it enabled free labor for the benefit of the landowners, as in the case of the various forms of the *repartimiento* regime in the Spanish empire (*cuatequiles* in New Spain, *mita* in Peru, *mandamientos* in Central America). Indirectly, because it enabled the wages of the workforce enrolled in the *repartimientos* (a forced labor system) to be set at levels systematically lower than those that would prevail in a "free" labor market. In all cases, the possibility of such wage setting methods lay in the fact that the reproduction of the social labor-power depended fundamentally on domestic forms of production (collective lands and family plots). In the same way, the spaces of domestic production served as a condition for the rise of surplus labor in the plantations. For example, the owners could stop giving their slaves means of subsistence, increasing thereby the degree of exploitation to the maximum (Hector and Moïse 1990). Cornerstone of colonial economic regimes and transition periods to capitalism, super-exploitation of labor is also a principle of intelligibility of the various forms of class struggle during colonialism, as shown, for example, by historian Severo Martínez Peláez (1985).

During the process of formation of capitalist conditions, the role of these domestic production spaces in setting wages gained importance. This can be explained schematically on the basis of a problem defined by the Arthur Lewis model: the representation of a capitalist modernization process led by a "modern urban sector" that obtains an "unlimited supply of labour" from a "rural and archaic sector." By putting pressure on wages, the "unlimited" flow of labor creates a virtuous circle characterized by a retroactive relationship between high rates of profit, saving, investment, and employment. This way of determining wages lasts as long as the sociodemographic structures of the archaic sector remain; that is, before the so-called Lewis turn. The essential facts of this problem remain unchanged if we abandon Lewis's approach to adopt a non-dualistic conception of the coexistence of the backward and the modern.[5] Thus, the Lewis model shows how the conversion of labor conditions into capital and its correlate, the conversion of the mass of the population into wage earners, are supported by domestic spaces of production that define the level and modes of fluctuation of wages, during the so-called primitive accumulations. It indicates the possibility—especially during the so-called take-off and intensification periods of the rural exodus—of prolonged intervals of accumulation during which the increase in the employed wage labor force does not necessarily entail an upward pressure on wages. This situation is an important cause of differentiation of "the general law of accumulation" in the social formations of the center and the periphery. In the former, a prolonged accumulation without fundamental disturbances to the technical base of production can be accompanied by an increase in the standard of living among the working-class: these are the conditions of accumulation "most favourable to the labourers" writes Marx. Here, "their relation of dependence upon capital takes on an endurable form," and "they can extend the circle of their enjoyments; can make some additions to their consumption fund of clothes, furniture, & c., and can lay by small reserve funds of money" (Marx 1867, 625).[6] In the latter, comparable accumulation conditions—in terms of the growth rate of the absolute and relative shares of variable capital—does not drive an increase in wages. Here again, the differentiation is because capital has not yet completely subverted the set of objective conditions of production.

CONCLUSION

For Marini, super-exploitation defined as permanent remuneration of the labor force below its value constitutes a "structural mechanism" of accumulation in dependent capitalism. This chapter demonstrates the unsustainability of this hypothesis in the conditions of fully developed waged labor. Super-exploitation as a "structural mechanism" necessarily implies the existence of forms of production not yet subject to the law of value. We circumscribe the scope of Marini's thesis to the colonial and transition to capitalism periods of the economic and social history of these social formations.

NOTES

1. Although Frank does not officially belong to Marxism, his political position is indicative of the distance that separates the two groups.

2. The notion of super-exploitation was common in the Third World literature of the 1960s, both among economists and noneconomists. Sartre, for example, defines super-exploitation as one of the "three levels" of colonization (Sartre, 1960: 808 y ss). Among economists, and prior to Marini's work, the concept was used in Latin America as a metaphor for the brutality of the modes of exploitation of labor.

3. Project that inspired Maurice Dobb's *Wages* (1928).

4. See Sotelo (2017), Osorio (2018), and a new response by Katz (2018).

5. Examination of these approaches goes beyond the scope of this chapter. In the history of Marxist thought, these are mainly inspired by Constantin Dobrogeanu-Gherea's (1910) and Leon Trotsky's works on the originality and unequal rhythms of capitalist development in backward formations. Trotsky's (1930: 40–41) "law of combined development" shares a certain kinship with "the law of backward societies" outlined by Dobrogeanu-Gherea, author of an important study on the transformations of agrarian structures in Eastern Europe, the interactions between the backward and the modern in these countries, as well as their implications for the "unique" nature of the emerging economic regimes (Love, 1996).

6. The rise in real wages, considered in these social and technique circumstances, "only means, in fact, that the length and weight of the golden chain the wage worker has already forged for himself, allow of a relaxation of the tension" (Marx, 1867: 625).

BIBLIOGRAPHY

Amin Samir (1970). *L'accumulation à l'échelle mondiale*. Paris: Anthropos, Ifan-Dakar.

Bagu Sergio (1949) 1992. *Economía de la sociedad colonial. Ensayo de historia comparada de América Latina*. México: Grijalbo.

Baran Paul (1957). *La economía política del crecimiento*. 1964 México: Fce.

Beigel Fernanda (2006). "Vida, muerte y resurrección de las "teorías de la dependencia." In VV. AA., *Crítica y teoría en el pensamiento social latinoamericano*. Buenos Aires: CLACSO.

Bambira Vania (1978). *Teoría de la dependencia: una anticrítica*. Mexico: Era.

Brewer Anthony (1980). *Marxist theories of imperialism. A critical Survey*. London: Routledge.

Cardoso Fernando H. (1972). "Notas sobre el estado actual de los estudios sobre dependencia," *Revista Latinoamericana de Ciencias Sociales*, No. 4, Santiago de Chile, pp. 3–31.

Cardoso Fernando H. and FALETTO Enzo (1969). *Dependencia y subdesarrollo en América Latina*. México: Siglo XXI.

Cardoso Fernando H. and MAGNANI J. G. C. (1974). "Las contradicciones del desarrollo asociado" *Desarrollo económico*, pp. 3–32.
Cardoso Fernando H. and SERRA José (1978). "Las desventuras de la dialéctica de la dependencia" *Revista Mexicana de Sociología*, p. 40.
Carton De Grammont Hubert (1985). "Venta de fuerza de trabajo de los campesinos pobres y acumulación de capital," *Revista Mexicana de Sociología*, Vol. 47, No. 3 (Jul.- Sep.), pp. 85–98.
Cueva Agustín (1977) 1980. *El desarrollo del capitalismo en América Latina.* Mexico: Siglo XXI.
Dias Carcahnolo, M. y Correa, H. (2021). "Ruy Mauro Marini (1932–1997)" en *Routledge Handbook of Marxism and Post-Marxism.* London: Routledge.
Dobb Maurice (1928) 1970. *Wages.* Mexico: FCE.
Dobrogeanu-Gherea Constantin [1910] (2010). *Neo-Serfdom (*excerpts*).* In Ersoy,
Górny, Kechriotis, Kopeček, Manchev, Trencsényi, Turda (eds.). *Modernism: The Creation of Nation-States: Discourses of Collective Identity in Central and Southeast Europe 1770–1945: Texts and Commentaries,* Volume III/1, pp. 419–425. Budapest: Central European University Press.
———. (1946) 1981. *Estudios sobre el desarrollo del capitalismo.* Mexico: Siglo XXI.
———. (1980). Prólogo a "El sistema señorial europeo y la hacienda latinoamericana" de C. Kay. Mexico: Era.
Dos santos Theotônio (2003). *Teoría de la dependencia. Balances y perspectivas.* Barcelona Plaza y Janés.
Emmanuel Arghiri (1959) 1969. *L'échange inégal.* Paris: Maspero.
Frank André G. (1967). *Capitalismo y subdesarrollo en América Latina.* Mexico: Siglo XXI.
———. (1968). Latin America Subdesarrollo capitalista o revolución socialista," *Pensamiento Crítico*, No. 13, La Habana.
Haring Clarens (1947) 1990. *El imperio español en América.* Mexico: CONACULTA.
Hector Michel and Moïse Claude (1990). *Colonisation et esclavage en Haïti. Le régime colonial français à Saint-Domingue (1625–1789).* Port-au-Prince: Henry Deschamps.
Howard Michael. C. and KING John. E. (1992). *A history of Marxian economics.* Vol. II (1929–1990). London: MacMillan.
Kay Cristobal (1989). *Latin American Theories of Development and Underdevelopment.* London: Routledge.
Katz Claudio (2017). "Aciertos y problemas de la superexplotación" https://katz.lahaine.org/b2-img/ACIERTOSYPROBLEMASDELASUPEREXPLOTACIN.pdf.
Katz Claudio (2018). "Actualización o veneración de la teoría de la dependencia" https://katz.lahaine.org/b2img/ACTUALIZACINOVENERACINDELATEORIADELADEPE.pdf.
Laclau Ernesto (1968). "Feudalismo y capitalismo en América Latina." In Sempat.
Assadourian, Carlos et al (1979), *Modos de producción en América Latina.* Mexico Siglo XXI, 1979.

Lewis Arthur (1954) 1960. "Desarrollo económico con oferta ilimitada de mano de obra," *El trimestre económico,* Vol. XXVIII, No. 4, Oct.–Dec, Mexico, pp. 629–675.

Love Joseph. L. (1996). *Crafting the third world: theorizing underdevelopment in Rumania and Brazil.* Redwood: Stanford University Press.

Marini Ruy Mauro (1973). *La dialéctica de la dependencia.* Mexico: ERA.

———. 1978. "Las razones del neodesarrollismo (respuesta a F. H. Cardoso y J. Serra)," *Revista mexicana de sociología*, Special number.

———. (2012). *Maestro en blanco y negro.* Quito: IAEN.

———. (1994). "La crisis del desarrollismo." In Marini, R. M. and Millán M. (eds.) (1994). *La teoría social latinoamericana.* México, El Caballito.

Marx Karl (2012). *El Capital.* Mexico: FCE.

———. (1979). *Manuscrits de 1861–1863. Cahiers I à V.* Paris: Editions Sociales.

Marx Karl (1863) [2010]. *Theories of surplus value.* In Marx and Engels, *Collected Woks.* Vol. 31. London: Lawrence and Wishard.

Marx Karl (1867) [2010]. *Capital* Book I. In Marx and Engels, *Collected Woks*, Vol. 35. London: Lawrence and Wishard.

Martinez Pelaez Severo (1985) 2011. *Motines de indios. La violencia colonial en Centroamérica y Chiapas.* Guatemala: F&G editores.

Osorio Jaime (1994). "Fuentes y tendencias de la teoría de la dependencia." In Marini and Millán, *La teoría social latinoamericana* (Tomo II). México: El caballito.

Osorio, Jaime (2018). "Los avatares de una nueva interpretación sobre el subdesarrollo y la dependencia. Notas críticas a la propuesta de Claudio Katz," diciembre,

Herramienta Web 24, https://herramienta.com.ar/articulo.php?id=2942 Peemans Jean-Philippe (2002). *Le développement des peuples face à la modernization du monde. Les théories du développement «réel» dans la seconde moitié du XXIe siècle.* Paris: L'Harmattan.

Puiggrós Rodolfo (1965) [1974]. "Los modos de producción en Iberoamérica." In Puiggrós, Frank, and Ramos, *Polémica sobre los modos de producción en Iberoamérica.* Buenos Aires: Agrupación Universitaria Nacional.

Sartre Jean Paul (1960) [1985]. *Critique de la raison dialectique (*Tome I : *Théorie des ensembles pratiques).* Paris : Gallimard.

Sotelo Valencia Adrián (2012). "Dependencia y superexplotación: la perspectiva de Marini," *Revista de la facultad de economía*, BUAP, year XVII, No. 44. January–April.

Sotelo, A. (2017). ¿Una teoría de la dependencia sin superexplotación? Mejor una teoría de la dependencia con superexplotación revisitada y actualizada, 19–12, https://www.lahaine.org/mundo.php/critica-a-la-critica-de.

Sweezy Paul M. (1976). "Crítica." In Hilton, *La transición del feudalismo al capitalismo*. Barcelona: Crítica.

Takahashi Kohachiro (1976). "Contribución al debate." In Hilton, *La transición del feudalismo al capitalismo.* Barcelona: Crítica.

Trotsky Léon (1930) [1995]. *Histoire de la révolution russe* (Tome 1). Paris: Seuil.

Valenzuela Feijóo José (1997). "Sobrexplotación y dependencia," *Investigación económica*, Vol. 57, No. 221 (July-September), pp. 105–127.

Chapter 9

Global Inequalities, Digital Capitalism, and Marx's General Law of Capitalist Accumulation

William I. Robinson

> One thing I've been hearing from a lot of very wealthy people these days, since the [U.S.] election [in 2016 of Donald Trump], is that they all have escape plans. There was a very interesting story in the New Yorker by Evan Osnos. He covered the ways in which rich people are buying up ranches in New Zealand and creating bunkers in the Bahamas, or wherever they're going, thinking that they're somehow going to be able to avoid the apocalypse when it comes. There's actually a business that operates in New York. It's a boat that will come, you can apparently pre-buy tickets, if there's some political crisis or some danger moment, and they'll come and pick you up and whisk you up the Hudson.
>
> —Interview with Rana Foroohar,
> Associate Editor of Financial Times
> and CNN Economic Analyst[1]

> Society and governments need to be amenable to disproportionately allow/encourage the few to retain that fatter profit share. The Managerial Aristocracy, like in the Gilded Age, the Roaring Twenties, and the thriving nineties, needs to commandeer a vast chunk of that rising profit share, either through capital income, or simply paying itself a lot.
>
> —Citigroup report on the "plutonomy"[2]

Speaking at a "Business of Luxury Summit" in Monaco in 2015, the billionaire owner of the luxury jewelry company Cartier, Johann Rupert, told the audience that the prospect of robots replacing workers and the poor rising up "keeps me awake at night." Equally as frightening, he went on to say, is that in the face of imminent social upheaval, the middle classes would no longer want to buy luxury goods for fear of exposing their wealth (Withnall 2015). The transnational capitalist class (TCC) to which Rupert belongs has good reason to be frightened. The data on global inequality has by now been widely disseminated. Capitalist globalization has resulted in unprecedented social polarization worldwide. In 2015, just 1% of humanity owned over half of the world's wealth and the top 20% own 94.5% of that wealth, while the remaining 80% must make do with just 4.5%.[3] What is more, this polarization continues to intensify. The British House of Commons released a report in 2018, which warned that the richest 1% of humanity are on course to control as much as two-thirds of the world's wealth by 2030 (Savage 2018).

If such savage inequalities keep the TCC up at night, they impose untold hardships on billions of people who face daily struggles for survival and uncertain futures. Yet they also reflect a crisis of global capitalism that is as much political as it is structural. Capitalist globalization has undermined redistributive policies that came into being following the Great Depression of the 1930s, themselves the result of widespread social and class struggles from below that forced such redistribution on capitalist states. But now digitalization is driving a new round of worldwide restructuring that promises to expand the ranks of surplus labor and extend the "precariatization" of work. The more global inequalities expand, the more constricted is the world market and the more the system faces a structural crisis of overaccumulation.

But escalating inequalities and the inability of global capitalism to assure the survival of billions of people throw states into crises of legitimacy and push the system toward more openly repressive means of social control and domination that exacerbate political and social conflict. The system is approaching an organic crisis; a general crisis of capitalist rule. We have entered a fluid period of great uncertainly that opens up the dangers of neo-fascism and war but also new possibilities for emancipatory projects. Part of the struggle for a counter-hegemony from below involves understanding the nature of the new global capitalism; how it has reshaped global class relations, the terrain of class and social struggles, forms of consciousness, and prospects for transnational class solidarities.

THE CRISIS OF GLOBAL CAPITALISM

What accounts for escalating worldwide inequalities that have so alarmed the likes of Johann Rupert? As Marx analyzed in *Capital*, polarization is inherent to the capitalist system since capitalists own the means of producing wealth and therefore appropriate as profits as much wealth as possible that society collectively produces. But such inequalities end up undermining the stability of the system since the mass of working people cannot purchase the wealth that pours out of the capitalist economy to the extent that capitalists and the well-off retain more and more of total income relative to that which goes to labor. If capitalists cannot actually sell (or "unload") the products of their plantations, factories, and offices, then they cannot make ("realize") profit. This is what in critical political economy constitutes the underlying internal contradiction of capitalism, or the *overaccumulation* problem. Capitalists accumulate huge amounts of surplus but do not find outlets to continue to profitably invest that surplus. Hence, if left unchecked, the expanding social polarization that is endemic to capitalism results in crisis—in stagnation, recessions, depressions, social upheavals, and war.

The Fordist-Keynesian social order that took shape in the decades following the 1930s' Great Depression involved high growth rates, a rise in living standards for substantial sectors of the working class, and a decrease in inequalities in the developed core of world capitalism. Why "Fordist-Keynesian"? It was Henry Ford who first recognized that the new system of mass, standardized production ("Fordism") could not be sustained without introducing mass, standardized consumption. This meant establishing a stable employment arrangement—or capital-labor relation—for a significant portion of the working classes and wages high enough for the working class to actually consume the goods and services that their labor produced—in exchange for workers' obedience to capital. In turn, John Keynes analyzed that the Great Depression owed to insufficient demand as a result of the concentration of wealth. The state needed in Keynes' view to intervene in the economy in order to regulate the market (especially financial markets) and to boost demand through state spending on public projects such as infrastructure and social services as well as through the establishment of minimum wages, unemployment insurance, pensions, and so forth.[4]

These Fordist-Keynesian arrangements came about because of the mass struggles of working and popular classes from the late 1800s into the 1930s, including worker, populist, and socialist movements; the Bolshevik revolution, and the anticolonial and national liberation struggles in the Third World. The period of post–World War II prosperity in the core countries owed a great deal to this combination of Fordist production and regulated capital-labor relations and Keynesian monetary, budgetary, and regulatory policies. State intervention in the capitalist market and a component of redistribution came to define economic policy in the mid-20th century in the then First World, as well as in the then Third World in the wake of decolonization. Redistributive nation-state capitalism evolved, therefore, from capital's accommodation to mass upheavals from below in the wake of the crisis of the two world wars and the Great Depression.

In the wake of the next great crisis, that of the 1970s, emergent transnational capital went global as a strategy of an emergent TCC to reconstitute its social power by breaking free of nation-state constraints to accumulation, and to do away with the Fordist-Keynesian arrangement. The post–World War II "class compromise" served capital well for several decades. Corporate profits rose sharply from 1945 to 1968, and then declined until the early 1980s, when it again rose very rapidly, this time as a result of globalization (Piketty 2014, 227).[5] The corporate class and its agents identified the mass struggles and demands of popular and working classes and state regulation as fetters to its freedom to make profits and accumulate wealth as the rate of profit declined in the 1970s. As the TCC congealed, it forged what became known as the "Washington Consensus," or the agreement around sweeping worldwide economic restructuring through neoliberalism to put in place a new transnational corporate order and go on the offensive in its class warfare against working and popular classes.

Globalization enhanced the structural power of transnational capital over states and popular classes worldwide. Popular and working classes have been less effective in defending wages in the face of capital's newfound global mobility. And states have seen the erosion of their ability to capture and redistribute surpluses given the privatization of public assets, ever more regressive tax systems and prospects for corporate tax evasion, mounting debt to transnational finance capital, inter-state competition to attract transnational capital, and the ability of the TCC to transfer money instantaneously around the world through new digital financial circuits. Behind this alleged "loss of state sovereignty," capitalist globalization changed the correlation of class forces worldwide in favor of the TCC. Transnational capital has been able to exercise a newfound structural power over states and territorially bound working classes, which has undermining the ability of states to capture and redistribute surpluses.

However, by escalating global social polarization and inequality, globalization fueled the chronic problem of overaccumulation. By the late 1990s, stagnation once again set in and the system faced renewed crisis as privatizations dried up, the conquered regions were brought into the system, global markets became saturated, and new technologies reached the limits of fixed capital expansion. Given the extreme polarization of wealth and income, the global market cannot absorb the output of the global economy. The Great Recession of 2008 marked the onset of a new structural crisis of overaccumulation. Transnational corporations are awash in cash. Corporations have reported record profits yet don't find opportunities to profitably reinvest these profits (Robinson 2018).

The TCC turned to several mechanisms to sustain accumulation in the face of stagnation. One is militarized accumulation, as the TCC acquires a vested interest in war, conflict, and repression as a means of accumulation. A second is the sacking and pillaging of public finances and cycles of public debt, reflecting a more general transformation of capitalist state finance. Predatory transnational finance capital extracts ever-greater amounts of surplus value from labor via public finances recycled as bailouts, subsidies, and the issuance of bonds. Capitalist state finance has been reconfigured to reduce or even eliminate the state's role in social reproduction and to expand its role in facilitating transnational capital accumulation. A third mechanism is frenetic financial speculation in the global financial casino. Fictitious capital now so exceeds the real output of goods and services that a new collapse of devastating proportions would appear all but assured. Although they helped keep the global economy sputtering forward, all three of these mechanisms have further aggravated inequalities, overaccumulation, and political conflict as the social fabric collapses around the world. But now it appears that the TCC has placed its bets on a new round of worldwide economic restructuring and profit making through digitalization. What effect will digitalization have on inequality and overaccumulation?

DIGITALIZATION, THE GLOBAL PRECARIAT, AND SURPLUS HUMANITY

Proletarianization worldwide has accelerated through new waves of primitive accumulation as billions of people have been dispossessed and thrown into the global labor market (see further). The global wage labor force doubled from some 1.5 billion in 1980 to some 3 billion in 2006, as workers from China, India, and the former Soviet bloc entered the global labor pool (Freeman 2010). These workers have entered the wage labor force at a time when labor markets have been deregulated. Spatial reorganization has helped transnational capital to break the territorial-bound power of organized labor and impose new capital-labor relations based on fragmentation, flexibilization, and the cheapening of labor. As workers become "flexible," they joined the ranks of a new global "precariat" of proletarians who labor under part-time, temporary, informalized, non-unionized, contract, and other forms of precarious work.[6]

This fragmentation of labor markets has been made possible, in part, by digitalization. The tech sector is now at the cutting edge of capitalist globalization, driving the digitalization of the entire global economy on the basis of a more advanced computer and information technology (CIT), the collection, processing, analysis of data ("big data"), and the application of digitalization to every aspect of the global economy, including to production, services, and finance, as well as to systems of warfare, social control, and repression. This rise of the digital economy responds in important part to earlier cycles of capitalist development and crisis, especially the downturn of the 1970s, then the boom of the 1990s followed by the dot-com bust and global recession in 2000–2001, and then the global financial collapse of 2008 and its aftermath. The tech sector has become a major new outlet for uninvested capital in the face of stagnation and overaccumulation. Investment in the IT sector jumped from $17 billion in 1970s to $175 billion in 1990, then to $496 billion in 2000. It then dipped following the turn-of-century dot-com bust, only to climb up to new heights after 2008, surpassing $700 billion as 2017 drew to a close.[7]

The first generation of capitalist globalization from the 1980s on involved the creation of a globally integrated production and financial system, whereas more recently digitalization and the rise of "platforms" have facilitated a very rapid transnationalization of services. Platforms refer to digital infrastructures that enable two or more groups to interact. As the dependence of economic activity on platforms spreads, the tech sector becomes ever more strategic to global capitalism. Trade in CIT goods in 2015 exceeded $2 trillion, according to United Nations data, while CIT services exports rose by 40% between 2010 and 2015. In that year, production of CIT goods and services represented 6.5% of global GDP and 100 million people were employed in the CIT service sector. Moreover, global e-commerce sales reached $25 trillion as 380 million people made purchases on overseas websites (UNCTAD 2017, 17). By 2017, services accounted for some 70% of the total gross world produce (Mariois 2017) and included communications, informatics, digital and platform technology, e-commerce, financial services, professional and technical work, and a host of other nontangible products such as film and music.

We are set for the digital decimation of major sectors of the global economy. Anything can be digitalized, and this is increasingly almost everything. Automation is now spreading from industry and finance to all branches of services, even to fast food and agriculture. Neoliberal economists and policymakers claim that the digital economy will bring high-skilled and high-paid jobs. Yet, evidence suggests that digitalization will accelerate the trend toward mass un- and under-employment as near laborless production expands throughout the economy alongside increased precarious and casualized forms of employment for those that continue to work, as members of the TCC seek to lower wages, to eliminate workers, and to out-compete one another. In the short term, digitalization may expand opportunities for accumulation and allow for a new round of fixed capital expansion. But ultimately, digitalization to the extent that it replaces labor with technology pushes costs down toward zero. All of the contradictions of capitalism become intensified. The rate of profit decreases. The realization problem is aggravated. Hence, the emerging digital economy cannot resolve the problem of overaccumulation.

In the United States, for instance, the net increase in jobs since 2005 has been almost exclusively in unstable and usually low paid work arrangements.

Precarious labor is predicated on so-called flextime, which as Starzmann notes, often means nothing other than a non-stop work schedule. On-call temp workers are rapidly replacing regular staff in retail, delivery, restaurant, and hospitality work in the United States (Bhattarai 2018). Amazon, with a workforce of 230,000 and tens of thousands of seasonal workers, is notorious for brutal sweatshop-like labor conditions in its warehouses and logistical networks, described as "the future of low-wage work" (meanwhile, Amazon chief executive officer (CEO) Jeff Bezos became the richest man in the world in 2017, with a net worth of over $100 billion, while thousands of Amazon employees require food stamps to make ends meet) (Jamieson 2015; Edwards 2013).[8] Indeed, digital-driven production seeks to lower wage, capital, and overhead costs—ultimately to achieve what the Nike Corporation refers to as "engineering the labor out of the product" (Ford 2015).[9] Revealingly, the U.S. labor market added 9.1 million jobs between 2005 and 2015, including 9.4 million precarious jobs, so that the net increase in jobs since 2005 has been solely in these unstable work arrangements (Srnicek 2017, 79). A billion dollar data center build in 2011 by Apple in North Carolina created a mere 50 full-time positions (Ford 2015, 107). In the Philippines, 100,000 outsourced workers earn a few hundred dollars a month searching through the content on social media such as Google and Facebook and in cloud storage to remove offensive images (Chen 2014). Yet they too stand to be replaced by digital technology, as do millions of call center, data entry and software workers around the world, along with their counterparts in manufacturing and in other service sector jobs.[10]

It had already become evident in the late 20th century that the restructuring of world capitalism associated with globalization and CIT has involved a polarization of the working class between those whose work has been deskilled and routinized and those who moved into the ranks of so-called knowledge workers engaged in high-skilled (and allegedly high-paid) labor. These workers are what Robert Reich called "symbolic analysts" and others have referred to as those performing immaterial labor (Reich 1992). However, digitalization brings about the expanded commodification of cognitive labor and the proletarianization and precariatization of those who perform such labor. This process involves the real subsumption of cognitive labor. Formal subsumption refers to the process by which people are separated from their means of survival or production, such as land or small businesses, so that they are forced to work for capital, whereas real subsumption refers to the subordination of workers into the capitalist production process as it is directly controlled by capital in the factory, the plantation, service sector, or in this case, through control over immaterial labor through the internet. Real subsumption involves the total corporeal discipline, oppression, and domination of labor, so that one loses whatever is left of individual power and autonomy, incorporated, in Marx's words, as a "living appendage" into the production process.

There is an important generational dimension to these new capital-labor relations insofar as the "millennial generation" is the first to be born into a digital world in which precarious work is becoming the norm and which could become *normalized* in the absent a class-conscious movement against precariatization. The 20th-century social contract that regulated work is a thing of the past for many, perhaps most of the millennial generation born between 1980 and the turn of century, and even more so the next generation that some have referred to as "Generation Y,"[11] this at a time when the global working class increasingly resembles a global army of youth. "While countries across Europe and East Asia are grappling with declining birthrates and aging populations, societies across the Middle East, Africa, and South Asia are experiencing youth booms of staggering proportions," noted one 2016 report. "More than half of Egypt's labor force is younger than age 30. Half of Nigeria's population of 167 million is between the ages of 15 and 34. In Afghanistan, Chad, East Timor, Niger, Somalia, and Uganda, more than two-thirds of the population is under the age of 25" and 300 million Indians were under the age of 15 (Lord 2016). The global youth face a wave of labor-replacing technology and the real prospects of laborless production. At the same time, global marketing tantalizes youth with an endless stream of products and services. How will the youth of today respond politically to the contradiction of being swept up in this ubiquitous "culture-ideology of consumerism" and the reality of unemployment and poverty?[12]

Young knowledge workers in particular are set to swell the ranks of the increasingly impoverished and alienated digital proletariat. An increasing portion of this proletariat labors by supplying "on-demand" digital services online, what is sometimes dubbed the "human cloud." While neoliberal economists and policymakers refer to them as "self-employed entrepreneurs," they are in effect outsourced contract workers laboring in the absence of any job stability or income security, entirely at the whim of those who contract them. Firms such as Freelancer.com and UpWork contracted more than five million people to work remotely online in 2017. Such "micro-work" sites as Mechanical Turk, a service operated by Amazon, contracts some 500,000 "Turkers" who earn a few cents for each task performed (*The Economist* 2017).[13] "All across the world," notes Starzmann, "uncountable solitary figures have committed themselves to lives in front of screens, fingers moving across keyboards ceaselessly—thinking, typing, producting" (Starzmann 2018). And Bradley and Lee warn that the "revolutionary energy [of this young digital proletariat] is spent elsewhere—on computer games, porn, gambling, endless forms of intoxication to escape the reality of the working day" (Bradley and Taek-Gwan 2018, 642).

Here we need to explore the implications of such a shift for consciousness and for what Pierre Bourdieu has termed habitus, as "an acquired system of generative schemes" adjusted to a given set of social conditions (Bordieu 1977, 95). The development of inter-subjectivities and class consciousness is impeded by the individuated and isolated nature of much cognitive labor. What type of a worldview may come out of this work absent in some political mobilization outside of the work process? Cognitive workers may be more inclined to identify with middle and professional strata rather than with the global working class to which most belong. Fragmentation of the labor process and of work into scattered and irregular moments of labor-power throws up new challenges to the organization of the working class and to the development of working-class consciousness. Certainly, any emancipatory project in order for it to succeed would have to bring together surplus humanity and their struggles in the margins and at points of social reproduction with those formally inserted into the circuits of global capital under precarious work arrangements.

FROM LUPENPROLETARIAT TO LUMPENPRECARIAT

In the broader picture, the global working class brings together those exploited more intensively through precarious and casualized employment with those excluded. Digitalization, in addition to generating precarious forms of employment, is expected to exponentially increase the surplus labor population. The "jobless future" and the "rise of robots" that replace human workers are the commonplace topics among academics, journalists, and politicians. Millions of people expelled from formal employment have managed to scratch out a living through Uber and other "platform companies" as informal and "self-employed" workers. But in 2016, Uber announced that it would replace one million drivers with autonomously driven vehicles (Mitchell and Lien 2016). Foxcomm, the Taiwanese-based conglomerate that assembles Ipads and other electronic devices, announced in 2012 following a wave of strikes by its workers in China that it would replace one million workers with robots. As productivity increases the system sheds more and more workers. In 1990, the top three carmakers in Detroit had a market capitalization of $36 billion and 1.2 million employees. In 2014, the top three firms in Silicon Valley, with a market capitalization of over $1 trillion, had only 137,000 employees (The Economist 2016, 9).

As digitalization concentrates capital and heightens polarization and inequality, the process expands the ranks of surplus labor. Surplus humanity toils in all sorts of survival strategies in the informal world of a "planet of slums." The informal sector has always been functionally linked to the formal sector in a myriad of ways, including as a bastion of social reproduction and for the provision of services to the formal sector (Manuel and Portes 1989).[14] Yet under globalization, the lines between formality and informality become ever more blurred. Surplus humanity is of no *direct* use to transnational capital. However, in the larger picture, surplus labor is crucial to global capitalism insofar as it places downward pressure on wages everywhere and allows transnational capital to impose heightened discipline over those who remain active in the labor market. "The overwork of the employed part of the working-class swells the ranks of the reserve," notes Marx, "whilst conversely the greater pressure that the latter by its competition exerts on the former, forces these to submit to over-work and to subjugation under the dictates of capital" (Marx 1972, 425). However, the restructuring of world capitalism through globalization has given rise to a new global army of superfluous labor that goes well beyond the traditional reserve army of labor that Marx discussed. The processes by which surplus labor is generated have accelerated under globalization.

Crises provide capital with the opportunity to restructure and to accelerate the process of forcing greater productivity out of fewer workers—a process that may increase exponentially through digitalization. At the same time, there has been a massive new round of primitive accumulation and displacement of hundreds of millions, perhaps billions, around the world. The TCC undertook hyper-accumulation in recent decades by applying new CIT technologies to organize a globally integrated production and financial system, and through neoliberal policies, and new modalities of mobilizing and exploiting a global labor force. The TCC conquered new markets in hothouse fashion in the former Soviet Union, Eastern Europe, and the Third World. Several hundred million new middle-class consumers in China, India, and elsewhere in the so-called emerging countries provided new global market segments that fueled growth. But at the same time, hundreds of millions, perhaps billions, of people, were displaced from the Third World countryside through new rounds of primitive accumulation brought about by neoliberal policies as well as social cleansing, and organized violence such as the "war on drugs" and the "war on terror," both of which have served as instruments of primitive accumulation and for the violent restructuring and integration of countries and regions into the new global economy (Paley 2014)[15] Banks and institutional investors began vast new land grabs around the world in the second decade of the 21st century in what amounts to a new round of global enclosures.

All this has generated a vast army of internal and transnational immigrants who have swelled the ranks of the unemployed and the structurally marginalized. In 2015, there were 232 million international migrants and 740 internal migrants, according to the International Organization on Migration.[16] Some of the uprooted millions are super-exploited through incorporation into the global factories, farms, and offices as precarious labor, while others are marginalized and converted into surplus humanity, relegated to a "planet of slums" (Davis 2006).[17] The ILO reported that 1.53 billion workers around the world were in such "vulnerable" employment arrangements in 2009, representing more than 50% of the global workforce, while another one-third of the global labor forces have been made superfluous and locked out of the global economy.[18] Together, some 80% of the global labor force is either surplus or employed precariously.

Let us revisit accumulation crisis and link it to this expansion of surplus labor worldwide. Capitalist competition and class struggle push capital to reduce costs or increase productivity by increasing the organic composition of capital, which leads to the tendency for the rate of profit to fall (Marx 1978). This tendency, the "most fundamental law" of political economy, is expressed as overaccumulation crisis. It is worth quoting Marx at length with regard to how capitalist production of necessity constantly reproduces an "industrial reserve army" or "surplus population" because the creation and expansion of this surplus population is the central background factor to understanding unprecedented inequality worldwide, the expansion of surplus humanity through a new round of global capitalist restructuring based on digitalization, and looming global crisis:

> It is capitalistic accumulation itself that constantly produces, and produces in direct ratio of its own energy and extent, a relatively redundant population of laborers, i.e., a population of greater extent than suffices for the average needs of the self-expansion of capital, and therefore a surplus population. The laboring population therefore produces, along with the accumulation of capital produced by it, the means by which itself is made relatively superfluous, is turned into a relative surplus population; and it does this to an always increasing extent. . . . This increase is effected by the simple process that constantly "sets free" a part of the laborers; by methods which lessen the number of laborers employed in proportion to the increased production. The whole form of the movement of modern industry depends, therefore, upon the constant transformation of a part of the laboring population into unemployed or half-employed hands. . . . But the greater this reserve army in proportion to the active labor-army, the greater is the mass of a consolidated surplus-population, whose misery is in inverse ratio to its torment of labor. The more extensive, finally, the lazarus-layers of the working-class, and the industrial reserve army, the greater is official pauperism. *This is the absolute general law of capitalist accumulation.* (Marx 1972, 422–430)

The constantly replenished reserve army of labor to the pulse of capital accumulation is for Marx "the general law of capitalist accumulation." Marx goes on to identify three forms of surplus labor: floating, latent, and stagnant. The first two were seen as those who weave in and out of the production process in accordance with the cycles of capital accumulation and changes in the division of labor. The third, however, is a group that has been pushed structurally outside of the production process, that is, which is of no *direct* use to capital over entire historical epochs. Marx tended to denigrate those in this latter category as lumpenproletariat. But given that digitalization, to the extent that it replaces labor with technology, has the potential to drastically reduce the need for labor ("variable capital" in Marx's lexicon) and to push costs toward zero, it may be that the expansion worldwide of the ranks of surplus humanity worldwide is a permanent structural phenomenon of global capitalism rather than a transitory dislocation pending absorption into new circuits of accumulation.

The concept of the lumpenproletariat has an important etiology in the history of capitalism. Marx first discussed the lumpenproletariat in derogatory terms as a *déclassé* and degenerated element among the proletariat—prostitutes, vagabonds, petty criminals—an underclass without a class consciousness and prone to serving as "a bribed tool of reactionary intrigue." In *The Eighteenth Brumaire of Louis Napoleon*, he describes the lumpenproletariat as "vagabonds, discharged soldiers, discharged jailbirds, escaped galley slaves, swindlers, mountebanks, lazzaroni, pickpockets, tricksters, gamblers, pimps, brothel keepers, porters, literati, organ grinders, ragpickers, knife grinders, tinkers, beggars—in short, the whole indefinite, disintegrated mass, thrown hither and thither" by capitalism (Marx 1952, 38). However, some of the negative connotations of the lumpenproletariat fell away in the mid-20th century as it became clear that racism, colonialism, and imperialism thrust hundreds of millions of their victims into the ranks of the displaced, the unemployed, and the excluded. Lumpenproletariat now appeared as a structural (and sometimes legal) location of marginality and informality in the world capitalist system with a contingent political agency. In *The Wretched of the Earth*, Franz Fanon referred to the lumpenproletariat as displaced peasants who constituted a potentially revolutionary force against the colonial system, although he warned that it is unpredictable and could as well turn into hired soldiers of the colonialists (Fanon 1963, 130). In the United States, the Black Panthers sought to organize the black lumpenproletariat as a mass social base, although this strategy was not without its limitations and its critics (Booker 2005).[19]

But now in this age of capitalist globalization, surplus humanity may be an analytically as well as politically superior concept to make sense of that mass of humanity thrown into the margins of the system. While there is certainly a delinquent element among the mass of humanity that has been "thrown hither and tither" by the destabilization of global capital, surplus humanity appears to be a structural category thrown up by an accelerated restructuring and a more advanced stage of global capital accumulation. Surplus humanity includes those who suffer from long-term structural un- and under-employment; the mass of people who eke out a living (or don't even manage to do so) in the informal economy of the slums of the world's megacities, as well as international refugees, those internally displaced by wars, repression, and natural disasters; and migrant workers who may be forced underground and unable to enter the formal labor market, among others, who exist in what Bradley and Lee call the "non-places of the world." In this regard, surplus humanity exists in conjunction with the precariat and may weave in and out of more formal yet precarious employment. "It is clear that 200 years after the birth of Marx, the composition of the lumpenproletariat has changed from 'vagabonds, criminals, prostitutes,' pariahs and untouchables, to precarious workers, a working poor, to contract staff, day staff, zero hour contract staff, and more desperately to the underclass or permanent underclass," observe Bradley and Lee. I concur with their political assessment: "Marx's distinction between the revolutionary laboring poor and the reactionary lumpenproletariat no longer holds under the global conditions of contemporary exploitation" (Bradley and Taek-Gwan 2018, 639–646). *Lumpenprecariat* captures the idea of a global working class that brings the precariat together with surplus humanity.

CONCLUSION: THE STRUGGLE AGAINST GLOBAL POLICE STATE

It is this lumpenprecariat that so terrifies the likes of Johann Rupert and the TCC and that gives impetus to a global police state to contain the real and potential rebellion of the lumpenprecariat. Savage global inequalities are politically explosive and to the extent that the system is simply unable to incorporate surplus humanity, it turns to every more violent forms of containment, captured in the concept of global police state.[20] Global police state refers to three interrelated developments. First is the ever more omnipresent systems of mass social control, repression, and warfare promoted by the ruling groups to contain the real and the potential rebellion of the global working class and surplus humanity. In this regard, global police state is centrally aimed at *coercive exclusion* of surplus humanity. Second is how the global economy is itself based more and more on the development and deployment of these systems of warfare, social control, and repression simply as a means of making profit and continuing to accumulate capital in the face of stagnation—what I have termed *militarized accumulation* or *accumulation by repression*—and that now goes well beyond military

Keynesianism. And third is the increasing move toward political systems that can be characterized as 21st-century fascism, or even in a broader sense, as totalitarian.

There is a critical spatial dimension to capitalist restructuring worldwide and to global police state. The restructuring of space facilitated by digitalization is captured by the notion of global green zoning. "Green zone" refers to the nearly impenetrable area in central Baghdad that U.S. occupation forces established in the wake of the 2003 invasion of Iraq. The command center of the occupation and select Iraqi elite inside that green zone were protected from the violence and chaos that engulfed the country. Urban areas around the world are now green zoned through gentrification, gated communities, surveillance systems, and state and private violence. Inside the world's green zones, elites and privileged middle and professional strata avail themselves of privatized social services, consumption, and entertainment. They can work and communicate through internet and satellite sealed off under the protection of armies of soldiers, police, and private security forces.

In between green zones and those of outright warfare, policing and other forms of containment become normalized against the lumpenprecariat subject to repressive discipline. This is the so-called *gray zone*, where much of humanity is coming to reside. Global police state centers around the gray zone. Here is where we find the prison-industrial complexes, immigration and refugee control systems, mass surveillance, ubiquitous, often paramilitarized policing, and the mobilization of the culture industries and state ideological apparatuses that dehumanize victims of global capitalism as dangerous, depraved, and undeserving at the same time as they inculcate petty consumerism and flight into fantasy. A neofascist culture emerges through militarism, misogyny, extreme masculinization, and racism. Such a culture generates a climate conducive to mass violence, often directed against the racially oppressed, ethnically persecuted, religious minorities, immigrants, refugees, and other vulnerable communities.

Ruling groups have turned to the social cleansing of surplus humanity through criminalization, as is the case with the bogus wars on drugs and terror. In many cases, criminalization makes surplus humanity *both* a structural and a legal location, as in the legal criminalization of immigrant workers in the United States. In Denmark, the government announced in 2018 plans to legalize discrimination against poor and immigrant communities through a bill that would set apart as "ghettos" communities where more than 50% of residents are non-Western immigrants, where unemployment is above 40%, and where the average income is less than 55% of the average for the region.[21] The United Nations Special Rapporteur on Extreme Poverty and Human Rights, Philip Alston, warned in a 2017 report on poverty and inequality in the United States:

> In many cities, homeless persons are effectively criminalized for the situation in which they find themselves. Sleeping rough, sitting in public spaces, panhandling, public urination and a myriad of other offenses have been devised to attach the 'blight' of homelessness. Even more demanding and intrusive regulations lead to infraction notices, which rapidly turn into misdemeanors, leading to the issuance of warrants, incarceration, the incurring of unpayable fines, and the stigma of a criminal conviction that in turn virtually prevents subsequent employment and access to most housing. (Alston 2018)

There is a dangerous spiral here in the contradiction between a digitalization that throws ever more workers into the ranks of surplus humanity and the need for the system to unload ever-greater amounts of accumulated surplus. Once masses of people are no longer needed on a long term and even permanent basis, there arises the political problem of how to control this expanded mass of surplus humanity. Greater discipline is required, both for those who manage to secure work under new regimes of precarious employment and super-exploitation and for those expelled and made surplus. The global order as a unity becomes increasingly repressive and authoritarian as a project of 21st-century fascism gains traction.[22]

But the fears of Rupert and the TCC are not unfounded. There has been an upsurge of workers struggles and strike activities around the world in recent years. Yet as we have seen, the global working class looks nothing like it did in the mid-20th century. Its lumpenprecariat position changes the terms of its struggles and the challenges of regenerating working-class consciousness and a collective action capacity. Any fight back will have to challenge exclusion and struggle against precarious work arrangements alongside the more traditional struggles of those that may be formally employed. The repertoire of global working-class struggles must involve strategies, in addition to strike activity, for the widespread disruption of the system, as those excluded cannot fight by withdrawing their labor. The conditions that the lumpenprecariat face, combined with the isolation and individuated nature of cognitive workers, suggest that the axis of class consciousness and collective agency surely must involve a shift from isolated points of production to communities and the political system. The challenge for emancipatory projects is how to achieve solidarity among workers who experience such individuated isolation along with those who are not in a position to withdraw their labor and those who face extreme vulnerability in precarious employment.

There is both a danger and a silver lining to the restructuring of the global working class and the devastation wrought on it by capitalist globalization. Those sectors that saw rising standards of living in the post–World War II period are now experiencing under capitalist globalization downward mobility, heightened insecurity, and precariatization that threaten to undo the hegemonic blocs forged in the 20th century in the rich countries through the incorporation of these sectors. When reform-oriented transnational elites bemoan the "loss of the middle class," they are referring to the destabilization of these formerly privileged sectors among the working class and to the erosion of the earlier hegemonic blocs. The erosion of such hegemonic blocs creates fertile ground for counter-hegemonic struggles but it also creates ground for the recruitment of such destabilized sectors into right-wing populist and neofascist projects. The threat of neofascism poses the need for broad class alliances, or united front politics. Historically such fronts have subordinated the left to the reform-oriented and "democratic" bourgeoisie. This time around, in my view, any strategy of broad antifascist alliances must foreground a clear and sharp analysis of global capitalism and its crisis, and strive for popular and working-class forces to exercise their hegemony over such alliances.

Splits and infighting within the ruling groups are escalating as the global capitalist historic bloc unravels. Reformists among the transnational elite, concerned over the fragility of the global economy, have called for mildly redistributive measures and introduction of transnational regulation of the global financial system.[23] They have also expressed concern over the prospects of 21st-century fascism and alarm that extreme levels of inequality will undermine the prospects for growth and profit making and fuel popular revolt. "Doing nothing, in the current model around capitalism, will destroy capitalism," warned in 2017 Mark Bertolini, the CEO of Aetna, a $250 billion healthcare company. "When 65 percent of people under the age of 35 believe that socialism is a better model, we have a problem. So unless we change it, it will change—and maybe not in a good way" (Leaf 2018). These concerns may become more widespread as the systems spirals into deeper crisis. "A crisis exists, sometimes lasting for decades," observed Gramsci. "This means that incurable contradictions have come to light within the structure and that the political force positively working to preserve the structure itself are nevertheless striving to heal these contradictions, within certain limits" (Gramsci 2016, 23–24).

Yet these reformists seem to be losing ground as the crisis intensifies. Rather than reform, the principal transnational capitalist conglomerates seem to be searching for how to turn crisis into new opportunities for accumulation. "The world is dividing into two blocs—the Plutonomy and the rest," noted the 2005 Citigroup report mentioned earlier. This plutonomy "is here, is going to get stronger, its membership swelling from globalized enclaves in the emerging world" (Citigroup 2005). Yet the report by one of the largest financial conglomerates in the world was written not as a warning over the social or political consequences of global inequalities but in order to unabashedly highlight investment opportunities made possible by concentration of the world's wealth among a tiny portion of humanity. Inequality, domination, and immiseration lead to new accumulation strategies for transnational capital. Similarly, in her book, *The Shock Doctrine*, Klein has shown how the TCC intervenes in natural and social catastrophes to dispossess communities and further its control (Klein 2008).

While alliances with reformers among the transnational elite may be important, so too is pushing beyond the reformist approach to global inequality. This approach is entirely inadequate because it bypasses the questions of *power* and of corporate control over the planet's productive resources that are at the very heart of global capitalism and its crisis. Any resolution to this crisis requires a radical redistribution of wealth and power downward to the poor majority of humanity. Social justice requires a measure of transnational social governance over the global production and financial system as a necessary first step in this radical redistribution, which, in turn, must be linked to the transformation of class and property relations and a struggle for what ultimately be an eco-socialism While I cannot take up here these larger matters, part of counter-hegemonic struggle is the interrogation of how forms of class and social consciousness have been shaped by exclusion, precariatization, and the individuated nature of work and life under digital capitalism, as well as the challenges to emancipatory struggles posed these capital-labor relations.

NOTES

1. Transcript of interview by *Real News Network*, 9 May 2018, accessed on 17 June 2018 at https://therealnews.com/stories/the-rich-have-escape-plan.

2. Citigroup, "Plutonomy: Buying Luxury, Explaining Global Imbalances," 16 October 2005, pp. 10, accessed on 17 June 2018 at https://delong.typepad.com/plutonomy-1.pdf.

3. Oxfam (London), *Wealth: Having It All and Wanting More*, on line report accessed on 4 March 2018, at the Oxfam website, http://policy-practice.oxfam.org.uk/publications/wealth-having-it-all-and-wanting-more-338125.

4. There is a great deal of good literature on Fordism and Keynesianism. David Harvey's *The Condition of Post-Modernity* (Cambridge, MA: Blackwell, 1990), although somewhat outdated, remains for me an important statement on the subject. See also: Ash Amin, ed., *Post-Fordism: A Reader* (Cambridge, MA: Blackwell, 1994), Robert W. Cox, *Production, Power, and World Order: Social Forces in the Making of History* (New York: Colombia University Press, 1987); William I. Robinson, *Global Capitalism and the Crisis of Humanity* (New York: Cambridge University Press, 2014).

5. Thomas Piketty demonstrates these swings in the profit rate in *Capital in the Twenty-First Century* (Cambridge, MA: Harvard University Press, 2014), figure 6.8, p. 227.

6. Guy Standing, *The Precariat: The New Dangerous Class* (New York: Bloomsbury, 2011) popularized but did not coin this term. But Standing's social democratic conception is seriously flawed. He suggests that the precariat is "a new class" rather than part of the working class experiencing a condition faced by expanding sectors of the working class. He does not conceive of this condition as an instance of the capital-labor relation. He takes a First World/Eurocentric view of the global precariat—what we could call "methodological Westernism"—and appears unable to combine class with racial, ethnic, and cultural analysis. His liberal orientation does not critique *capital* as a relation causal to the rise of the precariat as much as the state as an inadequate regulator of the market and its social consequences.

7. "Private Fixed Investment in Information Processing Equipment and Software," Federal Reserve Bank of St. Louis, 2017, graph compiled from U.S. Bureau of Economic Analysis, accessed on 2 February 2018 at https://fred.stlouisfed.org/series/A679RC1Q027SBEA.

8. See, for example: Dave Jamieson, "The Life and Death of an Amazon Warehouse Temp," *The Huffington Post*, 21 October 2015, accessed on 2 September 2017 at http://highline.huffingtonpost.com/articles/en/life-and-death-amazon-temp/; Jim Edwards "Brutal Conditions in Amazon's Warehouses Threaten to Ruin the Company's Image," *Business Insider*, 5 August 2013, accessed on 2 September 2017 at http://www.businessinsider.com/brutal-conditions-in-amazons-warehouses-2013-8.

9. As cited in Martin Ford, *The Rise of the Robots* (New York: Basic Books, 2015)

10. The report by the United Nations Conference on Trade and Development (UNCTAD*), Information Economy Report, 2017* (UNCTAD: Geneva, 2017), estimated (p. 62) that more than 85% of all retails and service workers in Indonesia and the Philippines were at risk of losing their jobs to digital automation.

11. See "The Trials of Generation Y," *The Guardian*, series published in March and April 2016, multi-authored, accessed on June 17 2018 at https://www.theguardian.com/world/series/millennials-the-trials-of-generation-y.

12. In the United States and perhaps elsewhere, higher education is becoming a strategy for deferring unemployment. There has been an unprecedented increase in university enrollment of over five million since 2001 and enrollment numbers are expected to climb another 15% by 2015, while the price for tuition and fees has jumped 157% in private institutions and 237% in public schools (see Maresi Starzmann, "Academic Alienation: Freeing Cognitive Labor from the Grip of Capitalism," *ROAR Magazine*, 2 June 2018, accessed on 15 June 2018 from https://roarmag.org/essays/academic-alienation-cognitive-labor-capitalism/). Student debt approached $1.5 trillion in 2018, over twice the total U.S. credit card debt (this figure for 2018 is from unauthored, "A Look at the Shocking Student Loan Debt Statistics for 2018," *Student Loan Hero*, accessed on 15 June 2018 from https://studentloanhero.com/student-loan-debt-statistics/. See Susanne Soederberg's brilliant analysis in *Debtfare States and the Poverty Industry: Money, Discipline, and the Surplus Population* (New York: Routledge, 2014), chapter 5, "Debtfarism and the Student Loan Industry."). This debt is a claim on the future wages of these students, and in at least 20 states, debtors can be denied drivers licenses and professional licenses if they

do not maintain debt payments. Their precarious situation creates the conditions for lives as precarious workers in the future.

13. For these details, see "Digital Labor: The Human Cumulus," *The Economist*, 2017.

14. See, inter alia, discussion in Manuel Castells and Alejandro Portes, eds., *The Informal Economy: Studies in Advanced and Less Developed Countries* (Baltimore: Johns Hopkins University Press, 1989).

15. See, for example, Dawn Paley, *Drug War Capitalism* (Oakland: AK Press, 2014).

16. *World Migration Report 2015* (IOM: Geneva, 2015), p. 2.

17. The phrase is from Mike Davis, *Planet of Slums* (London: Verso, 2006).

18. For the figure on those in vulnerable employment, see International Labor Organization, *Global Employment Trends 2011: The Challenge of Job Recovery* (Geneva, ILO, 2011). For the figure on the unemployed, see International Labor Organization (ILO), *World Employment Report 1996–97,* (Geneva: ILO/United Nations, 1997).

19. See Chris Booker, "Lumpenization: A Critical Error of the Black Panther Party," in Charles E. Jones, *The Black Panther Party Reconsidered* (Baltimore: Black Classic Press, 2005).

20. I have developed this concept in: William I. Robinson, "Accumulation Crisis and Global Police State," *Critical Sociology*, March 2018, on-line edition available here: http://journals.sagepub.com/doi/abs/10.1177/0896920518757054; William I. Robinson, "The Next Economic Crisis: Digital Capitalism and Global Police State," *Race and Class*, May 2018, on-line edition, available here: http://journals.sagepub.com/doi/abs/10.1177/0306396818769016.

21. "Denmark Plans Double Punishment for Ghetto Crime" *BBC News*, 27 February 2018, accessed on 16 June 2018 at https://www.bbc.com/news/world-europe-43214596.

22. See Robinson, *Global Capitalism and the Crisis of Humanity*, Chapter five, "Policing Global Capitalism."

23. For detailed discussion, see William I. Robinson, "Capital*ism* in the Twenty-First Century: Global Inequality, Piketty, and the Transnational Capitalist Class," in Lauren Langman and David A. Smith (eds.), *Piketty, Inequality and 21st Century Capitalism* (Boston: Brill, 2018).

BIBLIOGRAPHY

Bhattarai, Abha. 2018. "Side Hustles Go Mainstream," *Los Angeles Times*, 21 May 2018, p. A10.

Booker, Chris. 2005. "Lumpenization: A Critical Error of the Black Panther Party," in Charles E. Jones, *The Black Panther Party Reconsidered* (Baltimore: Black Classic Press, 2005), pp. 337–362.

Bourdieu, Pierre. 1977. *Outline of a Theory of Practice* (Cambridge: Cambridge University Press, 1977), p. 95.

Bradley, Joff P.N. and Alex Taek-Gwan. 2018. "On the Lumpen-Precariat-To-Come," *TripleC*, 16(2), 2018: 639–646, quote from p. 642.

Castells, Manuel and Alejandro Portes. 1989. eds., The Informal Economy: Studies in Advanced and Less Developed Countries (Baltimore: Johns Hopkins University Press, 1989).

Chen, Adrian. 2014. "The Laborers who Keep Dick Pics and Beheadings Out of Your Facebook Feed," Wired, 23 October 2014, accessed on 2 September 2017 at https://www.wired.com/2014/10/content-moderation/.

Citigroup. 2005. "Plutonomy: Buying Luxury, Explaining Global Imbalances," 16 October 2005, p. 2, accessed on 17 June 2018, at https://delong.typepad.com/plutonomy-1.pdf.

Davis, Mike. 2006. Planet of Slums (London: Verso, 2006).

Fanon, Franz. 1963. *The Wretched of the Earth* (New York: Grove Press, 1963), p. 130.

Ford, Martin. 2015. The Rise of the Robots (New York: Basic Books, 2015), pp. 107, 19, 12.

Freeman, Richard. 2010. "The Great Doubling: The Challenge of the New Global Labor Market," The Globalist online magazine, March 5, 2010. Online: http://www.theglobalist.com/StoryId.aspx?StoryId=4542.

Gramsci, Antonio. 2016. as cited in Marco Fonseca, *Gramsci's Critique of Civil Society* (New York: Routledge, 2016), pp. 23–24.

Jamieson, Dave. 2017."The Life and Death of an Amazon Warehouse Temp," *The Huffington Post*, 21 October 2015, accessed on 2 September 2017 at http://highline.huffingtonpost.com/articles/en/life-and-death-amazon-temp/; Jim Edwards. 2017 "Brutal Conditions in Amazon's Warehouses Threaten to Ruin the Company's Image," *Business Insider*, 5 August 2013, accessed on 2 September 2017 at http://www.businessinsider.com/brutal-conditions-in-amazons-warehouses-2013-8.

Lord, Kristin. 2016. "Here Come the Young," *Foreign Policy*, 12 August 2016, accessed on 16 June 2018 at http://foreignpolicy.com/2016/08/12/here-comes-the-young-youth-bulge-demographics/.

Mariois, Thomas. 2017"TiSA and the Threat to Public Banks," *Transnational Institute* (Amsterdam), April 2017, accessed on 2 February 2018 at https://www.tni.org/files/publication-downloads/tisa_and_the_threat_to_public_banks.pdf.

Marx, Karl. 1972. *Capital, Volume I*, in Robert C. Tucker, ed., *The Marx-Engels Reader* (New York: W.W. Norton, 1972), p. 425.

Marx, Karl. 1978. *Capital, Vol. III* (excerpt), in Robert C. Tucker, ed., *The Marx-Engels Reader*, 2nd Edition (New York: W.W. Norton, 1978).

Marx, Karl. 1972. *Capital, Volume I*, in Robert C. Tucker, ed., *The Marx-Engels Reader* (New York: W.W. Norton, 1972), pp. 422, 424, 429–430.

Marx, Karl. 1952. *The Eighteenth Brumaire of Louis Napoleon*, 1952, p. 38, pdf of internet edition from Marxist Internet Archive, available here: https://www.marxists.org/archive/marx/works/download/pdf/18th-Brumaire.pdf.

Mitchell, Russ and Tracey Lien. 2016. "Rides in Uber Robot Vehicles at Hand," *Los Angeles Times*, 19 August 2016, p. A1.

Paley, Dawn. 2014. *Drug War Capitalism* (Oakland: AK Press, 2014).

Piketty, Thomas. 2014. Capital in the Twenty-First Century (Cambridge, MA: Harvard University Press, 2014), figure 6.8, p. 227.

Reich, Robert. 1992. The Work of Nations: Preparing Ourselves for 21st Century Capitalism (New York: Vintage, 1992); Michael Hardt and Antonio Negri, Empire (Cambridge: Harvard University Press, 2001).

Savage, Michael. 2018 "Richest 1% on Target to Own Two-Thirds of All Wealth by 2030," The Guardian, retrieved on 9 April 2018 at https://www.theguardian.com/business/2018/apr/07/global-inequality-tipping-point-2030.

Srnicek, Nick. 2017. *Platform Capitalism* (Cambridge: Polity, 2017), pp. 79, 18.

Starzmann, Maresi. 2018. "Academic Alienation: Freeing Cognitive Labor from the Grip of Capitalism," *ROAR Magazine*, 2 June 2018, accessed on 15 June 2018 from https://roarmag.org/essays/academic-alienation-cognitive-labor-capitalism/.

The Economist. 2017. "Digital Labor: The Human Cumulus," *The Economist*, 26 August 2017, p. 55.

The Economist. 2016. "A Giant Problem," 17 September 2016, p. 9.

United Nations Conference on Trade and Development (UNCTAD). 2017. *Information Economy Report, 2017* (UNCTAD: Geneva, 2017), p. 17.

William I. Robinson. 2018. "Accumulation Crisis and Global Police State," *Critical Sociology*, March 2018, on-line edition available here: http://journals.sagepub.com/doi/abs/10.1177/0896920518757054.

Withnall, Adam. 2018. "Cartier Boss with $7.5bn Fortune Says Prospect of the Poor Rising Up 'Keeps Him Awake at Night,'" *Independent*, 10 June 2015, accessed on 12 June 2018 at https://www.independent.co.uk/news/business/cartier-boss-with-75bn-fortune-says-prospect-poor-rising-up-keeps-him-awake-at-night-10307485.html.

Chapter 10

The Industrial Reserve Army in the 21st Century

An Approach to the Case of Mexico

Luis Felipe Docoa Hernández

INTRODUCTION

Nowadays, the consensus prevails that four great technological revolutions were driven by the capitalist production system. According to Schwab (2016), the Fourth Industrial Revolution is due to the implementation of: artificial intelligence, robotics, electronic commerce, autonomous vehicles, 3D printing, nanotechnology, biotechnology, materials science, energy storage, and quantum computing. Likewise, the third revolution was sparked by digital technology and instantaneous telecommunications, the second by electrification and mass production, and the first occurred with the implementation of the steam engine and the mechanization of textile production. These technological changes notably modified the participation of the labor force within production of goods and services processes, either because they intensify the labor process (e.g., early manufacturing industrialization) or because they end up completely replacing the labor force (e.g., the use of *Robotic Pickers*[1] in agricultural activities). Both processes, in general, have worsened the employment conditions of the working class, regardless of the conditions of economic development present in each nation (Smith 2016). This worsening is expressed by increased rate and duration of unemployment, lower wages, migration, greater precariousness of work, informal work, impoverishment, and so forth.

The purpose of this chapter is to update the key element of regulation in the labor market within the Marxist political economy: the *Industrial reserve army* (IRA). This category, proposed more than 150 years ago, is significant in exposing the *general law of capitalist accumulation*. The goal of this chapter is therefore to prove the continued relevance of both elements to understanding the structural dynamics of the modern labor market.

The text is divided into two parts. In the first, we set out the fundamental technical and productive relationships that determine both the level of employment and the systematic training of the IRA. Subsequently, we present the specific characteristics of the subpopulations (stagnant, floating and latent) that make up the IRA and their expression in modern employment conditions. The second part refers to the empirical aspect. This section presents a proposal to estimate the size of the IRA. The results of the model, when applied to the case of Mexico, reveal that one-third of the working-age population belongs to the IRA. Although the absolute growth of the IRA does not follow the increase of the labor force, the precariousness prevailing in both working class groups is a remarkable constant in this century.

THE RESERVE ARMY OF LABOR: TOPICALITY AND RELEVANCE

The Labor Market and the IRA

In the capitalist production system, the *social productivity of labor*, expressed in greater mechanization, is the result of competition between the different capitalists in "the struggle" to reduce the unit costs of commodities. This mechanization is understood as "a process to increase labor productivity through the use of larger quantities of machines and materials per worker" (Shaikh 2006, 414) that encourages the formation of a *relative surplus population*.

Mathematically, the increase in mechanization in the long term[2] is expressed as the increase in the elements that compose and uplift the dimension of what Marx called the *technical composition of capital*:

$$T = K/N \tag{1}$$

Where K is an index of the stock of production means and N is the number of workers who can make use of that stock (Shaikh 2006, 481). The *technical composition of capital* is decisive for the understanding, within the workplace, of: (i) the *structural and secular* trend in the employment of workforce, (ii) its relationship with technological innovations, and (iii) the volume of total employment. In this sense, Gouverneur (2005) proposes that labor productivity (π) can be estimated as the relationship between the quantity produced in a period (Q) and the number of *present* working hours (T) dedicated to production. Likewise, T is the result of the product of occupied workers *(L)* (level of employment) times the average working day *(t)*:

$$\pi = \frac{Q}{T} = \frac{Q}{L * t} \tag{2}$$

By modifying equation (2) in terms of the level of employment, we obtain:

$$Q = \pi * L * t \tag{3}$$

and

$$L = Q * \frac{1}{\pi} * \frac{1}{t} \tag{4}$$

Thus, following the author, the level of employment *(L)* of an economy will fluctuate, in the first instance, due to the movements of Q and π, with the consequence that the level of employment will be higher when production increases, and will decrease with productivity growth. Likewise, L varies according to the length of the working day *(t)* and, having an inversely proportional relationship, it is argued that the employment level (number of jobs) in an economy can increase *ceteris paribus* when the working day is reduced. In this sense, Paul Lafargue's thesis (1883)[3] gains strength since growth in productivity *(π)* can lead to moderate growth in production accompanied by a substantial reduction in working hours without affecting the level of full employment, that is, without creating unemployment. However, in the capitalist production system, a combination of full employment and reduction of the working day goes against the logic of the system itself: such a combination restricts profit and dominance over wage earners (Gouverneur 2005), negatively impacting the appropriation of surplus value and its consequent decrease in the profit rate.

In this sense, just like the *general law of capitalist accumulation*, the *law of the falling tendency of the general rate of profit*, proposed by Marx, expresses the intrinsic and necessary existence of a relative surplus population that favors the reproduction of the capitalist system. In this way, by defining the rate of profit as:

$$g = \frac{P}{c + v} \tag{5}$$

and the *organic composition of capital* as:

$$\theta = \frac{c}{c + v} \tag{6}$$

it is easy to illustrate the negative impact generated by the increase in the *organic composition of capital* (OCC)—which allows us to understand the evolution of the *technical composition* both in terms of production and in terms of value—on the profitability of production processes. Multiplying by *v* both the numerator and in the denominator, in equation 5, the results are:

$$g = \frac{P * v}{(c + v) * v} \tag{7}$$

Furthermore, if we add and subtract the product ($P * c$) in the numerator, we obtain equation 8:

$$g = \frac{P(c + v) - Pc}{(c + v) * v}$$

$$g = \frac{P}{v} - \frac{Pc}{(c + v) * v}$$

$$g = p'(1 - \theta) \tag{8}$$

In this context, as Marx pointed out in volume III, relative surplus population operates as a counteracting cause toward the *decreasing trend of the general rate of profit* thanks to the low wage costs invested in employing this surplus population; in other words, the unemployment and the general precariousness of employment conditions are necessary to guarantee minimum levels of profitability in the production of goods and services. The intensification, both in unemployment and in the precariousness of existing jobs (increase in p'), is vital to neutralize the growth of the OCC; however, as argued by Mendieta (2011), the growth of the OCC overrides in the long term the increases in the capital gain rate, *ergo* the *downward trend of the general profit rate* is confirmed.[4]

The IRA and Marx's General Law of Capitalist Accumulation

In section 4 of chapter 23 of *Capital*, entitled "Different forms of the relative surplus population: The general law of capitalist accumulation," Marx presents what can justly be understood as a labor market theory from the perspective of supply. Thus, the industrial reserve army is a theory totally in accordance with the characteristics and dynamics that the workforce presents in the development of the general law of capital accumulation to this day.

In this same chapter, Marx also argues that "every special historic mode of production has its own special laws of population, historically valid within its limits" (Marx 2013, 786). Thus—capitalism being only one mode of production among many—the labor force could present different dynamics: the labor force could be in surplus, as it is in the capitalist system; it could be null as it would be in a planned, socialist, communist economy, and so forth. And it could even be negative, as it happened at the beginning of capitalism.[5]

The relative surplus population present in capitalism was coined by Marx as the IRA; however, following the Da Silva's reasoning (2010), "the availability of work does not occur only in that sector, so the qualitative 'industrial' may be suppressed, since the important factor to highlight is the existence of workers available to hire" (p.74). Perhaps the most practical thing is to think plainly of a "reserve army" (Shaikh 2009, 84; Shaikh 2006, 67).

Traditionally, the IRA theory is the key element to explain the fluctuations of the wage quota. Oscillations, that as a general trend, always point toward a detriment in the purchasing power of actual wages, such as the direct function of the IRA. In this regard, Carcanholo (2002) describes how: "any entrepreneur knows from experience that what defines the salary they must pay is not that marginal productivity, but the length of the unemployed line waiting at their factory's, workshop's or office's door" (Carcanholo 2002, 225).

Another insight suggests that we not only address the IRA as a "result" of the capitalist accumulation process but also understand it as an essential component of this process. As Marx put it in the abovementioned chapter:

> The surplus population of workers is the necessary product of wealth accumulation or development on the capitalist basis. This overpopulation becomes, in turn, a lever for capitalist accumulation, and even a *condition of existence of the capitalist mode of production*. It constitutes an Industrial reserve army at the disposal of capital, and it belongs to it as absolutely as if it had raised it at its own expense. (Marx 2013, 786)

In our view, and taking up Singer's appraisal (1980),[6] the study of the IRA reveals a modern comprehensive theory of the labor market subject to the subpopulations (latent, floating, and stagnant populations) that comprise it. We refer to this analysis further.

Today's IRA Subpopulations

In the attempt to update the activities carried out by the subpopulations that make up the IRA, and continuing with Marx's approach, various investigations (Basu 2012; Granatto 2013; Docoa 2018) have managed to identify the different contemporary occupations performed by the IRA subpopulations, as well as their interaction with the employed population also named in *Capital* as the *Active Army*.

Thus, the *floating* population corresponds exclusively to unemployed personnel who seek to enter the labor market and whose magnitude varies according to the economic cycle: it decreases in boom times and increases during crises.[7] For its part, the *latent* population brings together, to a large extent, workers engaged in noncapitalist mercantile activities (mainly producers of self-made commodities), that is, this subpopulation includes the active labor force that is not yet fully incorporated into the capitalistic mercantile production, the same appreciation by which Marx observed the absorption of the peasant population into the manufacturing industry. In addition, the working class that would be willing to be hired under the current wages is considered within this population (migrants, prisoners, a significant part of the female workforce, etc.). Particularly in the case of the prison population, Basu (2012) argues that it deserves to be considered as part of the IRA:

> We must also look at another, often overlooked, category of workers: those undergoing incarceration. . . . This forms a small but significant part of the relative surplus population because this population is potentially available to capital; by removing them off the labor market, pressure on wages is reduced. Hence, one must include some measure of the population in prisons and jails to get a more accurate measure of the Reserve Army of Labor. (Basu 2012)

On the other hand, the *stagnant* population, which is characterized by "the maximum working time and the minimum wage" (Marx 2013, 801), is employed in activities typically belonging to what is conventionally understood by the "informal economic sector":

> The stagnant layer of the IRA is made up of all those workers with irregular occupations, almost always in the form of self-employment, as a survival strategy for prolonged or permanent periods of unemployment. The workers of the stagnant IRA are engaged in activities aimed at the capitalist market both in commerce and in industry, which differentiates them from the workers of the latent IRA. (Granato 2013, 50)

Thus, while for many Marxists, the stagnant subpopulation is equivalent to the population employed in the informal sector,[8] for the economic mainstream, this population is constituted from an opportunistic practice of a certain fraction of the working class, according to Mankiw (2015): "In deciding whether to work in the informal economy or in a legitimate job, these offenders compare what they could earn by breaking the law with the salary they could legally earn" (p. 163).

If we could in some way identify the qualitative changes in the way the various subpopulations of the IRA are employed today, it would be by assuming that the modern structure of occupation is concentrated in the service sector and not in the manufacturing sector, as Marx observed. In this sense, the expansion of mercantile-capitalist production toward other economic activities (agricultural and service industrialization)[9] reveals a greater proletarianization of the labor force, and therefore a greater number of workers in IRA conditions.

Although Marx addressed the relationship of the different subpopulations of the IRA with the needs of the accumulation process of the manufacturing sector (the most industrialized at that time), today we can understand that the IRA serves every contemporary industrial activity, be it agricultural, manufacturing, or services. In the same way, although far from being the maximum, today the worker's *formal* freedom[10] is further involved in deciding, for the sake of better living conditions, in which activity he wants to be exploited, or to become specialized. Does the young worker want to be an agronomist, a lawyer, a *gamer*, a doctor? Furthermore, each of these increasingly specialized modern activities undeniably reveals the larger gap in the division of labor that absorbs and expels labor force according to the needs of the specific accumulation process of each economic sector; thus creating a kind of RIA for each economic activity: there is an unemployed doctor (floating population), there is another doctor employed autonomously (latent population), another who is immersed in poverty (stagnant population).

In the maelstrom of *technological revolutions*, and their consecutive *labor revolutions*, it is difficult to imagine that the subpopulations of the IRA are static. We can assume certain flows between these subpopulations, the most notable of which would be the flow from unemployment (floating population) to the condition of very precarious work (stagnant population) or to the lumpenproletariat,[11] or—in the best of cases—their reentry into the Active Army (figure 10.1).

Thanks to computer and statistical advances, we can currently identify the different subpopulations that make up the IRA. This is the case of the latent population and its expression as "self-employed workers" or "employers"—conditions that have maintained an intrinsic evolution within the capital accumulation process in recent decades. However, these employment conditions work, according to Shaikh (2009), more like an army of small (or very small) individual capitals adapted to the very specific needs of large capitalist companies: the proliferation of these small capitals in different economic sectors, as Marx put it in volume III (chapter 15, section 3), are another perspective of the growth of the IRA, and not a threat to large corporations.

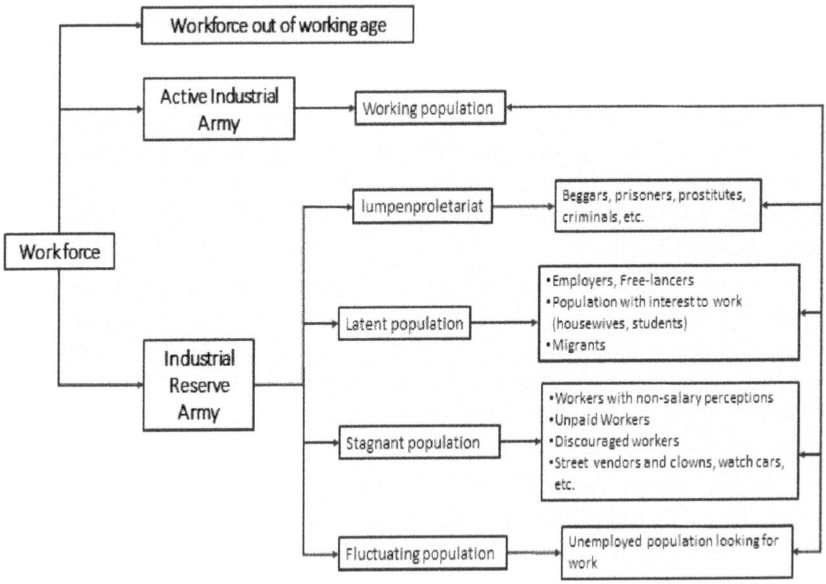

Figure 10.1 Taxonomy of the Labor Force. *Source*: Created by the author.

THE INDUSTRIAL RESERVE ARMY IN MEXICO

The Industrial Reserve Army and National Accounts

Unemployment is a luxury in Latin America. According to Pliego (1997), this situation is due to the fact that in countries with low capitalist development, the unsuccessful search for a job for a long period is an experience that few people can endure. This population, since these people do not have alternative forms of income—such as unemployment insurance or the protection of a sufficient level of savings to cover periods of unemployment—is generally forced to engage in activities in the "informal sector" that allow them to obtain an income, however insignificant it may be; a process that ends up reducing employment pressure in the formal sector. In this sense, 20 years after Pliego's investigation (1997), his conclusions have not lost their validity:

> Conventional indicators adapted to measure employment in countries like Mexico do not show the true behavior of the labor market, hence the need to thoroughly review both the international indicators used to explain the categories of employment and the theories themselves about the behavior of the labor market. (Pliego 1997, 90–91)

Such a suggestion may explain why the unemployment rate in countries like Mexico has traditionally maintained a more or less stable and low level. According to World Bank data, a sample of the unemployment rate in developed countries and Latin America corroborates the lower incidence of unemployment in the latter: from 1991 to 2019, the average was 7.6% and 4.7%, respectively.

A considerable number of researchers, such as Contreras (2015), argue that employment in the informal sector is par excellence the escape valve for unemployment; hence, this process helps to explain the reason for the downward trend in the rate of unemployment in Mexico: from 8.1% in 1977 to 3.3% in 2019.

Faced with such difficulties in studying the labor market, especially in "underdeveloped" countries, the IRA estimation allows a more comprehensive analysis of the composition of the labor force. Thus, in the first place, the IRA considers the population over 15 years of age, regardless of their status as Economically Active Population (EAP) or Economically Inactive Population (EIP). This gives rise to the following scheme in accordance with the various jobs considered in the different conditions of occupation of the population:

(1) Army-Active: Salaried staff (EAP)
(2) Reserve Army of Labor:
   a. Floating Population: Unemployed population looking for work (EAP)
   b. Latent Population: Employers (EAP), Freelancers (EAP), and people with an interest to work, but in a context that prevents them from doing so (EIP Not Available)
   c. Stagnant Population: Population that is not looking for a job because it considers that it has no chance of finding it or because it has stopped looking for it (EIP Available: street vendors and clowns, car watchers, etc.), Workers with non-salary incomes (EAP), unpaid workers (EAP), and domestic employees (EIP Not Available).

The period for the analysis of the IRA was from 2005 to the first quarter of 2020. Methodological changes in the employment surveys in Mexico restrict us to addressing only this period of time. The results are presented in the next section.

The Industrial Reserve Army in Mexico

Under the criteria set forth in the last section, the IRA in the case of Mexico is just over a third of the workforce (33.4%), while the salaried population represented 37.6% and the rest is made up of young students and housewives, that is, people "without interest to work because of other obligations" (EIP Not-Available) and of people with physical disabilities for work.

Thus, in Mexican capitalism, it is the *latent* population that represents the highest proportion within the IRA, and that, together with the *stagnant*, makes up 95% of the IRA. As previously noted with regard to Mexico, unemployment (the *floating* population) seems not to be a chronic problem, although it is sensitive to periods of crisis. In this sense, when considering the first quarter of 2020 within the series, the beginning of the consequences of the pandemic on the employment level is coming into sight: a period identified as the one with the greatest loss of employment in the economic history of Mexico (figure 10.2).

Although the changes in the proportions of each IRA subpopulation are not significant during the study period—a fact that makes the structural character of each of the IRA subpopulations remarkable—the modifications in the activities that make up such populations are significant.

Under the assumption that the people who make up the *latent* population did not move to another IRA population nor joined the Active Army, this subpopulation remained in its same proportion during the study period as a result of the null effect generated by the decrease in persons "with interest to work" in the face of the growth of both employers and self-employed workers.

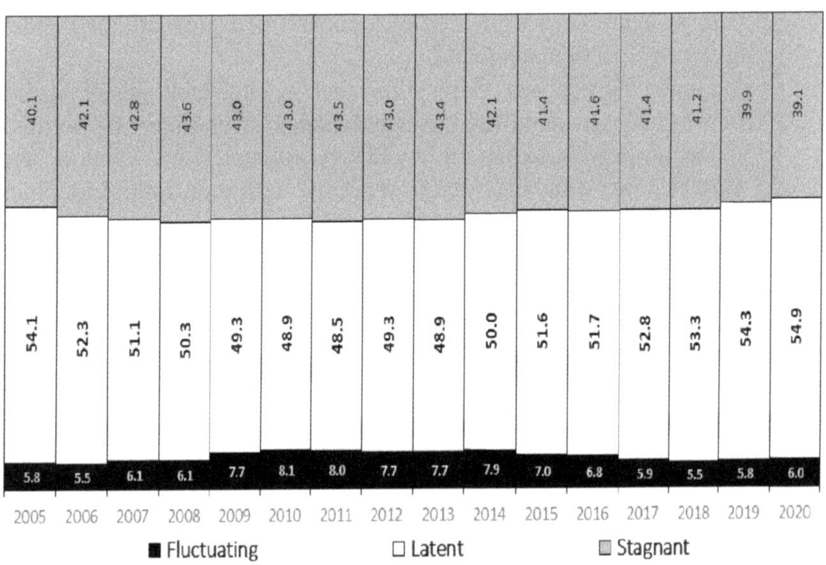

Figure 10.2 Composition of the IRA. *Note*: All results correspond to the first quarter of each year. *Source*: Created by the author with data obtain from INEGI (2020.a).

A similar pattern is to be observed in the case of the *stagnant* population: an increase in the number of persons engaged in typical informal sector activities, compared to the decrease in the population without a salary income and unpaid workers.

Likewise, during the study period (2005–2020), an IRA growth not in proportion with the workforce was noticeable: while the IRA grew 15% in absolute terms, the workforce and the Active Army saw an increase of 30% and 45%, respectively. Therefore, the IRA growth with respect to the labor force fell by 12%; nevertheless, during the crisis years (2008–2010) a greater absolute growth of the IRA was observed with respect to the labor force.

Is it legitimate to think that in Mexican capitalism, employment conditions have improved as a result of a slow decrease in the IRA with respect to the total workforce? In addition to the empirical limitations to this work, we may argue that the greater flexibility in the contracting terms under which contemporary capitalism operates, particularly in Mexico, allows the Active Army to grow without a corresponding improvement in working conditions or a real (absolute) decrease in relative surplus population, which increased from 28.6 to 32.9 million people. In this sense, there are many indicators showing the increase in job insecurity in Mexico. To begin with, the contrast between the growth rate of temporary employment versus permanent employment created so far during this century is widely disproportionate: 235% and 73%, respectively, for the 1997–2020 period.

Likewise, there is a record of a sustained increases in jobs in micro-businesses without fixed facilities, a heterogeneous stagnant productive structure that only employs 11% of the employed population in large companies and 65.4% in micro and small businesses; this goes hand-in-hand with a loss of high-paying jobs.

Another indicator that reveals the precariousness of jobs par excellence is the working shift. This has undergone a general increase in the different official segmentations, in particular, the increase in the most precarious shifts, either due to excess work (shifts amounting to more than 48 hours a week) or due to lack of it (shifts of less than 15 hours per week).

Apparently, the struggle to reduce the working shift has historically resulted in more defeats than victories, as described by Galeano (2012):

> In 1998, France passed the law that reduced working hours to 35 hours a week. Working less, living more: Thomas More, in his Utopia, had dreamed of it, but it took five centuries for a nation to finally dare to commit such an act of common sense. After all, what are machines for, if not to reduce working time and expand our spaces of freedom? Why does technological progress have to give us unemployment and anguish? For once, at least, there was a country that dared to

> challenge such unreason. But sanity did not last long. The thirty-five-hour law died at age ten. (Galeano 2012, 166)

Thus, the increase in working hours is an element that clearly shows the greater precariousness in Mexico's Active Army (formal wage earners). In addition to being hard data, this increase is presented as a subjective incentive not to try to become part of it.

CONCLUSION

The results of this study show a systematic deterioration in the general employment conditions in Mexico. This is a trend very much in line with the fundamentals on which the *general law of capitalist accumulation* was drawn up. However, the progression of the capitalist system in more and more personal and social activities poses a theoretical and empirical effort for those of us who consider the full theoretical and empirical functionality of this law.

The analysis of the IRA allows us to identify the composition of the workforce based on its structural (productive) character, thus obtaining a diagnosis of the most structural movements of contemporary capitalist economies. This is a much-needed diagnosis to try to understand the political and social perspectives of the working class.

For the particular case of Mexico, it was calculated that the total of the IRA is one-third of the population of working age; it was also identified that a large part of the IRA (latent and stagnant subpopulation) is poorly linked to modern capitalist production. These results point to a *long-term* path to reducing, in absolute terms, the proportion of the IRA within the total workforce; a purpose that suffers, sooner rather than later, the inherent recessions and economic crises of the capitalist system. In this sense, the stoppage, due to confinement, of a large number of economic activities caused an absolute decrease in the minimum (financial and organizational) conditions of employment. These conditions were already configuring a scenario in which the dilemma between being part of the Active Army or part of the IRA tends to be a very tenuous and ephemeral border.

The gradual extension of weekly working hours dispels the theoretical hypothesis that these would decrease as technological progress reaches different areas of socioeconomic activity, while also dispelling the presence of an inverse reactionary working class in "self-employed jobs" that increases the IRA in absolute terms.

NOTES

1. *Fruit Picking Robots* (Intorobotics, n.d.) perform the picking and collection of such small fruits as strawberries and coffee beans. Their image-processing algorithms may detect rotten, infected, damaged, or ripe fruits; they feature a GPS system and are fully autonomous.

2. According to Mariña (2007):

> The long term thus defined, although it has a real existence for the different sectors that make up the system, only has a figurative meaning for the system as a whole, since the times of concretion of accumulation decisions in each sector are generally different, while technical barriers to a free intersectoral mobility of capital and accumulation funds, although tending to disappear, also tend to reproduce over time. . . . The analytical delimitation of the long term is justified because . . . it allows to define the system's tendencies, which is essential to examine its dynamics. (p. 65)

3. "That work will only become a condiment for the pleasure of laziness, a beneficial exercise for the human organism, a useful passion for the social organism when it is wisely regulated and limited to a maximum of three hours per day" (Lafargue 1883, 29).

4. Mendieta's argument (2011) is as follows:

> Higher levels of OCC reduce the elasticity or exploitation rate of the profit rate (that is, they reduce the sensitivity of the profit rate with respect to the exploitation rate) and, therefore, they force the necessary increases in the exploitation rate to compensate for the increases in the COC level to be ever greater. (Mendieta 211, 185)

5. It is nowadays unconceivable that capitalists fear a labor shortage. But Maurice Dobb tells us how—approximately in 1563—England faced the shortage of workers:

> *The Statute of Artificers* made work in agriculture compulsory for any person who lacked another occupation. . . . When, even under these conditions, the supply of workers for a new company was insufficient—in mining, for example—it was not uncommon for the Crown to grant the employer the right of forced recruitment or to assign convicts to that work, under penalty of hanging in case they rebelled or escaped. . . . Tudor legislation imposed compulsory labor for the unemployed, and at the same time made unemployment a crime punishable with extraordinary brutality. (Dobb 1977, 278–279)

6. According to Singer (1980, 27):

> It is interesting to note that Marx conceives of the Industrial reserve army in the same way that modern unemployment analysis does. It would be composed of unmistakable unemployed ("floating" form), disguised unemployed in the countryside ("latent" form) and unemployed disguised as urban underemployed ("stagnant" form).

7. It is surprising how the economic mainstream today even romanticizes unemployment. In the study by Rifkin (1996), opinions are collected from such a perspective, for example: "the availability of the unemployed is no worse than the situation in which firefighters find themselves waiting in their facilities for a fire alarm, or that of the police waiting for the next call" (p. 39).

8. Not all Marxist economic approaches address the study of the subpopulations that make up the IRA. For example, the Monthly Review School, traditionally—from the studies of Paul Sweezy, Bellamy, McChesney and Jamil, and more recently in Smith (2016)—has omitted, when not approached tangentially, the analysis of the subpopulations of the IRA.

9. Shortly before this century, it was already notable that the genuine capitalist spirit was no longer exclusive to manufacturing entrepreneurs, as one agricultural entrepreneur put it: "We are no longer growing wheat, we manufacture it. . . . We are not peasants, not even are we farmers. We make a product to be sold" (Rifkin 1996, 139).

10. According to the work by Valenzuela (2006), *freedom* acquires a dual character: "a) *Formal freedom*: absence of prohibitions and/or obligations to carry out this or that activity; b) *substantive freedom*: ability to carry out this or that activity; in other words, to translate the will into effective action for success" (Valenzuela 2006, 143). Thus, "Substantive freedom supposes, as a prerequisite, that there is formal freedom. But the existence of the latter does not ensure the presence of the second" (Valenzuela 2006, 144) therefore "[the] wage earners [operate] with formal but not substantive freedom" (Valenzuela 2006, 144)

11. The lumpemproletariat may well be classified as the fourth subpopulation of the EIR, although Guerrero (2009) proposes five: floating, stagnant, latent, pauperism, and lumpemproletariat. It is empirically difficult to estimate the magnitude of the lumpemproletariat: statistical departments hardly give serious attention to tracking such a group, a difficult task in itself. Although such a lumpemproletariat concept appears in the *law* studied in this book, Marx gave little treatment to this population in his following books.

BIBLIOGRAPHY

The World Bank. "Indicadores del desarrollo mundial." Accessed June 25, 2020. https://databank.bancomundial.org/source/world-development-indicators.

Basu, Deepankar. 2012. "The Reserve Army of Labour in the Postwar U.S. Economy: Some Stock and Flow Estimates." In *Economics Department Working Paper Series*, 143, United States: University of Massachusetts.

Carcanholo, Reinaldo. 2002. "Ejército Industrial de Reserva." In *Lecturas de Economía Política,* edited by Diego Guerrero, 225–226, Madrid: Editorial Síntesis.

Contreras *Carbajal, José Javier*. 2015. *Enfoque crítico sobre las teorías del sector informal urbano en América Latina*. México: Universidad Autónoma Metropolitana.

Da Silva Ferraz, Deise Luiza. 2010. "Desemprego, exército de reserva, mercado formal-informal: rediscutiendo categorías." PhD diss., Universidad Federal del Río Grande del Sur.

Dobb, Maurice. 1977. "Crecimiento del proletariado" In *Estudios sobre el desarrollo del capitalismo*, 263–302. Mexico: Siglo Veintiuno Editores.

Docoa, Luis Felipe. 2018. "Excedente de fuerza de trabajo como principio del Sector Informal en México (2005–2017)." MSc diss., Universidad Autónoma Metropolitana.

Galeano, Eduardo. 2012. *Los hijos de los días*. Mexico: Siglo Veintiuno Editores.

Granato Neto, Nelson Nei. 2013. "Exército Industrial de Reserva: conceito e mensuração." MSc diss., Universidad Federal de Paraná.

Guerrero, Diego. 2009. *Un resumen completo de El Capital de Marx*. España: Ediciones Maia.

Gouverneur, Jacques.2005. *Comprender la economía. La cara oculta de los fenómenos económicos*. Francia: La librairie des documents scientifiques. https://www.i6doc.com/fr/book/?GCOI=28001100746330

Inrobotics. 2017. "Fruit Picking Robots." Accessed April 14, 2021. https://www.intorobotics.com/fruit-harvesting-robots/.

Instituto Nacional de Estadística y Geografía. 2020a. "Encuesta Nacional de Ocupación y Empleo (ENOE)." Accessed Aug 30, 2020. https://www.inegi.org.mx/programas/enoe/15ymas/ .

Instituto Nacional de Estadística y Geografía. 2020b. "Encuesta Telefónica de Ocupación y Empleo (ETOE)." Accessed 31 July, 2020. https://www.inegi.org.mx/investigacion/etoe/ .

Lafargue, Paul. 2010. *El derecho a la pereza*. España: Editorial Sol 90.

Mankwin, Gregory. 2015. *Microeconomía. Versión para América Latina*. México: CEANGAGE Learning.

Mariña Flores, Abelardo. 2007. "La determinación del valor como precio de producción de mercado en un marco de desequilibrio intersectorial de mediano plazo: un modelo marxista de capital circulante." PhD diss., Universidad Nacional Autónoma de México.

Marx, Karl.2013. *El Capital. Crítica de la economía política*. México: Siglo Veintiuno Editores.

Mendieta, Ivan. 2011. "La tendencia al descenso de la tasa de ganancia y el nivel de la composición orgánica de capital." *Revista Problemas del Desarrollo* 167, no. 42 (October): 175–186.

Pliego Quintana, Mónica. 1997. "La evolución del empleo en México: 1982–1995, desempleo, participación de la fuerza laboral y ocupación informal." In *Macroecononomía del empleo y políticas de pleno empleo para México*, edited by Julio López Gallardo, 13–94. México: Universidad Nacional Autónoma de México and Miguel Ángel Porrúa.

Rifkin, Jeremy. 1996. *El fin del trabajo. Nuevas tecnologías contra puestos de trabajo: el nacimiento de una nueva era*. España: Editorial Páidos.

Schwab, Klaus. (2016). "Cuatro principios de liderazgo de la Cuarta Revolución Industrial" In World Economic Forum. Accessed 26 Dec, 2020. https://es.weforum.org/agenda/2016/10/cuatro-principios-de-liderazgo-de-la-cuarta-revolucion-industrial/.

Shaikh, Anwar. 2009. *Teorías del comercio internacional*. Spain: Ediciones Maia.

———. 2006. *Valor, acumulación y crisis. Ensayos de Economía Política*. Argentina: Ediciones ryr.

Singer, Paul. 1980. *Economía política del trabajo. Elementos par aun análisis histórico-estructural del empleo y de la fuerza de trabajo en el desarrollo capitalista*. Mexico: Siglo Veintiuno Editores.

Smith, John. 2016. *Imperialism in the Twenty-First Century. Globalization, Super-exploitation, and Capitalism's Final Crisis*. New York: Monthly Review Press.

Valenzuela Feijóo, José Carlos. 2006. *Libertad y razón. Rousseau, Hegel, Marx*. Chile: Universidad Autónoma Metropolita y LOM Ediciones.

Chapter 11

Unpaid Housework, Social Reproduction, and Accumulation of Capital

A Theoretical Framework and Empirical Evidence from Mexico

Carlos Alberto Duque Garcia

This chapter presents a theoretical framework that integrates the dynamics of social reproduction and unpaid housework within Marx's *general law of capitalist accumulation* as well an empirical illustration for México. As it has been pointed out by several authors, the social reproduction of the labor-power is a wide and complex process that covers the wage relation, biological reproduction, unpaid housework, the "social wage" provided by the capitalist state, geographical flows of labor-power (migration), and so on. In this chapter, we focus only on the wage relation and the unpaid housework.

The first section focuses on the *general relationship* between the reproduction of capital and the social reproduction of the labor-power. In the second section, we explore a new approach to the Marxist analysis of unpaid housework. In this approach, the *magnitude* and *distribution* of unpaid housework are two separate and sequential problems. First, the mass of unpaid housework (at household or aggregate level) is determined by a deficit of means of subsistence. This deficit occurs when the household wage income is below the value of labor-power, a situation that could be associated with the notion of "super-exploitation of labor-power." Then, the mass of unpaid housework is distributed among the members of the working-class households according to several criteria in which the sex is one of the most important. Although the focus of this chapter is the first problem, we provide some theoretical and empirical insights on the second problem.

In the first two sections, we operate under a *short-run* time horizon, that is, we consider the value of labor-power, the wages (individual and aggregate), and the employment *as given*. Here, the structural deficit of means of subsistence (super-exploitation of labor-power) is a case *presupposed.* On the contrary, the core model of unpaid housework and the accumulation of capital, presented in the third section, is built under a *long-run* horizon. In that context, the value of labor-power, the wages, and the employment are *endogenously* determined by the accumulation of capital. Here, the super-exploitation of labor-power is *explained* from the conditions of accumulation of capital instead of unequal international exchange as in Mauro Marini's approach.

Finally, section fourth presents the empirical analysis for Mexico in the years 2003–2016 based on official-time-use data. This section provides preliminary empirical support for the theoretical predictions suggested in the third section. Finally, we set up the conclusions.

REPRODUCTION OF CAPITAL AND SOCIAL REPRODUCTION

In contrast with the static and physical neoclassical definition, *Capital* is defined by Marx in monetary and dynamic terms like "money which begets money" (Marx [1867]1990, 257). This definition is condensed in the *circuit of capital, M-C...P...C´- (M +ΔM)*, which also represents the general movement of capital, its different stages, forms, and its driving force. Likewise, the circuit of capital is suitable representing both the movement of a *particular* capital (firm level) and the *total social* capital (macro level).

In the first stage (*M-C*) capital assumes the form of *money-capital*, which is spent by the capitalists in the purchase of *means of production*, *Mp*, and *labor-power*, *L.* This stage occurs in the sphere of circulation: the capitalists are the buyers and workers the sellers. Then, in the second stage (*C...P...C'*), circulation is interrupted, capital takes the form of *productive-capital*, and the *labor process* is carried out: inputs are transformed in outputs. Meanwhile, a *valorization process* takes place simultaneously: labor-power is productively consumed and become *living labor* which, as such, conserves and transfers the value of the means of production (constant capital) at the same time that aggregate *new value.* This new value aggregated by labor reproduces the variable capital or wages, and creates, besides, a *surplus value.* According to Marx (1990 [1867]), the *source* of the surplus value is the exploitation of wage labor, that is, the monetary expression of the *surplus-labor.*

Finally, in the third stage (*C´- M + ΔM*), all types of commodities are launched to the market. *If* they overcome the "commodity's *salto mortale*," that is, they are sold successfully, the capitalists recover their initial advanced money (*M*) and *realize* the potential surplus value (*ΔM*) embodied in the final commodities (*C'*). Therefore, at the end of the cycle, the capitalists are in conditions to restart the circuit of capital again and again, in the same or an expanded scale. Thus, *the valorization of capital becomes a process of reproduction of capital.*

The circuit of capital also shows that "the driving motive and determining purpose of capitalist production [and reproduction] is the self-valorization of capital to the greatest possible extent, i.e. the greatest possible production of surplus value, [not in mass, but its ratio to capital advanced] hence the greatest possible exploitation of labor-power by the capitalist" (Marx [1867] 1990, 449). Without exploitation of labor-power, there will be no surplus value either self-valorization. Consequently, the existence and reproduction of the labor-power plays a central role in the reproduction of capital.

Labor-power and Reproduction of Capital

In Marx's theory, there is a crucial difference between *labor* and *labor-power*. Labor is the substance and source of both value and surplus value. On the other hand, labor-power is the "labour-capacity, the aggregate of those mental and physical capabilities existing in the physical form, the living personality, of a human being, capabilities which he sets in motion whenever he produces a use-value of any kind" (Marx 1990, 270).

As we can infer from the circuit of capital, *M-C...P...C'-M'*, the reproduction of capital depends crucially on the labor-power at every stage. In the first stage (*M-C*), it is absolutely necessary that the labor-power exist as a commodity, in the *quantity* and *quality* required by the capitalists, that is, as determined population without means of production and, therefore, of means of subsistence, but with the physical, mental, and social skills required by the capitalist production. Thus, this "mass of human material always ready for exploitation by capital" is a *necessary condition* for the beginning of the valorization process and the continuous reproduction of capital. Consequently, this permanent labor-power supply implies the daily and generational reproduction of the labor-power.

In the second stage (*C...P...C'*), the purchased labor-power is exploited by capital and creates a surplus value. This implies necessarily the capitalists' control of the labor process (technical methods, division of labor, length of the working day, intensity of labor, etc.) as well as the obedience and subordination of labor-power. Therefore, the capitalist authority over the workers in the production process is also a necessary condition for both the valorization process and the reproduction of capital. Finally, in the third stage (*C'-M'*), the normal reproduction of capital involves three aspects. First, worker's consumption must be enough to allow the continuous reproduction of labor-power in a daily and generational basis. Second, the bulk of the working class must be given full expense of the wages in order to sell again their labor-power, that is, they cannot be allowed to hoard enough money to become capitalists. Third, the full expense of the wages is also a condition for the realization of the value of the sectors that produce wage goods.

Hence, the role played by labor-power in the reproduction of capital allows us to understand how the capital is also a *social relation of exploitation*. The circuit of capital is organized upon the continuous economic exploitation of the working class by the capitalists. Furthermore, the reproduction of capital also creates the conditions for the continuous reproduction of the two main classes in the capitalist society: the owners of capital and the dispossessed working population.

Social Reproduction of the Labor-Power

The social reproduction of labor-power can be modeling in the *circuit of labor-power: L-M-C*, where *L* is the labor-power, *M* is the wage money, and *C* the wage goods. According to Marx ([1884]1992, 119): "The wage-labourer lives only from the sale of his labour-power. Its maintenance—his own maintenance—requires daily consumption. His payment must therefore be constantly repeated at short intervals, to enable him to repeat the purchases—the act *L-M-C* or *C-M-C*—that are needed for this self-maintenance." Consequently, while the capitalists' reproduction follows the circuit of capital (*M-C-M'*), the labor-power reproduction follows the circuit of simple commodities production (*L-M-C*). While the driving motive of the circuit of capital is the greatest possible production of surplus value, the driving motive of the circuit of labor-power is the satisfaction of human needs (Lebowitz 2003). The circuit of labor-power has *three stages* and takes place in three social spheres: the markets, the capitalist workplace, and the household. Furthermore, *the basic unit of reproduction of labor-power is the household instead of the individual.*

First Stage (L-M)

In the first stage, households' labor-power is offered in the market. Like other commodities in circulation, the labor-power must also go through the *salto mortale*. If a working-class household can sell the labor-power of its members, that household will be integrated into capitalist production and will get a wage income. On the contrary, if a working-class household is unable to sell the labor-power of any of its members, that household will be enlisted in the industrial reserve army with its social reproduction compromised.

In *Capital*, volume I, Marx ([1867]1990, 269) made the explicit *assumption* of equality between prices and values. This assumption implies that the *price of labor-power* (wages) are equal to the *value of labor-power* (V_{LP}). In aggregate terms, this implies:

$$V_{LP} = W = wL \tag{1}$$

Where W is the mass of wages, w the average wage per worker, and L the number of workers. In turn, the (monetary) value of labor-power (VLP) is determined by "the value of the means of subsistence necessary for the maintenance of its owner" (Marx 1990, 274). These means of subsistence not only cover physiological needs but also "moral and historical" needs, as well as education/training costs. In addition, "the sum of means of subsistence necessary for the production of labour-power must include the means necessary for the worker's replacements, i.e. his children, in order that this race of peculiar commodity-owners may perpetuate its presence on the market" (Marx 1990, 275). Therefore, the VLP is determined at the *household* instead of the individual level. Thus, at the aggregate level, the VLP can be represented in the following way:

$$V_{LP} = pX_{LP} \tag{2}$$

Where V_{LP} is the aggregate (monetary) value of labor-power; X_{LP} the mass of all consumption goods (and services) required for the reproduction of the whole working class; and p the vector of prices, *at a certain point in time*. If we assume, for simplicity, that each working household has only one worker, we can define the following variables at the household level:

$$v_{LP} = \frac{V_{LP}}{L} \tag{3}$$

$$x_{LP} = \frac{X_{LP}}{L} \tag{4}$$

Where v_{LP} is the VLP for an *average* working-class household, and x_{LP} is the bundle of consumption goods required for the reproduction of an *average* working-class household. In this chapter, we assume that the bundle of goods x_{LP} is enough for the complete satisfaction of requirements of household social reproduction *without any additional requirement for unpaid housework*. From (1) and (4), we obtain the following relation:

$$w = v_{LP} \tag{5}$$

Equation (5) indicates that, under Marx's assumption (equation 1), the wage per worker, *w*, is equal to the VLP at household level (this assumption is reconsidered in the third section).

Second Stage (M-C)

The second stage in the circuit of labor-power takes place in the market of goods: the working-class households spend their wages on *wage-goods*. Marx's assumption on the equality between the V_{LP} and wages (equations 1 and 5) implies that the bundle of wage-goods purchased by an average household, x_w, are enough to guarantee its social reproduction. In consequence:

$$x_w = x_{LP} \tag{6}$$

Third Stage (C...H...L)

Finally, in the third stage, the wage-goods bundle is consumed and the labor-power is reproduced. This stage occurs inside the working-class households and presents several special features. First, since the majority of working-class households are families, the reproduction of labor-power is mediated *by gender, generational, and emotional relationships among the family members and among the families* (Bhattacharya 2017). This implies several gender gaps and inequalities in the process of reproduction of labor-power like the sexual division of labor.

Second, the *reproduction* of labor-power refers to two different but simultaneous processes: *daily reproduction* and *generational reproduction* (Seccombe 1974). The daily reproduction means the *daily restoration* of the labor-power consumed by capitalist production. This reproduction is related to not only certain basic needs as feeding, shelter, sleeping, transportation, and so on but also emotional and more complex social needs. On the other hand, the generational reproduction refers to the continuous replacement of old/worn labor-power by new labor-power. The generational reproduction includes the biological reproduction of human beings, childbearing, childcare, healthcare, education, training, and so on. As such, the generational reproduction of labor-power is also linked with demographical issues as birth rates, mortality rates, life expectancy, and so on. If we consider the role of capitalist state, generational reproduction of labor-power also includes services provides by public education, health and pensions systems (Bhattacharya 2017; Sarıtaş Oran 2017).

Third, in this stage, the unpaid housework, *H*, plays a central role. Unpaid housework includes all the *private labor* made by household members to bear daily and generational reproduction of labor-power: meal preparation, housecleaning, laundry, childbearing, childcare, eldercare, emotional support, educational support, and so on. As such, unpaid domestic labor contributes to the physical reproduction of labor-power as well as to its ideological reproduction (Seccombe 1974; Gimenez 2019; Vogel 2000). Mathematically:

$$X_w,\ H \Rightarrow N \tag{7}$$

$$N = L + L_F + R \tag{8}$$

Where X_w is the mass of wage-goods consumed by the whole working-class, H is the aggregate mass of unpaid housework, and N is the total labor-power reproduced. In turn, N is composed of L, the active labor-power employed in capitalist production; L_F the future labor-power under current breeding/education (children, teenagers, students, etc.), and R the relative surplus population or industrial reserve army. However, under the assumption of equality between the V_{LP} and wages, the magnitude of unpaid housework would tend to zero since the wage goods would be enough for the complete satisfaction of household social reproduction needs without any additional requirement for unpaid housework. In this case, a certain (and small) magnitude of unpaid housework is possible but associated only with extra-economic factors (e.g., cultural norms).

SUPER-EXPLOITATION OF LABOR, WAGES, AND UNPAID HOUSEWORK

The specific relation of unpaid housework with wages and the value of labor-power has been widely discussed by the Marxist and Feminist-Marxist literature (for a review, see: Vogel 2000; Arruzza 2013; Jefferson and King 2001). In this section, we explore a new approach to this controversy using the category of *super-exploitation of labor-power*. We suggest this category as one of the determinants of the *mass* of unpaid housework spent by working-class households. The introduction of super-exploitation of labor allows us to reformulate some of the assumptions made in the previous section and it is the conceptual base for the following section.

Determination of the Magnitude of Unpaid Housework

In the chapter prior to the presentation of his general law of capitalist accumulation, Marx makes the following claim:

> In the chapters on the production of surplus-value we constantly assumed that wages were at least equal to the value of labour-power. But the forcible reduction of the wage of labour beneath its value plays too important a role in the practical movement of affairs for us not to stay with this phenomenon for a moment. In fact, it transforms the worker's necessary fund for consumption, within certain limits, into a fund for the accumulation of capital. (Marx 1990, 747–48)

From that claim, three important ideas can be inferred. First, the equality between wages and the VLP (equation 6) is only a theoretical assumption and not a rigorous law of wage determination. Thus, wages can be above or beneath the VLP. Second, in the practical movement of the capitalist economy, wages usually are reduced beneath VLP. Third, the reduction of wages below its value boosts the accumulation of capital.[1]

The reduction of wages beneath the VLP was called as *Super-Exploitation of Labor* (SEL) by Marini (1981) and other authors of the Latin-American Dependency School.[2] In our analytical framework, the SEL is defined as follows:

$$SEL = V_{LP} - W > 0 \tag{9}$$

The *SEL* has important effects on both the reproduction of capital and reproduction of labor-power. On the one hand, *SEL* implies a higher surplus value and, consequently, a higher potential mass of capital to accumulate. On the other hand, *SEL* implies a lower wage income for working-class households as well as lower wage-goods purchased. Therefore, in contrast with equation (6), *SEL* implies:

$$SEL > 0 \rightarrow x_w < x_{LP} \tag{10}$$

Equation (10) means that the average bundle of wage-goods purchased by the household, x_w, is *no* longer enough to guarantee its social reproduction. Therefore, *the SEL implies a deficit of subsistence goods in the working-class households*. We define this deficit bundle of goods for the average working-class household as:

$$x_d = x_{LP} - x_w \tag{11}$$

and the deficit-goods bundle, for the whole working-class as:

$$X_d = X_{LP} - X_w \tag{12}$$

We claim that unpaid housework is one of the *survival mechanisms* used by working-class households to face, within certain limits, wages beneath the VLP. Given X_d the working-class households will try to produce these "missing" goods/services using unpaid domestic labor. Therefore, the magnitude of unpaid housework will depend on X_d:

$$H = H_0 + d(X_d) \tag{13}$$

Equation (13) is a general function of unpaid housework, at aggregate level; where H_0 is the autonomous unpaid housework[3] and $d(.)$ a general function which relates X_d with *H*. We assume $d'(X_d) > 0$, that is, unpaid housework will increase with the deficit-goods bundle size.

Let us consider a numerical example. Let's suppose that the bundle of necessary goods, X_{LP}, is composed of only two kinds of goods/services. Goods *A* only can be purchased in the market (e.g., raw food). Goods *B* can be *both* purchased in the market and produced within the households with unpaid housework (e.g., care services). Let's suppose that the size of X_{LP}, in a certain period of time, is composed of 1,000 units of A, and 500 units of B. Assuming, for simplicity, that all prices are equal to one, we get $V_{LP} = \$1000 + \$500 = \$1500$. Now, let's suppose that the mass of wages, *W*, is only \$1300. In this case, the wages are beneath the VLP and there is super-exploitation of labor (see equation 9). The wage income only allows the working households to purchase the 1,000 units of A and only 300 units of B. Thus, there is a *deficit* of 200 units of B (see equation 12).

In this case, since B can be produced within the working-class households, they would use unpaid housework to produce those 200 units of B. Thus, if we assume a household production function $2H \rightarrow 1B$, the domestic production of the 200 deficit units of B would require 400 units of *H*. Therefore, the normal social reproduction of these working-class households under SEL implies a *magnitude* of 600 units of unpaid housework. Now, let's consider a case in which the mass of wages is only \$1,100. In that case, the SEL is even higher, the deficit is 400 units of B and the required *magnitude* of unpaid housework is 800 units. Thus, unpaid housework will increase with the deficit-goods bundle size and the SEL.

Now, on substituting (12) into (13), we obtain:

$$H = H_0 + b(X_{LP} - X_w) \tag{14}$$

Since $V_{LP} = pX_{LP}$ and $W = wL = pX_w$, we simplify the mathematical exposition normalizing prices: $p_i = 1, \ \forall i$. Consequently, we get: $X_{LP} - X_w = V_{LP} - W$. This allows us to express (14) as $H = H_o + b(V_{LP} - wL)$.

$$H = \begin{cases} H_o + b\left(V_{LP} - wL\right), & V_{LP} > wL \\ H_o, & V_{LP} \leq wL \end{cases} \tag{15}$$

Equation (15) is the key equation in our theoretical framework. It holds that, under SEL, the aggregate magnitude of unpaid housework spent by working-class households, H, will increase with the value of labor-power, V_{LP}, and will decrease with both the wage per worker, w, and the level of employment, L. On the other hand, if there is no SEL ($V_{LP} \leq wL$), the mass of unpaid housework will be H_0. Meanwhile, the magnitude of unpaid housework has an upper bound defined by:

$$H_{MAX} = T - \mu L - E \tag{16}$$

Where T is the total time per unit of time (e.g., daily, weekly, or yearly) for the whole working class, μ the average workday, μL the total time spend in wage labor, and E the time required to physiological needs (e.g., sleeping and eating) and transportation.[4]

Distribution of Unpaid Housework

In this theoretical framework, the *magnitude* and *distribution* of unpaid housework are analytically two different problems sequentially determined. First, the magnitude of unpaid housework required for social reproduction is determined by the super-exploitation of labor. Then, that mass of unpaid housework (at aggregate or household level) is distributed among the different members of the working-class households according to several factors (sex, age, occupational status, education level, relative income, etc.). Although the focus of this chapter is the determination and dynamics of the magnitude of unpaid housework, we will briefly comment on the gender gap in the distribution of unpaid housework.

Let's σ be the share the unpaid housework done by women and $(1-\sigma)$ the share of unpaid housework done by men; where $0 \leq \sigma \leq 1$. Thus, the gender-based distribution of the mass of unpaid housework is:

$$H_w = \sigma H \tag{17}$$

$$H_m = \left(1 - \sigma\right) H \tag{18}$$

Where H_w is the mass of unpaid housework done by working-class women and H_m the mass of unpaid housework done by working-class men. The parameter σ is an indicative of the gender gap *within* the working class: if $\sigma \approx 0.5$, there are gender equality in the distribution of *H*. However, the empirical research has shown that $\sigma \gg 0.5$ in all countries (Addati et al. 2018).

The parameter σ is determined by several factors: the social structure of the working-class families, birth rates, female education levels, female participation in wage labor, the relative strength of patriarchal hegemony, and the political effectiveness of feminism, among other social, cultural, and political factors. Although the parameter σ indicates to what extend *H* is divided between men and women, that parameter by itself does not determine the magnitude of *H*.

UNPAID HOUSEWORK AND THE GENERAL LAW OF CAPITALIST ACCUMULATION

In this section, we develop a model that incorporates the unpaid housework within the dynamics of Marx's general law of capitalist accumulation. This model is based on both the theoretical framework presented in first section and the model of SEL and unpaid housework introduced in second section. The main focus in this section is the dynamics of the *magnitude* of unpaid housework instead of its gender-based *distribution*. Also, in this section, we operate under a *long-run* time horizon, that is, the wages, the employment level, and the value of labor-power is endogenously determined by the dynamic accumulation of capital. Therefore, in this section, we explain the conditions that make SEL, as it was previously defined, possible. Finally, in this section, we assume a closed economy without government where accumulation is occurring in its normal way (without any reproduction problem), and the division of the surplus value (between profits, interest, rent, and taxes) has no impact.

A System of Variables

In figure 11.1, we present the system of variables that compose the model of unpaid housework and accumulation of capital. This system can be divided into three parts. The first part (in red color) is our point of departure; it summarizes the model seen in the previous section showing the immediate effects of SEL on unpaid housework, *H*, surplus value, *S*, and, indirectly, on capital's accumulation ΔK. The second part (in black color) synthetizes Marx's *general law* dynamics (accumulation of capital, technical change, employment and reserve army, wages, and productivity of labor). Finally, the third part (in blue color) points out the effects of the *general law* over the SEL and the magnitude of unpaid housework.

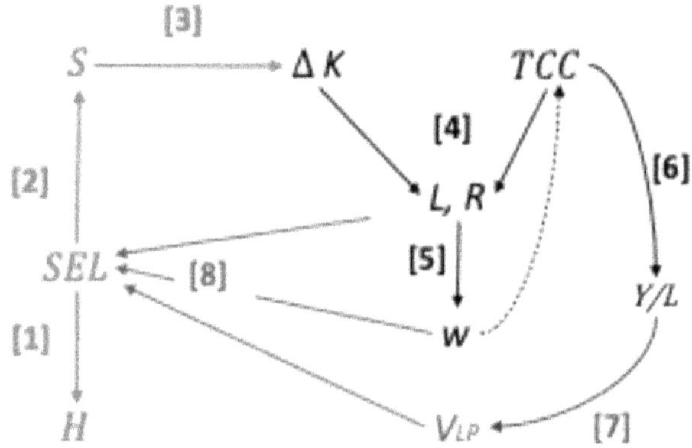

Figure 11.1 Unpaid Housework and Accumulation of Capital: System of Variables. *Note*: Arrows indicate causal relation. *Source*: Created by the author.

Super-exploitation of Labor and Its Immediate Effects ([1], [2], and [3])

A reduction of wages beneath the value of labor-power (SEL) will produce two simultaneous effects. First, an increase in the magnitude of unpaid domestic labor made by working-class households [1] (see equation 15). Second, an increase in the mass of surplus value [2]. Then, since the mass of capital accumulated is a share of the surplus value, the SEL will lead to an increase in the mass of capital accumulated[5] [3]. In that way, the SEL "transforms the worker's necessary fund for consumption, within certain limits, into a fund for the accumulation of capital" (Marx 1990, 747–48).

Dynamics of the General Law of Capitalist Accumulation ([4], [5], and [6])

The main objective of Marx's *general law* is to analyze the impact of capitalist accumulation on the living conditions of the working-class. Consequently, Marx focuses in the dynamic of three variables: employment, L, industrial reserve army, R, and wages, w. As can be seen in figure 11.1 (relation [4]), the level of (waged) employment is determined by the volume of constant capital, K, and the *technical composition of capital*, *TCC:*

$$L = L\left(K, TCC\right) \tag{19}$$

Both variables have contrary effects on the level of employment.[6] Given the TCC, the accumulation of capital will increase the capital stock, ΔK, and, with it, the required number of wage-laborers (Marx 1990 [1867]), that is, $L'(K) > 0$. On the other hand, given the stock of capital, technological change *a la Marx* (Duménil and Lévy 2003) will increase the technical composition of capital and, thus, replace workers by means of production (machinery, robots, software, etc.) decreasing the level of employment, that is, $L'(TCC) > 0$.

According to Marx (1990 [1867]), the market competition among profit-lead individual capitals will lead to both: a continuous accumulation of capital (centralization and concentration) and permanent technical change (growth in the technical composition of capital). Therefore, ΔK and TCC tend to growth endogenously. Hence, the net effect on the employment level will depend on the relative strength in the changes in ΔK (attraction) and TCC (repulsion).

A remarkable feature of Marx's *general law* is his analysis of *Industrial Reserve Army* (IRA): "it is capitalist accumulation itself that constantly produces and produces indeed in direct relation with its own energy and extent, a relatively redundant working population, i.e., a population which is superfluous to capital's average requirements for its own valorization, and is therefore a surplus population" (Marx 1990, 782). We define the IRA as follows:

$$R = N^* - L(K, TCC) \tag{20}$$

Where R is the mass of working population in the IRA and N^* the *effective* mass of working population available for work, $N^* = N - L_F$ (see equation 8). Equation (20) shows that technical change, which increases TCC, will lead to an increase in the redundant working population. This new redundant working population will, in turn, increase the "supply of labor." Thus:

> Capital acts on both sides at once. If its accumulation on the one hand increases the demand for labour, it increases on the other the supply of workers by "setting them free," while at the same time, the pressure of the unemployed compels those who are employed to furnish more labour, and therefore makes the supply of labour to a certain extent independent of the supply of workers. The movement of the law of supply and demand of labour on this basis completes the despotism of capital. (Marx [1867] 1990, 793)

The two-quadrant diagram depicted in figure 11.2 show the general interaction of accumulation of capital, technical change, employment, IRA, and wages. The left quadrant shows the level of employment as a function of the stock of capital, where the curve slope is the inverse of the TCC (see equation 19). On the other hand, the right quadrant depicts the wage per worker, w, as a function of the level of employment, L, and the size of the IRA, R. This quadrant is an adaptation of the diagram used by Goodwin (1967).

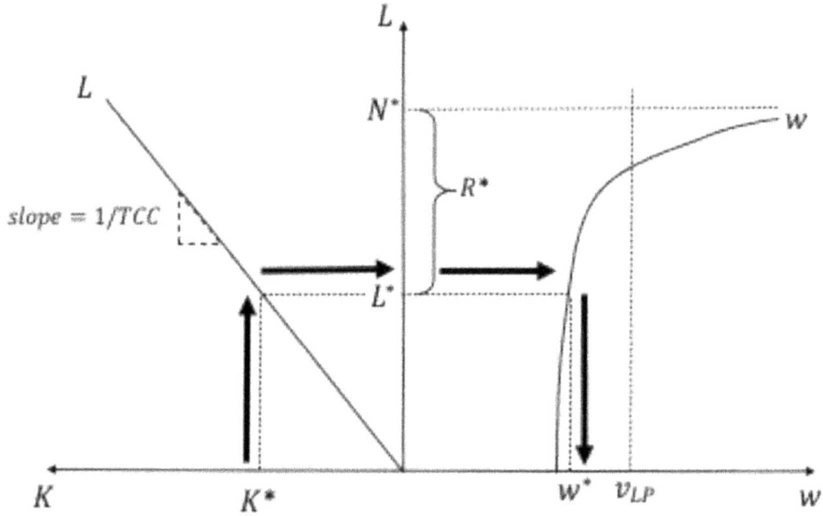

Figure 11.2 Accumulation of Capital, Employment, Reserve Army, and Wages. *Source*: Created by the author.

Thus, under a big IRA, *the pressure of the unemployed compels the active workers to accept wages beneath the VLP*. Therefore, for a wide range of low employment level, wages are relatively constant and below the VLP. Here, we suggest an alternative explanation to the SEL that differs from Mauro Marini's (1981) approach (where SEL is a compensation mechanism to international unequal exchange). On the other hand, as employment approaches full employment, wages begin to rise even to the extent of surpassing the VLP. In Marx's words: "the requirements of accumulating capital may exceed the growth in labour-power or in the number of workers; the demand for workers may outstrip the supply, and thus wages may rise" (Marx [1867]1990, 763). In figure 11.2, the bold arrows indicate causal relation. The stock of constant capital K^*, and the TCC, determines the level of employment, L^*. This, in turn, determines the size of the reserve army, R^*, and, finally, the wage per worker, w^*, which is beneath the VLP.

Finally, arrow [6] in figure 11.1 shows the direct relationship between the TCC and the productivity of labor, *Y/L*. According to Marx ([1867]1990, 773) "the level of the social productivity of labour is expressed in the relative extent of the means of production that one worker, during a given time, with the same degree of intensity of labour-power, turns into products. The mass of means of production with which he functions in this way increases with the productivity of his labour." The growth in the productivity of labor has several effects. On the one hand, a reduction in the individual prices of commodities (in both means of subsistence and means of production). On the other hand, an increase in the mass of surplus product and, with fixed real wages, an increase in the rate of surplus value (Marx 1990 [1867]). Therefore, increasing productivity of labor is both an outcome and a factor in the accumulation of capital.

Accumulation of Capital and Unpaid Housework ([7] and [8])

The third part of the system of variables depicted in figure 11.1 focus on the impacts of accumulation of capital on the SEL and the mass of unpaid housework spent by working-class households (see arrows [7], [8], and [1]). In general terms, the mass of unpaid housework decreases with the mass of wages, that is, it decreases with the level of employment and the wages per worker (see equation 15). On the other hand, the mass of unpaid housework increases with the VLP.

In figure 11.3, we show the integration of unpaid housework within the model of accumulation of capital previously developed (see figure 11.2). Panel B in figure 11.3 shows the detailed relation between the level of employment and the unpaid housework (integrating the effects of wages and the IRA). Curve H in panel B is based on equation (15); it shows that for levels of employment near to full employment, individual wages are above the VLP, there is no SEL and, consequently, the mass of unpaid housework is fixed at H_0. Thus, the curve H is vertical in its upper section. On the other hand, as the IRA expands, both employment level and individual wages contract. This, in turn, leads to a "fast" expansion of unpaid housework in the middle section of curve H. Finally, with a big IRA, the wages stagnate below the VLP and the curve H takes a linear shape in its lower section.

Meanwhile, curve H_{MAX} is based on equation (16). This curve represents the time restriction face by the whole working-class households: as employment rises, time available for unpaid housework reduces. The slope of this curve is determined by the extension of the workday (see equation 16).

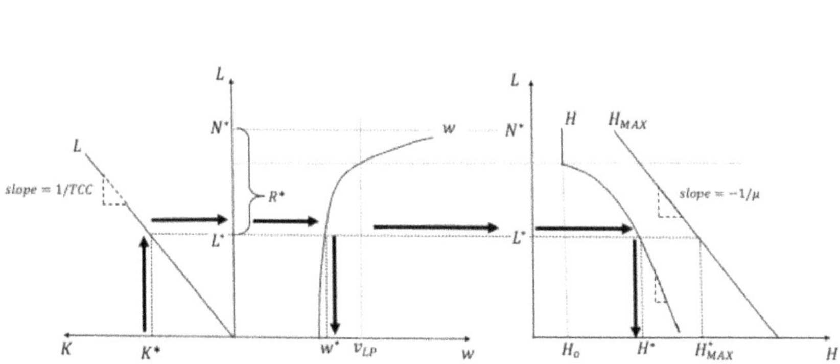

Figure 11.3 Unpaid Housework, Employment, and Wages. *Source*: Created by the author.

Thus, figure 11.3 shows that, given a stock of capital K^* and a technique TCC^*, the level of employment is L^*, and the wage per worker is w^* (beneath v_{LP}). In that circumstances, there is a goods-deficit bundle that working-class households try to produce using the quantity of unpaid housework H^* within the time-restriction H^*_{MAX}. Figure 11.3 allow us to predict the *ceteris paribus* effects of changes in capital stock and TCC:

$$\uparrow K \Rightarrow \uparrow L \Rightarrow \uparrow w \Rightarrow \downarrow H \Lambda \downarrow H_{MAX} \tag{21}$$

$$\uparrow TCC \Rightarrow \downarrow L \Rightarrow \downarrow w \Rightarrow \uparrow H \Lambda \uparrow H_{MAX} \tag{22}$$

In equation (21), we see that an increase in the capital stock will lead to employment and wages increase, which, in turn, will reduce both the required quantity of unpaid housework, H, and the time available for unpaid housework, H_{MAX}. This seemed to be the prediction of many Marxian authors at the beginning of the 20th century. According to Luxemburg, Engels, Lenin, Bebel, Bujarin, and Zetkin, the accumulation of capital leads to the gradual reduction of unpaid housework until its eventual disappearance (Jefferson and King 2001). Nevertheless, as can be seen in (22) the accumulation of capital has also a contrary effect on unpaid housework: *ceteris paribus* an increase in the TCC will lead to employment and wages reduction, which, in turn, will increase both the required quantity of unpaid housework, H, as well as the time available for unpaid housework, H_{MAX}.

Therefore, the accumulation of capital has a contradictory effect on the quantity of unpaid housework made in working-class households. The net effect will depend on the relative strength of capital growth and the technical change, as well as the size and dynamics of the industrial reserve army. In contexts of rapid growth, reduction of the industrial reserve army, and increasing real wages, our model predicts decreasing tendency in the quantity of unpaid housework. On the contrary, in contexts of economic recession or crisis, with an increasing industrial reserve army, and stagnate or decreasing real wages, our model predicts an increasing tendency in the quantity of unpaid housework.

In addition, the contradictory effect of accumulation of capital on the unpaid housework is strengthen by the dual role of the increasing productivity of labor. According to equation (2), the VLP depends on the size of the bundle of necessary goods/services, X_n, and their prices, p. As Marx (1990 [1867]) correctly pointed out, an increasing productivity of labor reduces the prices of commodities. Thus, an increasing productivity of labor will reduce the VLP and, consequently, the mass of unpaid housework:

$$\uparrow TCC \Rightarrow \uparrow (Y/L) \Rightarrow \downarrow p \Rightarrow \downarrow VLP \Rightarrow \downarrow H \quad (23)$$

But, on the other hand, an increasing productivity of labor tends to increase the quantity of *social needs* required by the social reproduction of labor-power. Thus, new goods are added to the bundle of necessary goods/services, X_n (e.g., TV, access to internet, or smartphones). Furthermore, as the increasing productivity of labor presupposes an increasing application of science and technology to the labor process, it also implies a growth in the costs of education and training of the labor-power. Finally, increasing productivity of labor is normally accompanied by improvements in health, medicine, and care, which resolve itself in an increasing life expectancy, which, in turn, increases the requirements of elder care within working-class households. In synthesis:

$$\uparrow TCC \Rightarrow \uparrow (Y/L) \Rightarrow \uparrow X_n \Rightarrow \uparrow VLP \Rightarrow \uparrow H \quad (24)$$

Geometrically, effect (23) can be depicted in figure 11.3 as a displacement of curve *H* to the left. On the contrary, effect (24) can be depicted in the same figure as a displacement of curve *H* to the right.

EMPIRICAL ILLUSTRATION: MEXICO 2003–2016

In contrast with economic variables as income, employment, or wages, whose measurement dates back to more than 100 years, the measurement of unpaid housework has only begun in recent decades. In Latin America, México holds the longest record of unpaid housework with consolidated data from 2003 to 2016.[7] In figure 11.4, we show the trend in the aggregate and per capita magnitude of unpaid housework for that country.

As we can see in figure 11.4, the mass of unpaid housework in Mexico, *H*, presented an increasing trend for the overall period. In 2003, the mass of *H* was estimated in 1,934 million hours per week, that is, the equivalent to the time spent by 40.3 million workers laboring 48 hours per week. Then, in 2016, *H* had increased to 2,633 million hours per week: the equivalent to the time spent by 54.8 million of workers. Thus, this huge and increasing amount of labor shows the *qualitative* and *quantitative* importance of unpaid housework for the social reproduction of Mexican households and their labor-power (see equation 7). Figure 11.4 also reports the dynamics in the unpaid housework per capita ($h = H/N$). This presented two different periods: from 2003 to 2009, a slow downward trend, where *h* decreased from 18.8 hours per week to 18.0. Then, the 2010–2016 period with an increasing trend, where *h* rose from 18.5 hours (in 2010) to 21.4 hours (in 2016).

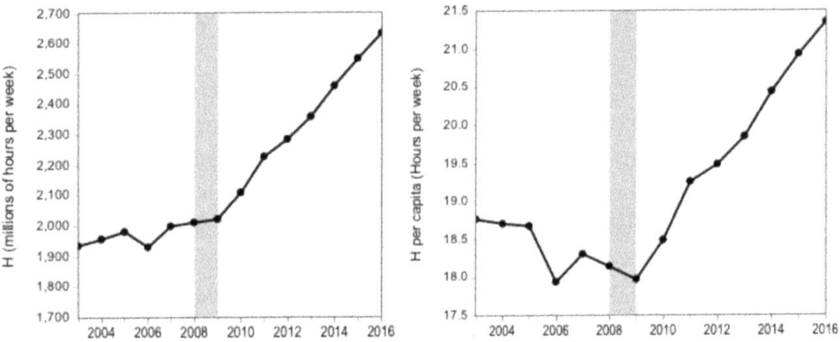

Figure 11.4 Unpaid Housework (Total and Per Capita), Mexico 2003–2016. *Note*: The shaded area corresponds to the crisis of 2008–2009. *Source*: Created by the author with data from INEGI (2019).

These variations in the magnitude of unpaid housework in Mexico seem to indicate the impact of changes in the accumulation of capital over the social reproduction of Mexican households. In fact, the great recession of 2008–2009 seems to be the breaking point in the dynamics of both H and h: the unemployment rate increased from 3.6% in 2007 to 5.4% in 2010; while the real average wages fell 4.1% between 2007 and 2010. Furthermore, the years after the great recession (2010–2016) were characterized by higher unemployment rates and lower wages in comparison with the years before the great recession (2003–2007). These empirical findings seem to support the theoretical predictions of our analytical model. In fact, equations 21 and 22 predict that reductions in both the average wages and the employment will lead to an increase in the deficit of subsistence goods and therefore to an increase in the mass of unpaid housework made by working-class households. This precisely was the scenario after the great recession (2009–2016). On the contrary, the years before the great recession (2003–2008) were characterized by high levels of employment and relatively high wages. In that context, the mass of unpaid housework (aggregate and per capita) was relatively low.

Gender Gap in the Distribution of Unpaid Housework in Mexico

During the overall period in study, Mexican women did most of the burden of unpaid housework (see figure 11.5). The average share of female unpaid housework, the parameter σ in equation (17), was 79.7% between 2003 and 2016. This shows a clear gender-based inequality in the distribution of unpaid housework within the Mexican working-class households. Even so, the right-side graph in figure 11.5 shows a slightly decreasing trend in the parameter σ.

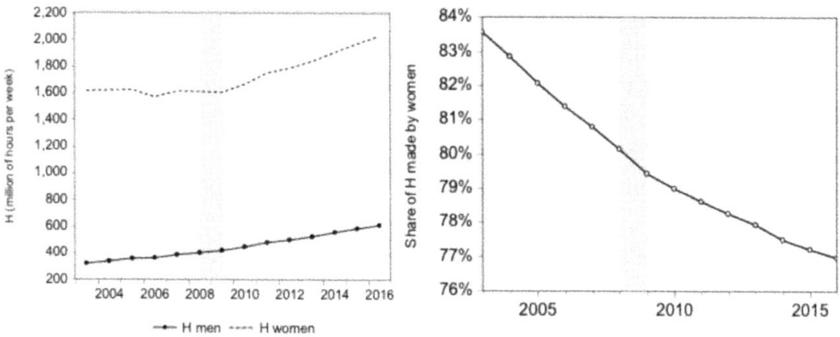

Figure 11.5 Mass of Unpaid Housework by Men and Women, Mexico, 2003–2016. *Note*: The shaded area corresponds to the crisis of 2008–2009. *Source*: Created by the author with data from INEGI (2019).

In 2003, Mexican women did 83.6% of the mass of unpaid housework, while in 2016 that percentage had decreased to 77%. Thus, men's participation in unpaid housework has slowly increased from only 16.4% in 2003 to 23% in 2016.

As we have seen at the end of section II, the evolution of the parameter σ obeys several social, cultural, and political factors that are out of the scope of this chapter. Nevertheless, the exploratory analysis of the available data suggests a possible relation between the dynamics of capital's accumulation and the gender-based distribution of the mass of unpaid housework. In the years before the great recession (2003–2008), the mass of female unpaid housework, H_w, was decreasing at an average annual rate of 0.05%, while the mass of male unpaid housework, H_m, was increasing at a rate of 4.7%. This double behavior led to an average annual reduction in the parameter σ in 0.68 percentage points. However, in the years after the great recession (2010–2016), H_w increased at an average annual rate of 3.4%, while H_m increased at a rate of 5.5%. The growth in H_w led to slow the annual reduction in the parameter σ, which in the second period was 0.35 percentage points (on average). Summing up, the great recession seemed to slow down the decreasing tendency in women's share of unpaid housework.

CONCLUDING REMARKS

The theoretical framework suggested in this chapter can be understood as both a contribution to the social reproduction literature as well as a new approach to the classical domestic labor debate. It explores an alternative conceptual linkage between wages, the value of labor-power, unpaid housework, and employment, not only in a "static" but also in a "dynamic" context.

The preliminary empirical findings for Mexico, despite the lack of information, support the theoretical predictions of our model: the mass of unpaid housework (at aggregate and per capita level) is affected by the dynamics of capital's accumulation, especially by the variations in the industrial reserve army, the average wages, and the productivity of labor.

Although we considered the *magnitude* and *distribution* of unpaid housework as two separate theoretical problems, the empirical evidence suggests that the dynamics of the accumulation of capital also can affect the gender gap in unpaid domestic labor. In the boom periods, with a decreasing reserve army and increasing wages, the mass of unpaid housework tends to decrease along with the women's share in that labor. This last effect can be explained by the combined effect of female employment and wages on the gender-based bargaining process on housework within households. On the contrary, in crisis or stagnate periods, with an increasing reserve army and decreasing wages, the mass of unpaid housework tends to increase while the bargaining power of women within working-class households results weakened. Hence, the possible relationship between the accumulation of capital and the gender-based distribution of unpaid housework requires further both theoretical and empirical research.

Finally, we suggest an alternative explanation of the super-exploitation of labor. While in Mauro Marini and the Dependency School the super-exploitation of labor is a compensation mechanism due to international unequal exchange, in this chapter, the super-exploitation of labor emerges as an *especial case* within Marx's general law of capitalist accumulation.

NOTES

1. In *Volume III*, Marx identify the reduction of wages below its value as one of the counteracting factors of the law of the tendential fall of the general rate of profit.
2. In this chapter, we employ the category of SEL with complete independence of the rest of the dependency theory framework (unequal exchange, value transferences, sub-imperialism, etc.).
3. This is the amount of unpaid housework when there is no SEL. It reflects the magnitude of unpaid housework determined *purely* by cultural patterns.
4. The difference between H_{MAX} and H is the *leisure* or free time available for the working-class.
5. A more formal analysis can be done using the "Cambridge equation," which expresses the growth rate as a function of the profit rate multiplied by the rate of accumulation. Given the rate of accumulation, a reduction of wages beneath the VLP (i.e., SEL) will increase the rate of profit and, in turn, the rate of growth of capital stock.
6. Equation (19) can be interpreted like a labor demand function. In an aggregate one-good model, like in Blecker and Setterfield (2019), equation (19) can be expressed in the following functional form: $L=K/TCC$. We use this functional form in figure 11.2.

7. There are also preliminary data for 2017 and 2018. However, we only use the consolidated data (2003–2016).

BIBLIOGRAPHY

Addati, Laura, Umberto Cattaneo, Valeria Esquivel, and Isabel Valarino. 2018. "Care Work and Care Jobs for the Future of Decent Work." International Labour Organization.

Arruzza, Cinzia. 2013. *Dangerous Liaisons: The Marriages and Divorces of Marxism and Feminism. IIRE Notebook for Study and Research*. Merlin Press.

Bhattacharya, Tithi. 2017. "How Not to Skip Class: Social Reproduction of Labor and the Global Working Class." *Social Reproduction Theory: Remapping Class, Recentering Oppression*, 68–93.

Blecker, Robert A, and Mark Setterfield. 2019. *Heterodox Macroeconomics: Models of Demand, Distribution and Growth*. Edward Elgar Publishing.

Duménil, Gérard, and Dominique Lévy. 2003. "Technology and Distribution: Historical Trajectories à La Marx." *Journal of Economic Behavior and Organization* 52 (2): 201–33. https://doi.org/10.1016/S0167-2681(03)00022-2.

Feenstra, Robert C, Robert Inklaar, and Marcel P Timmer. 2015. "The next Generation of the Penn World Table." *American Economic Review* 105 (10): 3150–82.

Gimenez, Martha E. 2019. *Marx, Women, and Capitalist Social Reproduction: Marxist-Feminist Essays*. Brill.

Goodwin, R. M. (1967). "A growth cycle". In "Socialism, Capitalism and Economic Growth". Edited by C. H. Feinstein. Cambridge University Press, Cambridge.

INEGI. 2019. "Trabajo No Remunerado de Los Hogares." Instituto Nacional de Estadística y Geografía (INEGI). https://www.inegi.org.mx/temas/tnrh/.

Jefferson, Therese, and John E King. 2001. "'Never Intended to Be a Theory Of Everything': Domestic Labor in Neoclassical and Marxian Economics." *Feminist Economics* 7 (3): 71–101.

Lebowitz, Michael. 2003. *Beyond Capital: Marx's Political Economy of the Working Class*. 2nd ed. Palgrave Macmillan.

Marini, R. M. 1981. *Dialéctica de La Dependencia*. México D.F.: Ediciones Era.

Marx, Karl. 1990. *Capital: A Critique of Political Economy, Volume 1*. 1867th ed. London: Penguin Classics.

Marx, Karl. 1992. *Capital: A Critique of Political Economy, Volume 2*. Edited by Friedrich Engels. 1884th ed. London: Penguin Classics.

Sarıtaş Oran, Serap. 2017. "Pensions and Social Reproduction." *Social Reproduction Theory. Remapping Class, Recentreing Oppression, Pluto Press London*, 148–71.

Seccombe, Wally. 1974. "The Housewife and Her Labour under Capitalism." *New Left Review*.

Vogel, Lise. 2000. "Domestic Labor Revisited." *Science and Society* 64 (2): 151.

World Bank. 2020. "World Bank Open Data." 2020. https://data.worldbank.org/country/colombia.

Index

About the Editors and Contributors

ABOUT THE EDITORS

Leinad Johan Alcalá Sandoval is a lecturer at the Universidad Nacional Autónoma de México (UNAM) and a PhD candidate in economic sciences at Universidad Autónoma Metropolitana (UAM). His research interests include political economy, Marxian labor theory of value, and Marx's method. His recent publications include "La lógica ínterna de valorización del capital. Un análisis crítico de la categoría capital ficticio," *Cuadernos de Economía* (2015) and "La lógica dialéctica como método para aprehender el modo de producción capitalista y el análisis de la crisis," *Revista Mexicana de Ciencias Agrícolas* (2018).

Lorenzo Fusaro holds a PhD in international political economy from King's College London and is associate professor of political economy at the Universidad Autónoma Metropolitnana, Mexico. He leads the economics departments' research group in political economy (*Área de Sociedad y Acumulación Capitalista, ASAC*) and his recent publications include *Crises and Hegemonic Transitions: From Gramsci's Quaderni to the Contemporary World Economy* (2019) and *Revisiting Gramsci's Notebooks* (2020, edited with Francesca Anotnini, Aaron Bernstein and Robert Jackson). He is currently working on a new monograph titled *Revolutions, Dependency and Geopolitical Autonomy: The Emergence of Hegemonic and Subordinated States* (forth. with Routledge).

ABOUT THE CONTRIBUTORS

Abelardo Mariña Flores, PhD in economics, is full professor within the Department of Economics at the Universidad Autónoma Metropolitana-Azcapotzalco. He has published widely on Marxist theories of value, accumulation, and crises.

Carlos Alberto Duque Garcia is a PhD candidate in economics at the Metropolitan Autonomous University (UAM) in Mexico City. His most recent publications include: "Unpaid housework and super-exploitation of labor: a suggested model and empirical evidence from Mexico and Colombia," *Review of Social Economy* (2021) and "Economic growth and the rate of profit in Colombia: a VAR time-series analysis," MPRA working paper (2021).

Lucia Pradella is a Senior Lecturer in International Political Economy at King's College London. She has written two monographs on Marx's *Capital (L'attualità del Capitale*, Il Poligrafo 2010, and *Globalisation and the Critique of Political Economy*, Routledge 2015) and she co-edited the *Routledge Handbook of Marxism and Post-Marxism* (2021). She has published extensively on migration, imperialism and new workers' movements.

Luis Felipe Docoa Hernández is a doctoral candidate in social economy under the postgraduate program in social studies at the UAM.

Matari Pierre is an economist and associated researcher at the Instituto de Investigaciones Sociales (IIS) of the Universidad Nacional Autónoma de Mexico (UNAM). His research interests include history of economic thought, finance capital, and state theory. Recently, he published "Finance capital and financialization: A comparative reading of Marx and Hilferding" (*Œconomia. History, Methodology, Philosophy*, 2020, no. 10–14), "Crédito al consumo: determinantes estructurales y rol en la gestión estatal de la fuerza de trabajo" *El Trimestre Económico* (julio–septiembre 2020), "James Steuart and the making of Karl Marx's monetary thought," *The European Journal of the History of Economic Thought* (2018, vol. 25, no. 5).

Roberto Fineschi has studied philosophy and economy. His main focus is the investigation and reconstruction of Marx's theory of the capitalist mode of production in the light of the new critical edition of Marx's and Engels' works (*Marx-Engels-Gesamtausgabe*, MEGA). He has written books and essays published in several languages, and edited a new Italian version of the first volume of *Capital* after the MEGA. He is a member of the International Symposium on Marxian Theory.

Rossana Cillo is a postgraduate researcher at the Ca' Foscari University of Venice and a PhD candidate in labour sociology at the Université Libre de Bruxelles. Her research interests include racial discrimination at work, immigrant union participation, labour mobility in the EU market, and youth and precariousness. Recently, she published "Mandatory mobility? The case of immigrant posted workers sent from Italy to Belgium in the construction sector" (*International Migration*, 2022), "Work-Based Learning Policies and Numbers. The Italian Case in a Broad Context" (with Iside Gjergji, Scuola Democratica, 2021) and "Remaking the labour movement in Italy: the revival of strikes at Fiat-Chrysler Automobiles in 2015–17" (with Lucia Pradella, *Globalizations*, 2019).

Sergio Cámara Izquierdo is a full-time tenured professor of political economy at the Universidad Autónoma Metropolitana-Azcapotzalco, Mexico City, where he is Head of the Department of Economics. He is a member of the Executive Council of the Latin American Society of Political Economy and Critical Thought (SEPLA) and the Council of the International Initiative for Promoting Political Economy (IIPPE), and serves on the Editorial Boards of *Review of Radical Political Economics* and *Análisis Económico*. He has been distinguished Level I researcher by the National System of Researchers (Conacyt) and Teacher with Desirable Profile within the Program of Professors' Professional Development (PRODEP-SEP). He holds PhD in applied economics from the Universidad Complutense de Madrid. His research interests include applied political economy and the Marxian labor theory of value.

Sibyl Italia Pineda Salazar is a visiting professor at Universidad Autónoma Metropolitana in Mexico City. She teaches political economy and researches labor economics and Marxist theory.

William I. Robinson is Distinguished Professor of sociology, global studies, and Latin American studies at the University of California at Santa Barbara. His most recent book is *Global Civil War: Capitalism Post-pandemic*.

www.ingramcontent.com/pod-product-compliance
Ingram Content Group UK Ltd.
Pitfield, Milton Keynes, MK11 3LW, UK
UKHW020840290926
15470UKWH00004B/1453

9 781793 638236